CONTEMPORARY'S

American History 1
Before 1865

Matthew T. Downey

McGraw Hill · Wright Group

The McGraw·Hill Companies

Author

Matthew T. Downey received his Ph.D. in American History from Princeton University. He served as Director of the Clio Project in History-Social Science Education in the Graduate School of Education at the University of California, Berkeley. He also directed the U.C. Berkeley site of the California History-Social Science Project. He has taught at the University of Colorado, the University of California at Los Angeles, and Louisiana State University. Currently, he directs the Social Science Program and the William E. Hewitt Institute for History and Social Science Education at the University of Northern Colorado.

Reading Consultant

Grace Sussman, Ed.D.
    University of Northern Colorado

Project Editor: Mitch Rosin
Executive Editor: Linda Kwil
Image Coordinator: Barbara Gamache
Cover Design: Tracy Sainz
Interior Design: Linda Chandler
Cartography and Graphics: Tim Piotrowski

Reviewers

Jeffrey J. Johll
    K–12 District Social Studies Supervisor
    Dubuque Community School District
    Dubuque, Iowa

Eleanor Nangle
    Social Studies Instructor
    Chicago, Illinois

Judy Novack-Hirsch
    Social Studies Instructor
    New York, New York

Brian Silva
    Social Studies Instructor
    Long Beach, California

Jill Smith
    Social Studies Instructor
    Giddings, Texas

About the Cover

The images on the cover include (from left to right): Ferdinand Magellan, Abigail Adams, Abraham Lincoln, Sequoya, Sojourner Truth, George Washington.

Photo credits are on page 364.

Wright Group

ISBN: 0-07-704435-5 (Student Softcover Edition)
ISBN: 0-07-704434-7 (Student Softcover Edition with CD)
ISBN: 0-07-704513-0 (Student Hardcover Edition)
ISBN: 0-07-704514-9 (Student Hardcover Edition with CD)

Send all inquiries to:
Wright Group/McGraw-Hill
P.O. Box 812960
Chicago, IL 60681

Printed in the United States of America.

1 2 3 4 5 6 7 8 9 QUE 09 08 07 06

Contents

To the Student

This textbook is the first part of the story of the American people. It includes Stone Age hunters, Native Americans, European settlers, African slaves, farm families, townspeople, statesmen, and Civil War soldiers.

The American story is not just one story, but many stories woven together. It is the story of ordinary people as well as the rich and famous. It is the story of politicians, merchants, farmers, sailors, servants, and frontier hunters. It is the story of people from different ethnic groups, races, and cultures that helped make America the country it is today.

American History 1 is the story of individuals as well as groups of people. This book includes biographies of men and women who left a mark on American society. Each chapter also includes first-hand accounts by individuals who lived at the time. These accounts are called primary sources.

Americans have not always agreed. At times, they fought each other in attempt to find "the good life." Some did not believe the country needed its independence from England. At other times, they divided into political parties and argued over slavery. Their biggest disagreement ended in a civil war. Despite their differences, they worked together to create a strong nation.

While Americans are very different people, most have one thing in common. Most people, or their ancestors, came to America from somewhere else with the hope of finding a better life. Even Native Americans' ancestors came from other areas of the world. Slaves were the exceptions because they did not come on their own accord. Yet they, too, helped America become a better place in which to live.

The people included in this book helped shape the society in which you live. I hope it helps you understand that you, too, can help shape the America of the future.

Matthew T. Downey

UNIT 1

THE NEW WORLD

In 1492, Christopher Columbus and his three ships anchored off an island in the Caribbean. However, they were not the first Europeans to explore the Western Hemisphere. About the year 1000, Vikings sailed along the coast of Newfoundland. They were probably the first Europeans to reach North America, but they were not the first to explore it.

The first people to reach the Western Hemisphere probably came from Siberia across the Bering Strait some 20,000 to 30,000 years ago. They explored this land from Alaska to the tip of South America. Christopher Columbus was a newcomer.

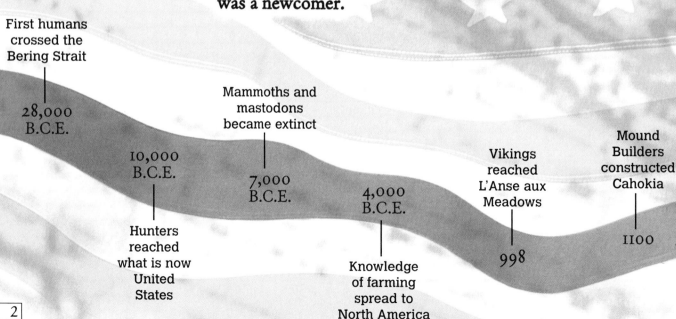

First humans crossed the Bering Strait

28,000 B.C.E.

10,000 B.C.E.

Hunters reached what is now United States

Mammoths and mastodons became extinct

7,000 B.C.E.

4,000 B.C.E.

Knowledge of farming spread to North America

Vikings reached L'Anse aux Meadows

998

Mound Builders constructed Cahokia

1100

How do scientists learn about early life in the Americas?

Why were spices so important to European merchants?

Why did European countries send explorers to the Americas?

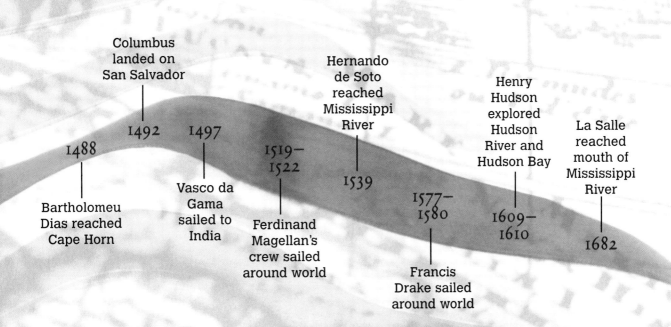

Columbus landed on San Salvador

Hernando de Soto reached Mississippi River

Henry Hudson explored Hudson River and Hudson Bay

La Salle reached mouth of Mississippi River

1488

1492

1497

1519–1522

1539

1577–1580

1609–1610

1682

Bartholomeu Dias reached Cape Horn

Vasco da Gama sailed to India

Ferdinand Magellan's crew sailed around world

Francis Drake sailed around world

Chapter 1

EARLY PEOPLE AND CULTURES

Getting Focused

Skim this chapter to predict what you will be learning.

- Read the lesson titles and subheadings.
- Look at the illustrations and read the captions.
- Examine the maps.
- Review the vocabulary words and terms.

Think about what you already know about the early people and cultures of North America. Write the questions you have about the topic before reading the chapter. Discuss your questions with a partner.

Early Hunters and Farmers

Thinking on Your Own

Read over the vocabulary. While you read, use each vocabulary word in a sentence of your own. Write the sentences in your notebook.

The first people to live in North America were big-game hunters. Many early settlers crossed the Bering Strait from Siberia around 20,000 to 30,000 years ago. They came to North America following herds of animals. Although the strait is now a body of water, during the last **Ice Age**, when portions of the oceans froze, it was a land bridge. The level of the Bering Sea was lower then because glaciers and ice sheets took up much of the world's water. In a few thousand years, descendants of these hunters occupied most of North and South America.

focus your reading

How did the first humans get to North America?

What animals did they hunt?

What kind of crops did early farmers raise?

vocabulary

Ice Age

archaeologists

hunters and gatherers

domesticate

Mound Builders

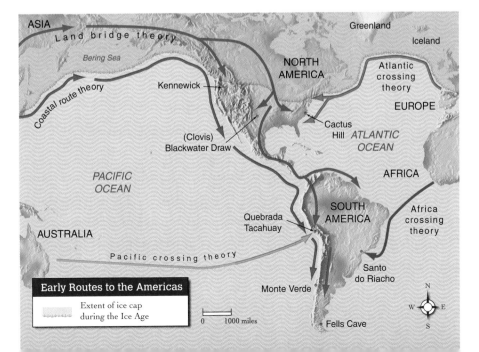

Early Routes to the Americas

Extent of ice cap during the Ice Age

0   1000 miles

Although many people came across the Bering Land Bridge, some scientists believe that people also came to the Americas from other parts of the world. Some scientists speculate that people came across the Pacific Ocean from Australia. Others believe groups of people came from Europe. Archaeological evidence even exists that shows some early settlers may have migrated from Africa.

Early people hunted mastodons with spears and rocks.

Hunters and Gatherers

Big-game hunters reached what is now the United States about 12,000 years ago. **Archaeologists**, scientists who study ancient people, have found stone spear points, or spear heads, in dozens of places. The points are mixed with the bones of mammoths, mastodons, and giant bison. In time, excessive hunting and climate changes wiped out these large animals. By about 9,000 years ago, the hunters had to rely mainly on elk, deer, and bison for meat. They were **hunters and gatherers**, as they also lived on the plants, roots, and seeds that they gathered.

Early Farmers

About 5,000 years ago, hunters and gatherers in Mexico learned to **domesticate**, or regulate the growth of, wild plants. Their main crops were corn, squash, and beans. By 2,000 years ago, knowledge of farming had spread north to what is now the United States. The Hohokam people in Arizona and the Anasazi, or Ancestral Puebloans, in Colorado had learned to grow these plants. People who lived east of the Mississippi River also took up farming.

Early North American spear heads

The Hohokam planted crops for food.

stop and think

On the basis of what you have read, write definitions for *Ice Age* and *archaeologist* in your own words. Then write one sentence about how these words are related to the topic of this chapter.

Mound Builders

The people east of the Mississippi that scientists have learned the most about are the **Mound Builders**. They are named after the mounds of earth that they built. These people were hunters and gatherers who also farmed. Farming allowed them to produce surplus, or extra, food. This let some people become priests, governors, and mound builders. The Adena people (3,000 to 1,200 years ago) built the Great Serpent Mound in Ohio. This snake-shaped mound extends for a quarter of a mile along the Ohio River. Later, the Hopewell people (2,300 to 1,300 years ago) built even larger mounds shaped like snakes, birds, and humans. Some mounds were used as burial places.

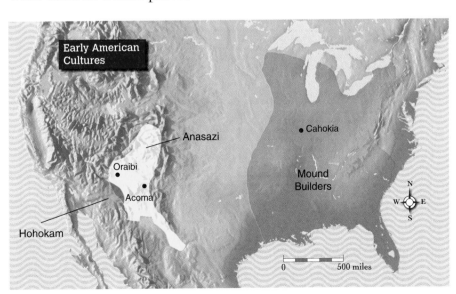

Early American Cultures

Anasazi

Oraibi

Acoma

Hohokam

Cahokia

Mound Builders

N
W   E
S

0   500 miles

Mound Builders known as the Mississippian people—900 years ago—built entire cities around earth mounds. The largest mounds were 100 feet high and would cover several present-day city blocks. On top they built temples, public buildings, and houses for important people. The largest mound complex was Cahokia in Illinois. It was a city of 20,000 to 30,000 people built around 1,000 mounds.

The Great Serpent Mound in Ohio

Putting It All Together

In your notebook, make a timeline that includes the dates 20,000; 9,000; 5,000; 2,000; and 900 years ago. Below each date explain how the people of each era spent their time. Then write a sentence or two that explains the timeline.

Biography

Ishi (1861?–1916)

In the summer of 1911, a lone Native American walked out of the hills of northern California. A crew of meat cutters working nearby saw him. They were puzzled, as they had not seen Native Americans in that part of the state for years.

When they asked the man what he wanted, they found that he did not speak English. The sheriff came and put him in handcuffs. He did not resist. "He had a big smile," one of the workmen remembered, "as much as to say, 'These are for me? Are you giving those to me?'"

The man in handcuffs was Ishi. He was believed to be the last Yahi person to survive in the backcountry of California. About fifty years old, Ishi was the last member of his family of four. The other three had recently died. Ishi could not survive on his own. He came out of the hills half-starved.

The Ishi story became front-page news. The local newspaper called him "the Wild Man of Deer Creek." The *San Francisco Examiner* described him as a "savage of the most primitive type." Alfred Kroeber, head of the University of California's Museum of Anthropology, offered Ishi a home.

Ishi spent the next five years living at the museum. He was amazed by light switches and other things most people took for granted. Getting used to large crowds took time. At a local bathing beach, he cried out, "Hansi salta!" or "So many white people!" Still, he adapted to civilized ways. He learned to eat at a table and sit on a chair. He liked doughnuts, ice cream sodas, and candy.

Although Ishi worked at the museum as a janitor, he also was a living museum exhibit. Visitors came to watch him make arrowheads and listen to him sing his native songs. He showed children how to catch birds with snares and trap fish by setting twigs close together in a stream bed. "He liked everybody, and everybody liked him," one of the professors said.

Ishi eventually became sick with tuberculosis. This was the leading killer disease of that time. He died of tuberculosis in 1916.

Woodland People

Thinking on Your Own

Read the Focus Your Reading questions. Make three columns in your notebook. Label them "Villages," "Food," and "Shelter." As you read, make notes in each column about what you learn about that topic.

When Europeans arrived 500 years ago, many cultures occupied North America. Many lived east of the Mississippi River in a region called the **Eastern Woodlands**. This was a vast region of forests, rivers, and lakes. The forests were broken by clearings and meadows where deer and other animals grazed. Wild plants, berries, and edible roots grew under the trees.

focus your reading

Why did Woodland People go to war?

What kind of food did they eat?

What kind of shelters did they build?

vocabulary

Eastern Woodlands

palisade

wigwams

longhouses

Groups and Villages

Several cultures lived in the Eastern Woodlands. The Iroquois were a powerful league, or confederation of groups, who lived in present-day New York State. The Powhatan Confederation occupied much of Virginia. The Miami, Shawnee, and smaller

The Iroquois used canoes as a means of travel.

groups hunted west of the Appalachian Mountains. Groups often were at war with one another. They fought to protect their hunting grounds and because warriors wanted to prove that they were brave. Sometimes war parties captured women and children, who were adopted into the tribe. The captives also helped replace losses a group had suffered during earlier raids.

The Woodland People lived in villages that usually were located along a creek or river. The streams provided water for everyday use and for canoe travel. Many villages were enclosed with a wall made of upright poles called a **palisade**. The wall helped protect the village from enemy raids.

stop and think

Discuss with a partner what Woodland People and people today have in common and what is different. Put your ideas on a chart labeled "Compare" and "Contrast." Write ideas for villages, food, and shelter.

Making a Living

The Woodland People lived mainly from the animals and plants of the forest. During the summer, women gathered seeds and berries. Men fished and left on hunting trips each autumn. The men hunted deer, bear, rabbits, and other small animals. Women did much of the work in the village. Each spring, they planted corn, beans, and squash known as "The Three Sisters." Women tended the fields and harvested the crops. They also cooked, made clothing, created pottery, and took care of young children.

Corn was a staple of the Woodland People's diet.

11

Clothing and Shelter

The Woodland People made clothing of woven grass or animal skins. Their clothing varied with the seasons. In summer, women wore wraparound skirts made of grass or deerskin. Men wore breechcloths fastened with a belt at their waists. During the winter, everyone wore robes made of animal skins.

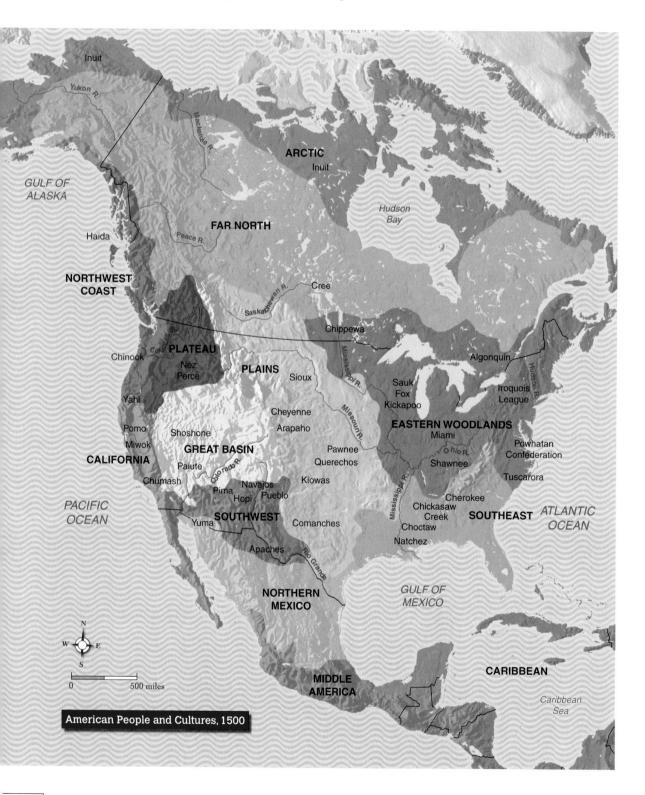

American People and Cultures, 1500

The wigwam provided shelter.

The types of shelters varied from group to group. Most groups built **wigwams** made of poles, reeds, and tree bark. Some were cone shaped; others were shaped like domes. In warmer climates, people built circular houses with roofs made of thatched grass. The Iroquois built **longhouses** with arched roofs. Each longhouse was large enough to house several families.

Longhouses were home to many families.

Putting It All Together

In Thinking on Your Own, you created a three-column list. Use the information from your list to write a short paragraph about the lives of the Woodland People.

Read a Primary Source

Coronado Describes the Querechos

In 1540, Spanish explorer Francisco Vásquez de Coronado marched north from Mexico with several hundred men. They were looking for the cities of gold that Indians said existed in the North. The following is his report about the Indians that he met on the plains in present-day Kansas.

reading for understanding

What did the Querechos use for food?

What kind of shelters did they live in?

How did they carry their belongings when they traveled?

"And after seventeen days' march I came to a settlement of Indians who are called Querechos, who travel around with these cows [bison], who do not plant, and who eat the raw flesh and drink the blood of the cows they kill, and they tan the skins of the cows, with which all the people of this country dress themselves here. They have little field tents made of the hide of the cows, tanned and greased, very well made, in which they live while they travel around near the cows, moving with these. They have dogs which they load, which carry their tents and poles and belongings."

G. P. Winship, *The Coronado Expedition, 1540–1542,* Smithsonian Institution, Bureau of American Ethnology, Fourteenth Report (1896).

Francisco Vásquez de Coronado explored Mexico.

Cultures of the West

Thinking on Your Own

Read the Focus Your Reading questions. What image comes to mind for each question? In your notebook, predict the answers before you read. After reading the lesson, compare your predictions with what you learned.

The land west of the Mississippi River was more thinly settled than regions in the East. It was a region of mountains, deserts, and plains, with few woodlands. The people who lived there had to adapt to many different environments. As a result, they developed more diverse ways of life than the eastern cultures.

> **focus your reading**
>
> How did horses change the Plains People's way of life?
>
> How did people farm in the desert?
>
> What food was most important to the Coastal People?
>
> **vocabulary**
>
> nomadic   arid
>
> Southwest   adobe
>
> irrigate

Plains Cultures

In 1540, the Spanish explorer Francisco Vásquez de Coronado found bands of **nomadic** people on the plains. The groups followed the bison herds. It was a hard life, as killing bison on foot was difficult. Two hundred years later the Apaches, Comanches, and Kiowas also hunted bison on the plains. But they hunted on horseback.

With horses bought or stolen from the Spanish, the Plains People adapted their way of life to create a new culture. With fast horses they killed all the bison they needed. These animals provided them with food, hides to make clothing and shelter, and bones to make tools. They lived in teepees that were easy to move as they followed the bison herds.

Bison were a source of food on the Great Plains.

Peoples of the Southwest

The oldest people of the **Southwest** are the Pima, Yuma, and Pueblo. They lived in the deserts and river valleys of southern California, Arizona, and New Mexico. Like their ancestors, the Hohokam and the Anasazi, these people were farmers. They had to **irrigate**, or bring water to their fields, as they lived in an **arid**, or dry, climate.

The Apaches and Navajos were newcomers to the Southwest. They migrated from Alaska and Canada some 600 years ago. The Apaches lived by hunting and gathering; the Navajos hunted and herded sheep. The Navajos later became widely known for their brightly colored wool blankets.

Their houses varied from group to group. Some lived in shelters made of woven grass. The Pueblo built large houses made of stone and **adobe**, or sun-dried bricks. They used ladders to enter the rooms through the roof.

stop and think

Imagine that you are a Plains person hunting on foot. During the hunt, you see hunters from another group hunting on horseback. Go back to your village and explain why you, too, need horses. Write the heading "Why We Need Horses" and use a number for each point.

Fishing for salmon provided food for the Chinook.

Cultures of the Far West

Several quite different groups lived in the Far West. The Piaute and Shoshone lived in the Great Basin, which is the desert country of Utah and Nevada. Most of the groups lived on or near the Pacific Coast. Among them were the Chinook, who lived in the forests near the mouth of the Columbia River. The Pomo and Chumash lived farther south along the California coast. Still other groups lived inland, such as the Miwok of the San Juaquin Valley of California.

The groups of the Far West lived quite different lives. The Coastal People depended heavily on fish. Salmon from the Columbia River was an important item in the Chinook diet. The groups farther south fished in the ocean with nets and gathered mussels and clams. Cultures living in the interior hunted deer and rabbits, and gathered acorns and grass seed.

The kinds of houses they built depended on local resources. The Chinook, who lived in the forests, built longhouses made of wooden planks. Each longhouse sheltered several families. The groups farther south lived in shelters made of thatched grass and reeds. Those living further inland and in the Great Basin also lived in reed huts and shelters covered with animal skins.

Putting It All Together

Create a Venn diagram with two interlocking circles. Label the circles "Southwest" and "Far West." Discuss the similarities and differences between the cultures with a partner. Then list differences in the outer circles and similarities in the overlapping area.

Chapter Summary

The first humans to live in North America arrived during the last **Ice Age**, some 20,000 to 30,000 years ago. They were **hunters and gatherers** who crossed a land bridge from Siberia. **Archaeologists** have discovered these hunters' stone spear points at dozens of places in the United States. About 5,000 years ago, these people learned how to **domesticate** plants. The early farmers who lived east of the Mississippi River are called the **Mound Builders**.

Many cultures lived in North America when Europeans arrived about 500 years ago. Most lived in the **Eastern Woodlands** east of the Mississippi River. Most groups built shelters called **wigwams** made of poles, reeds, and tree bark. The Iroquois built **longhouses** with arched roofs. They surrounded their shelters with **palisades**.

People also lived west of the Mississippi River. Some were **nomadic** bison hunters, but people of the **Southwest** were mostly farmers. Living in an **arid** desert climate, they had to **irrigate** their fields. The Pueblo lived in stone and **adobe** houses. Other tribes built shelters made of woven grass.

Most people of the Far West lived near the Pacific Coast. These coastal groups depended on fishing and hunting for food. Groups that were farther south lived in shelters made of thatched grass and reeds.

Chapter Review

1   In your notebook, explain how this chapter changed or confirmed your ideas about early American people and cultures.

2   Make a list of the vocabulary words for this chapter. Then arrange the words into categories. Label the categories. In two or three sentences explain why you chose these categories.

3   Create a two-column chart in your notebook. In the column on the left list the most important points made in this chapter. Use only one or two words for each. In the right-hand column write a brief explanation of each point.

Skill Builder

Primary and Secondary Sources

Historical writings consist of primary and secondary sources. A primary source is any firsthand account, document, artifact, photograph, or other piece of evidence created in the past. Secondary sources are accounts written later that are based on primary sources.

Coronado's Journey

In May 1541, Francisco Vásquez de Coronado led an army of Spanish explorers to the Great Plains. He kept a journal during the trip. An excerpt from this primary source is included on page 14.

In 1949, Herbert E. Bolton published a history of Coronado's journey, *Coronado: Knight of Pueblos and Plains.* To write this secondary source, Bolton relied heavily on Coronado's journal. The excerpt on the right is from Bolton's history.

"Soon after reaching the great herd of buffaloes . . . [Coronado's men] first encountered the interesting people who, with their families and all their belongings, gypsy-like, followed the buffaloes for a living. . . . The life of these nomads, who were apparently a branch of the great Apache people so conspicuous in the same region at a later date, was graphically pictured by members of the expedition. These wandering natives, whose physique Coronado described as 'the best . . . of any I have seen in the Indies,' were Querechos. . . . They lived with and off the buffalo, and by this animal their whole life was regulated."

Herbert E. Bolton, *Coronado: Knight of Pueblos and Plains* (New York: McGraw-Hill Book Company, Inc., 1949).

Compare the excerpt from Coronado's journal on page 14 with the one above from Bolton's history.

1 How do we know that Bolton read Coronado's journal?

2 To what extent is Bolton's conclusion in the last sentence based on the journal?

3 What information did Bolton add that was not part of Coronado's journal?

Chapter

2 European Explorers

Getting Focused

Skim this chapter to predict what you will be learning.

- Read the lesson titles and subheadings.
- Look at the illustrations and read the captions.
- Examine the maps.
- Review the vocabulary words and terms.

Some discoveries happen by accident. People find things while looking for something else. Recall a time when you found an item while searching for some other thing. Discuss this with a partner. Skim this chapter to see what that experience might have in common with European exploration. In your notebook, write one connection that you see.

Portuguese and Spanish Exploration

Thinking on Your Own

Read the Focus Your Reading questions. In your notebook write "Route to the Indies." As you read, make a list of all the explorers who looked for a route to the Indies.

In the late 1400s, Europeans searched for a new route to the **Indies**. The Indies, as East Asia and the islands of Indonesia were called, was the source of spices, gold, jewels, and perfume. They were known as the Spice Islands. The Arab merchants who controlled this trade charged high prices for their goods. Italian merchants bought the goods from the Arab merchants and shipped them to Europe. They also charged a fee for their service. People in Western Europe looked for ways to get these items at lower costs.

focus your reading

Why did Europeans look for a new route to the Indies?

What route did the Portuguese find?

Was Columbus's plan to sail west realistic?

vocabulary

Indies	cartographer
navigate	strait
caravel	

Marco Polo helped establish the spice trade.

Portuguese Explorers

The Portuguese were the first to set out to reach the Spice Islands by sailing around Africa's Cape of Good Hope. A Portuguese prince, Henry the Navigator, took the lead. He set up a school to help sea captains learn to **navigate** the African coast. In 1488, a Portuguese sea captain named Bartholomeu Dias reached the tip of Africa, known as the Cape of Good Hope. Nine years later, Vasco da Gama followed that route and sailed on to the west coast of India. In a short time, Portuguese ships reached Asia and the Spice Islands by sailing east. This was, however, a long and dangerous trip.

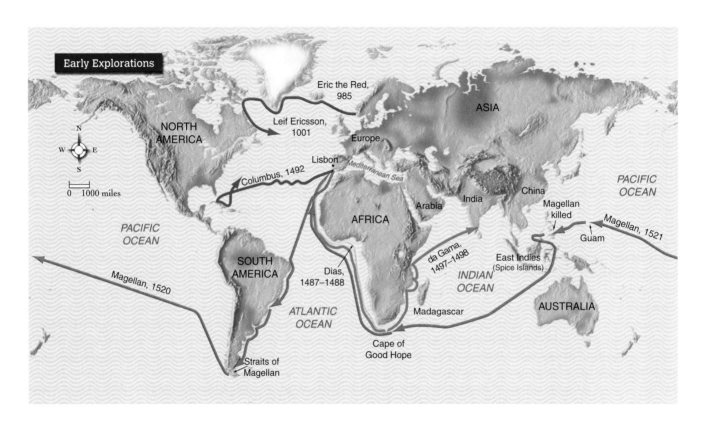

Early Explorations

Christopher Columbus

A sea captain from Genoa, Italy, named Christopher Columbus thought he could reach the Indies by sailing west. This route had never been tried. He persuaded King Ferdinand and Queen Isabella of Spain to finance his voyage. In August 1492, Columbus sailed from Spain with three ships: the *Niña*, the *Pinta*, and the *Santa Maria*. By his calculations, the distance between Europe and Asia was about 2,500 miles. That was well within the sailing range of a Spanish **caravel**, his choice of

King Ferdinand and Queen Isabella of Spain

ship. In fact, the actual distance to Asia is about 10,000 miles. Columbus miscalculated the length of his voyage by thousands of miles.

After two months at sea, the crew demanded that Columbus sail for home. He agreed to do so, if they did not find land within three days. On the third day, October 12, 1492, a lookout sighted land. It was an island in the Caribbean Sea that Columbus named San Salvador. Columbus was certain that he had reached the Indies. Until this time, no European, other than the Vikings, had set foot on North and South America. Columbus called the people he met on San Salvador "Indios," a name that later became "Indians."

Columbus made a total of four trips to the Caribbean. He explored its islands and the coast of South America. Contrary to popular belief, he never touched the land of what is now the United States. He died in 1506, convinced that these lands were part of Asia instead of an unknown hemisphere.

Christopher Columbus

He and his crew, however, were not the first Europeans to reach the Western Hemisphere. About the year 1000, a Viking named Leif Ericsson had sailed from Iceland to the coast of Newfoundland. The Vikings established a settlement at what is now the town of L'Anse aux Meadows, Newfoundland. Columbus knew nothing about that voyage or the Viking settlement.

Amerigo Vespucci and Vasco Nuñez de Balboa

Amerigo Vespucci was the first European to realize that Columbus had discovered a continent. He reached that conclusion in 1499, after exploring the coast of South America for Portugal. A **cartographer**, or mapmaker, later named the entire hemisphere America, after Amerigo Vespucci. Vasco Nuñez de Balboa, a Spanish explorer, was the first European to find the ocean that separates the Americas from Asia. In 1513, from the top of a hill in Panama, he saw the "South Sea." We know it today as the Pacific Ocean.

stop and think

In your notebook write a statement that describes each explorer's route to the Indies. Compare your statements with those of a partner.

Ferdinand Magellan

In 1519, Ferdinand Magellan set out to explore the Pacific Ocean. He crossed the Atlantic and sailed down the east coast of South America. At the tip of South America, known as Cape Horn, he discovered a **strait** that led to the Pacific. It is now called the Strait of Magellan. He sailed west to the Philippine Islands, where he was killed during a battle between two local groups. His crew sailed on to Asia. When they arrived in Spain in 1522, they were the first people to sail around the world.

Magellan's fleet off the tip of South America

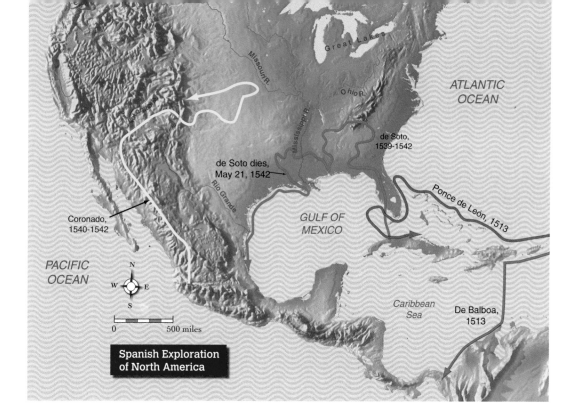

Spanish Exploration of North America

Later Explorers

Thereafter, Spain sent other explorers to learn more about the Americas. Juan Ponce de León explored the coast of Florida. He also stopped to search for the Fountain of Youth, a story of legend. In 1539, Hernando de Soto set out from Florida with 600 men to explore what is now the southern United States. They were the first Europeans to reach the Mississippi River. Francisco Coronado later explored the American Southwest.

Putting It All Together

Columbus and other explorers made several mistakes in their calculations about getting to the Indies. Find three mistakes they made and write them in your notebook. Compare your list with a partner.

Hernando de Soto

Read a Primary Source

Columbus Describes the Caribbean People

On October 12, 1492, Christopher Columbus landed on an island in the Caribbean. In the following journal entry, he describes the first people that he saw. Although Columbus and later settlers treated the local people harshly, their first meeting was welcoming.

reading for understanding

Why did Columbus give the people gifts?

How did they respond?

How did they react to European weapons?

❝I, that we might form great friendship, for I knew that they were a people who could be more easily freed and converted to our holy faith by love than by force, gave to some of them red caps, and glass beads to put round their necks, and many other things of little value. . . .

"They afterwards come to the ship's boats where we were, swimming and bringing us parrots, cotton threads in skeins, darts, and many other things. . . . In fine, they took all, and gave what they had with good will. . . .

"They are very well made, with very handsome bodies, and very good countenances. . . . They neither carry nor know anything of arms, for I showed them swords, and they took them by the blade and cut themselves through ignorance.❞

J. Franklin Jameson, ed., *Original Narratives of Early American History* (1909).

The English Search for a Northwest Passage

Thinking on Your Own

Read the Focus Your Reading questions. Think about the term *northwest passage*. Imagine that you are an English explorer in 1500 looking out at the Atlantic Ocean. Where might a northwest passage be located? Why would finding it be important to you? Write the answers to these two questions in your notebook.

News that Columbus had reached the Indies quickly reached England. King Henry VII did not want England to be shut out of the Indies. The result was a series of English voyages of exploration.

focus your reading

Why were John Cabot's voyages important to England?

What does the term *northwest passage* mean?

How were the "sea dogs" a different kind of explorer?

vocabulary

claimed

northwest passage

sea dogs

plundered

John Cabot

John Cabot was the first explorer to sail in search of land for England. Cabot believed he could find a shorter route to the Indies by sailing directly west from England. Henry VII gave him a small ship and a crew of eighteen men. In 1497, Cabot sailed to Newfoundland, a land which he **claimed**, or took, for England. Highly pleased, the king sent Cabot out again in 1498. On this voyage, he explored the coast of North America as far south as Delaware. He, too, thought he had reached the coast of China.

John Cabot

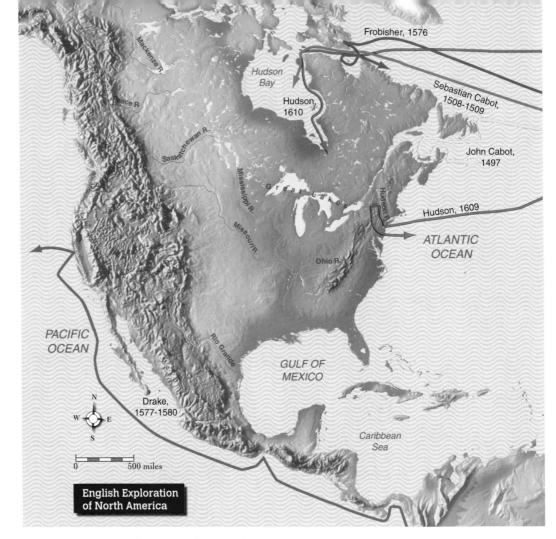

Frobisher, 1576

Mackenzie R.

Hudson Bay

Peace R.

Hudson, 1610

Saskatchewan R.

Sebastian Cabot, 1508-1509

John Cabot, 1497

Columbia R.

Mississippi R.

Great Lakes

Hudson R.

Hudson, 1609

ATLANTIC OCEAN

Missouri R.

Ohio R.

PACIFIC OCEAN

Rio Grande

GULF OF MEXICO

N W E S

Drake, 1577-1580

Caribbean Sea

0   500 miles

English Exploration of North America

Searching for the Northwest Passage

The next British explorers had a more definite purpose in mind. They knew that Columbus had not reached the Indies.

Explorers searched for a northwest passage during the sixteenth century.

They set out to find a **northwest passage**, a direct route to Asia through North America. In 1509, Sebastian Cabot, John Cabot's son, looked for it along the east coast of Canada. He claimed to have found the opening. Instead, he probably found the inlet to Hudson Bay. Later, in 1576, Martin Frobisher also searched in vain for a passage through the

In your notebook draw three interlocking circles with a common middle. Label the circles "Sebastian Cabot," "Martin Frobisher," and "Henry Hudson." In each circle write one interesting fact about that explorer. In the common middle write what the three had in common.

stop and think

continent. He returned with his ship loaded with ore that looked like silver. It turned out to be worthless. In 1610, Henry Hudson thought he had found the Northwest Passage. It was only a large inland sea that later was named Hudson Bay.

Francis Drake's Voyage Around the World

The reign of Queen Elizabeth I (1558–1603) produced a new kind of English explorer. These English **"sea dogs" plundered**, or stole from, Spanish ships while exploring new territory. The most daring of all was Francis Drake. Queen Elizabeth helped Drake outfit a fleet of ships for a voyage around the world. He crossed the Atlantic in 1577 and sailed through the Strait of Magellan. Then he sailed north to raid Spanish colonial towns along the Pacific coast of South America. After capturing a Spanish treasure ship near Panama, he sailed up the coast of Mexico and California. He was looking for a western entrance to the Northwest Passage. Drake arrived back in England in 1580. He spent nearly three years traveling 36,000 miles around the world, but did not find a shortcut to the Indies.

Francis Drake and the "sea dogs"

Putting It All Together

Sailors often told stories about their adventures at sea. Imagine that you are an English seaman who sailed with Martin Frobisher (1576) or Francis Drake (1577–1580). Write a story about your adventures. Include facts such as time of year, weather, conditions at sea.

Biography

Henry Hudson (1565–1611)

Few names are as prominent on the map of North America as Hudson. The longest river in New York State is the Hudson River. Hudson Bay is North America's largest inland body of water. The 500-mile strait leading to it is called Hudson Strait. The name is there because of Henry Hudson's explorations to find a northwest passage to the Indies.

Little is known about Henry Hudson's youth. Hudson probably spent his earlier years as a cabin boy on a ship. Hudson's grandfather helped found the Muscovy Company. This company, made up of merchants in London, traded with Russia for furs, hides, and lumber.

In April 1607, the Muscovy Company sent Hudson to search for a passage to the Indies north of Greenland. He found polar bears, whales, and icebergs, but no ice-free route to the Indies.

The next year the company asked Hudson to look for a "Northeast Passage." He sailed north and east from England to the Barents Sea, searching for a way around Russia to China. Icebergs there forced him to turn back.

In 1609, Henry Hudson tried the northeast route again. This time his voyage was financed by Holland. Again, the icebergs stopped him. He took a long way home, crossing the Atlantic to explore the coast of North America. On this leg of the voyage, he sailed into a long waterway. What he hoped was the Northwest Passage turned out to be the Hudson River.

In 1610, London merchants again sent Hudson to search for the northwest passage. This time he sailed to the icy north coast of Canada. Hudson found a long waterway—now Hudson Strait—that led inland to a huge bay, today called Hudson Bay. Then the ice closed in, stranding the ship for the winter. In the spring, the starving crew refused to go further. They set Hudson, his son John, and seven others adrift in a small boat. The crew returned to England, leaving the men to die.

French Explorers in North America

Thinking on Your Own

Read the Focus Your Reading questions. Then look at the map and pictures included in this lesson. What clues do they give you about French explorers in North America? Write three predictions in your notebook. Compare your predictions with those of a partner.

As explorers of North America, the French were latecomers. In 1492, France, not Spain, was Europe's most powerful nation. The French kings kept their attention focused on Europe. For a hundred years they spent little time or money exploring new lands. When France finally did take an interest in North America, its explorers staked out a vast **empire**.

focus your reading

What did early English and French explorers have in common?

What was Champlain's goal as an explorer?

How did La Salle's explorations benefit France?

vocabulary

empire   missionary

trading posts   Louisiana

Verrazzano and Cartier

The first French explorers set out to find a water route to the Indies. Like the early English sea captains, they hoped to find a northwest passage. In 1523, Giovanni da Verrazzano, an Italian living in France, led the first expedition. He explored the coastline from North Carolina to Newfoundland, but found no passageway. From 1534 to 1541, Jacques Cartier made three voyages to North America. On his second voyage in 1535, he sailed up the St. Lawrence River. That journey established France's claim to eastern Canada. Cartier also failed in his attempt to find the Northwest Passage.

Giovanni da Verrazzano

French Exploration of North America

Samuel de Champlain

The voyages of Samuel de Champlain opened a new chapter in French exploration. The main purpose of his eleven voyages (1603–1635) was to expand the fur trade with the people of America. The French exchanged brass kettles, iron pots, and knives for beaver, fox, bear, and wolf skins. Fur was used to make men's felt hats, to trim coats, and to make warm covers. Champlain explored the interior of Canada for places to set up **trading posts**. He also discovered a huge lake, which he named Lake Champlain.

Samuel de Champlain

stop and think

Create an ad for a French trading company that is trying to attract families to move to Canada. Include the advantages and rewards of making the move to Canada. You may have to do additional research to find specific information about different settlements.

Later French Explorers

Other French explorers followed Champlain's lead. Sieur de La Salle explored the Ohio River valley, claiming it for France. A French trader, Louis Joliet, and a **missionary** named Jacques Marquette traveled west to Lake Michigan. They also

Sieur de La Salle claimed land for France.

paddled down the Mississippi River to present-day Arkansas. In 1682, La Salle journeyed all the way down the Mississippi River, reaching the Gulf of Mexico. He claimed the entire Mississippi River valley for France, along with all the rivers that flowed into it. He named this vast area **Louisiana**, in honor of King Louis XIV.

Putting It All Together

With a partner review the sections describing the explorations of Verrazzano, Cartier, Champlain, and La Salle. Write questions about the explorers and quiz each other. Write the questions and the answers to them in your notebook.

Jacques Marquette

Chapter Summary

In the late 1400s, Europeans tried to find a new route to the **Indies**. They wanted more control over the spice trade with that region. A Portuguese prince, Henry the Navigator, helped explorers learn to **navigate** around the tip of Africa. In 1492, Columbus sailed from Spain in three **caravels** to an island in the Caribbean Sea. He thought he had reached the Indies. In 1519, Ferdinand Magellan found a way to the Indies through the **strait** south of South America. These explorations helped **cartographers** map the hemisphere.

England also wanted to find a route to the Indies. In 1497, John Cabot **claimed** the coast of North America for England. He thought he had reached the Indies. The English explorers who came after him knew better. They searched for a **northwest passage** through North America to Asia. Later, English **"sea dogs" plundered** Spanish ships while exploring land in the Western Hemisphere.

French explorers also looked for a route to the Indies. Jacques Cartier explored the St. Lawrence River and claimed land for the French **empire**. Samuel de Champlain established **trading posts** to sell furs to help pay the cost of his journeys. The French were the first Europeans to explore the Ohio River valley. A **missionary** named Marquette explored part of the Mississippi River. Later, La Salle claimed the river valley for France, naming it **Louisiana** for King Louis XIV.

Chapter Review

1 Create a crossword puzzle using key words from this chapter. Connect the words horizontally and vertically where they share the same letters. Write definitions in your own words under the puzzle.

2 Imagine that you are listening to a conversation. Write several lines of dialogue between the French traders and Native Americans. Keep in mind what they exchanged for the furs.

3 Create a newspaper ad for a merchant who has various items from the Indies for sale.

Skill Builder

Reading Maps

Maps link history to geography. They show where on the earth's surface past events and developments took place. Maps are valuable sources of information. However, to read the information one must understand the language and symbols of maps. These include the following:

- **Map Title.** It tells you what kind of information the map includes.

- **Map Labels.** They are words or names that identify places on the map.

- **Map Symbols.** The lines, arrows, dots, and icons present information.

- **Map Key or Legend.** The explanatory list, usually placed in a box, helps you interpret the information.

- **Compass Rose.** This indicator helps you find directions on the map.

- **Distance Scale.** It indicates the scale in miles on the map. Maps are drawn to different scales.

Use the map to answer the following questions:

1 What geographical area does this map include?

2 What part of North America did the first French explorer visit?

3 In what direction did Cartier sail when he explored the St. Lawrence River?

4 Who first explored the Mississippi River and in what year?

5 About how far did Joliet and Marquette travel down the Mississippi River?

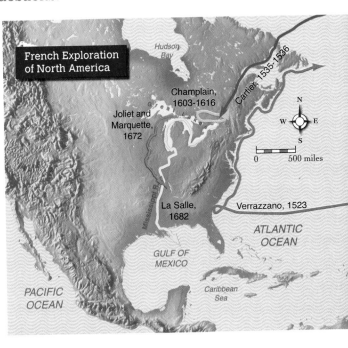

French Exploration of North America

2 UNIT

EUROPEAN COLONIZATION

For Europeans, the Western Hemisphere was a land of opportunity. It attracted people with many different ways of life. Soldiers came to conquer native empires. Adventurers came looking for gold. Priests arrived to Christianize the local people. Traders came to exchange goods with them. Farmers wanted their land. For whatever reasons the Europeans came, they came as colonists. They came to stay.

The Europeans divided up the Western Hemisphere among themselves. The Spanish and Portuguese, who were the first to arrive, staked out Mexico and Central and South America. English, French, and Dutch colonists took what was left. They colonized North America. Very few bothered to ask the local people for permission to occupy their land.

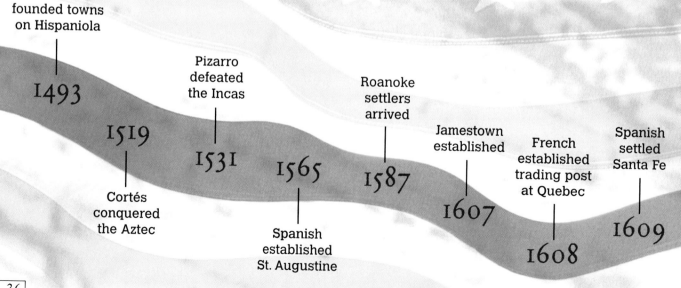

Columbus founded towns on Hispaniola
1493

Cortés conquered the Aztec
1519

Pizarro defeated the Incas
1531

Spanish established St. Augustine
1565

Roanoke settlers arrived
1587

Jamestown established
1607

French established trading post at Quebec
1608

Spanish settled Santa Fe
1609

What opportunities did the French and the Dutch find in North America?

How were the English colonies different from others?

What American empires did Spain conquer?

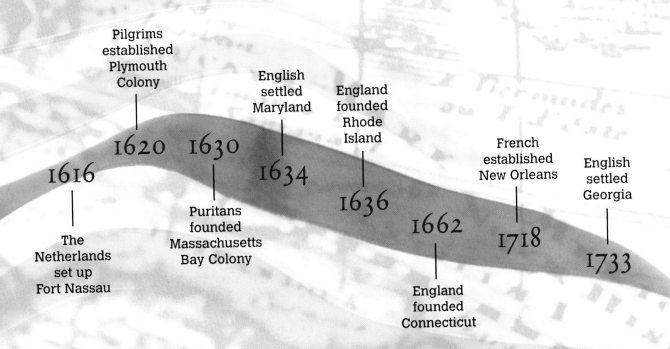

Pilgrims established Plymouth Colony

1620

English settled Maryland

1634

England founded Rhode Island

1636

French established New Orleans

1718

English settled Georgia

1733

1616

The Netherlands set up Fort Nassau

1630

Puritans founded Massachusetts Bay Colony

1662

England founded Connecticut

Chapter 3

Spanish, French, and Dutch Colonies

Getting Focused

Skim this chapter to predict what you will be learning.

- Read the lesson titles and subheadings.
- Look at the illustrations and read the captions.
- Examine the maps.
- Review the vocabulary words and terms.

Pick a photo from this chapter that you find interesting and examine it closely. What questions does it raise about the Spanish, French, or Dutch colonies? Share your ideas with a partner. Write a sentence in your notebook summarizing your ideas.

The Spanish Colonies

Thinking on Your Own

Read the Focus Your Reading questions. What do you expect to learn from this lesson? Write one sentence that predicts what you will learn. Then write the vocabulary words in your notebook. As you read each vocabulary word in the lesson, write a definition in your notebook.

Spain took the lead in establishing **colonies** in the Western Hemisphere. Columbus's discovery gave Spain a one-hundred-year head start. Its only rival was Portugal. Portugal established a colony in Brazil.

focus your reading

How did Spanish colonists treat the Native Americans?

How did Spain gain control over Mexico and Peru?

How did American colonies make Spain a rich nation?

vocabulary

colonies   smallpox

founded

The Spanish in the Caribbean

The first Spanish explorers set up colonies in the Caribbean. On his second voyage in 1493, Columbus brought 1,200 soldiers and colonists with him. They **founded**, or established, the towns of Isabela and Santo Domingo on the island of Hispaniola. Later explorers set up other colonies in the Caribbean.

Far from Europe, these first settlements struggled to survive. Most of the settlers were soldiers. They made slaves of the local people. The slaves did the hardest work. But the local people died by the thousands. They had no immunity to **smallpox** and other European diseases.

Diseases such as smallpox devastated many Native American groups.

When Columbus arrived at Hispaniola in 1493, about 250,000 native people lived on the island. Only fifty years later, none were left. The Spanish settlers imported slaves from Africa to replace local laborers.

Spanish Colonies in Mexico

From its base in the Caribbean, Spain set out to gain control of Mexico. The powerful Aztec emperor, Montezuma, ruled Mexico. In 1519, Hernando Cortés invaded the mainland with an army of 500 men. He captured the city of Tenochtitlan with the help of groups opposed to the Aztecs. Montezuma was killed in the fighting. Cortés emptied the Aztec treasure houses and sent the gold and silver back to Spain.

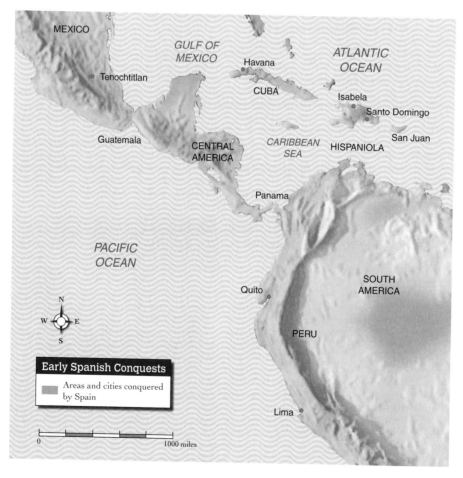

MEXICO

GULF OF MEXICO

ATLANTIC OCEAN

Havana

Tenochtitlan

CUBA

Isabela

Santo Domingo

Guatemala

CENTRAL AMERICA

CARIBBEAN SEA

HISPANIOLA

San Juan

Panama

PACIFIC OCEAN

Quito

SOUTH AMERICA

PERU

Early Spanish Conquests

Areas and cities conquered by Spain

Lima

0   1000 miles

Cortés's soldiers remained in Mexico as colonists. Spain gave individuals control over local villages. They put the local people to work as farmers. They raised cattle and mined silver. Spanish colonists in Mexico depended on the forced labor of local inhabitants.

Hernando Cortés meeting Aztec leader Montezuma

The Spanish in South America

Spain next turned its attention to South America. In 1531, Francisco Pizarro led a Spanish army against the Incas. The Inca People controlled a large empire in Peru. Pizarro captured the Incan ruler, Atahualpa, and demanded gold and silver in exchange for his life. After collecting twenty tons of precious metal, Pizarro murdered Atahualpa. The Spanish then destroyed the empire and took all the wealth from its cities.

Francisco Pizarro burning Incan chief Atahualpa

Spain sent colonists to settle in South America. They used the land for cattle ranches and took over the Incan silver mines. As in Mexico, the colonists forced the local people to do most of the work. In one silver mine in Peru, 58,000 locals worked as slaves. Silver shipped from Peru and Mexico made Spain the richest nation in Europe.

Putting It All Together

Create a three-column chart in your notebook. Label the columns "Spanish in the Caribbean," "Spanish in Mexico," and "Spanish in South America." In each column describe three or four things the Spanish did in each place.

Biography

Hernando Cortés (1485?–1547)

In August 1519, Hernando Cortés marched into Mexico to attack the Aztec Empire. He brought with him about 500 Spanish soldiers, seventy-five sailors, sixteen horses, and a few small cannons. His goal seemed impossible. To reach the Aztec capital, Tenochtitlan, Cortés had to lead his men through 250 miles of unknown territory. Waiting for him were Montezuma, the Aztec emperor, and thousands of warriors. However, Cortés did not doubt for a moment that he would conquer the Aztec Empire. The only question was how.

Cortés was a risk taker. He had left Spain in 1504, at age nineteen, looking for adventure. He went to the Caribbean. There he helped conquer Cuba, receiving land and slaves as his reward. He discovered gold on his property, but he wanted more. On a voyage across the Gulf of Mexico, he found local people wearing gold jewelry. It came, they said, from the land of the Aztec. So, with men and ships provided by the governor of Cuba, Cortés was determined to conquer the Aztec.

On his march through the mountains, Cortés discovered how to do it. Groups that the Aztec had conquered were ready to rebel against them. The emperor Montezuma had taxed them heavily, taking their corn and gold. He also demanded people for human sacrifice. Cortés reached Tenochtitlan with thousands of native warriors at his side.

The emperor opened the city to Cortés, believing that he was the Aztec's white god, Quetzelcoatl. Once inside, Cortés took Montezuma prisoner. When the Aztec attacked, the Spaniards and their local allies destroyed the city. Montezuma died in the fighting. With Montezuma's gold, Cortés built a Spanish city, Mexico City, in its place. He stayed there as the new and very wealthy governor of Mexico.

Spanish Settlements in North America

Thinking on Your Own

Spanish officials in Mexico thought of North America as a "borderland." What kind of borderlands exist today? Find the word in the Glossary and write a definition of *borderland* from your point of view.

N orth of Mexico were the **Spanish borderlands**. This vast area extended from Florida west to California. It was a poor country that had no gold or silver mines. Even so, Spanish officials in the late 1500s began to colonize this region. They needed to make a **barrier** in Florida against English and French settlers. They also wanted to bring Christianity to the native people who lived in this region.

focus your reading

Why did the Spanish set up a colony in Florida?

How did the Pueblo react to the Spanish settlements?

How were missions different from other settlements?

vocabulary

Spanish borderlands

barrier

imposed

missions

empire

The Spanish in Florida

In 1565, the Spanish built a fort and a town at St. Augustine on the Atlantic coast of Florida. It is the oldest continuous settlement in what is now the United States. The colony was a barrier in the east. French and British attacks upon the fort made it one of the most dangerous colonies. Not many farmers settled in St. Augustine. Spanish officials even had to import food for the soldiers at the fort.

St. Augustine was established by Spain in 1565.

Spanish Settlements in New Mexico

To protect Mexico's northern border and to Christianize the local people, Spanish officials decided to settle New Mexico. In 1598, Juan de Oñate led 400 settlers north from Mexico. They settled in present-day New Mexico and began farming. In 1609, Spanish officials founded the town of Santa Fe. From Santa Fe, colonial governors **imposed** Spanish rule over New Mexico's Pueblo Indians.

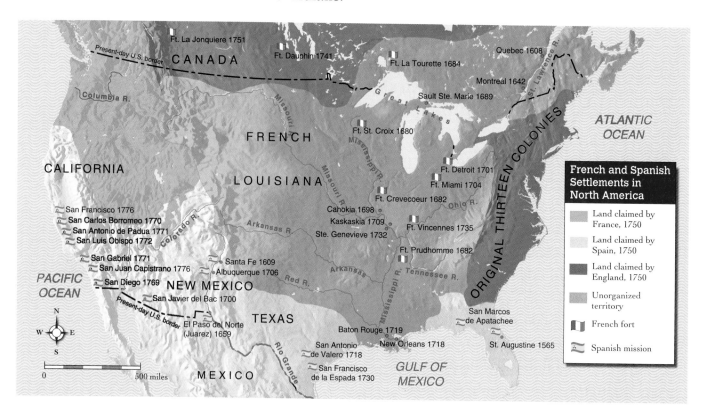

The early governors treated the Native Americans badly. They took away the Pueblo's corn to feed the settlers. They forced the Pueblo to weave cloth. Then, the governor sold the cloth and kept the money.

In 1680, the Pueblo rebelled. They killed several hundred Spanish colonists. They also drove the remaining colonists out of New Mexico. The Spanish returned in 1692. This time they stayed. They also realized that they had to treat the Pueblo more fairly.

stop and think

Make a list of the different kinds of Spanish settlements in North America. Add to the list as you read. Describe each in a sentence or two.

San Miguel was established as a Spanish mission in 1797.

Spanish Missions in Arizona and California

The first Spanish settlers in present-day Arizona and California were Catholic priests. They built **missions** instead of towns. In 1687, Father Eusebio Kino founded eight missions in Arizona. Almost a hundred years later, Father Junipero Serra set up more than twenty missions in California. The Spanish also built mission churches in New Mexico and Texas.

Each mission included a church, living quarters for several priests and soldiers, and shelters for the Native Americans. The priests invited the local people to live at the mission. They tried to convert those who came to Christianity. They taught the converts how to farm and raise cattle. They wanted the Native Americans to live near the missions so they would not return to their old ways. The Spanish priests often sent soldiers out to bring back those who tried to escape.

By 1600, Spain's **empire** extended nearly eight thousand miles from California to the tip of South America. It was the largest empire in the western world since the Roman Empire.

Putting It All Together

Imagine that you are a Native American living in the Spanish borderlands during the 1680s. What would you say to a Spanish settler or priest about the Spaniards' treatment of your people? How would you feel about being converted to Christianity? Write your thoughts in your notebook.

French and Dutch Colonies

Thinking on Your Own

Read this section with a partner. Decide whether you will read aloud together, take turns, or read silently. At the end of each paragraph, each partner must ask a question, say a thought, or state an opinion about the French and Dutch colonies. Write one of your ideas in your notebook.

France and the Netherlands were latecomers in colonizing America. Both had focused their attention elsewhere. The French were involved in European politics and wars. The Dutch were busy making money. The Netherlands produced many wealthy merchant families. Most of the colonists that France and the Netherlands finally sent overseas were traders rather than farmers. The French also sent priests to spread Christianity to the local people.

focus your reading

Why were France and the Netherlands late in establishing colonies?

What was the chief purpose of French settlements?

Why did the Dutch establish colonies along the Hudson River?

vocabulary

New France

New Netherland

New Amsterdam

patroon

The French in Canada

French colonies in North America were closely linked to the fur trade. The first French settlements in Canada were at Quebec (1608) and Montreal (1611). These were missions and fur trading posts. The French government tried to attract farmers to Canada. Very few farmers came to the colonies. Canada had to import food from Europe. The pioneers of **New France** were fur traders and priests, not farmers.

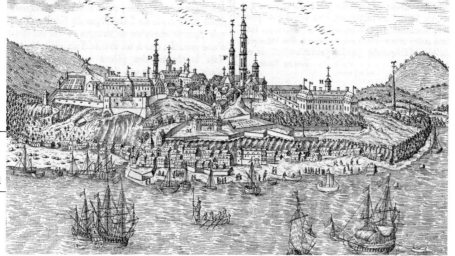

Early French settlement of Montreal

French fur traders set out in their canoes each year for Algonquin and Huron villages. At times they helped those groups fight their enemy, the Iroquois. The traders spent the winter swapping trade goods for beaver, mink, and otter pelts. In the spring, they paddled back to Quebec or Montreal with canoes filled with furs.

The French in the Mississippi Valley

The French officials also wanted to control the Mississippi River valley. This region was rich in animal pelts. They also wanted to create a barrier to protect against Spain's northward expansion from Mexico. In 1682, Sieur de la Salle had claimed the entire valley for France. But words were not enough to stop the Spanish.

stop and think

Write two or three sentences that describe New France. Include details about the early settlers.

The French lined the Mississippi River with Catholic missions and forts. In 1699, they built Fort Detroit at the

Quebec in the 17th century

upper end of the Mississippi valley. They built a fort and missions in present-day Illinois. They also established forts near the mouth of the Mississippi. The largest settlement was the town of New Orleans. It was settled on the lower Mississippi River in 1718.

New Netherland was settled in 1626.

The Dutch in New Netherland

The Dutch also wanted a share of the fur trade. Henry Hudson's voyage of 1609 gave the Netherlands a claim to present-day New York State and part of New Jersey. In 1616, the Dutch set up a trading post at Fort Nassau on the Hudson River. They used the fort to trade with the Iroquois. Located at the present site of Albany, New York, it became part of the Dutch colony of **New Netherland**.

In 1626, the Dutch founded a second settlement on Manhattan Island. Governor Peter Minuit bought the land from the local chiefs for about $24, paid in trade goods. He called the settlement **New Amsterdam**. In 1638, Peter Minuit helped Sweden set up a colony called New Sweden. It was located in present-day Delaware. The Dutch took it over in 1655.

The purchase of Manhattan Island

The Dutch worked hard to attract farmers to New Netherland. Anyone who brought over fifty families became a **patroon**. Patroons were landowners in New Netherland. The patroons were given large estates along the Hudson River in New York and New Jersey.

Putting It All Together

With your partner, make a list of words and phrases that best define or describe the French and Dutch colonies. Then try to agree on which are the three most important. Use each of the three terms in a sentence about colonization.

Read a Primary Source

A French Colonial Town

New Orleans was founded in 1718 as the capital of French Louisiana. In 1763, an early settler wrote the following description of the town.

reading for understanding

What was New Orleans' biggest advantage?

What are the town's main buildings?

What role did the Catholic Church play in early New Orleans?

"A better choice could not have been made, as the town [is] on the banks of the Mississippi, vessels, tho' of a thousand ton, may lay their sides close to the shore, even at low water. . . .

"The place of arms [parade ground] is in the middle of that part of the town which faces the river; in the middle of the ground of the place of arms stands the parish church, called St. Louis. . . . To the right stand the prison, or jail, and the guard-house. . . .

"The Governor's house stands in the middle of that part of the town, from which we go from the place of arms to the habitation of the Jesuits, which is near the town. . . . The House of the Ursilin Nuns is quite at the end of the town to the right; as is also the hospital of the sick, of which the Nuns have the inspection. . . . The greatest part of the houses is of brick: the rest are of timber and brick."

Le Page du Pratz, *The History of Louisiana I* (London, 1763).

Chapter Summary

Spain took the lead in setting up **colonies** in the Western Hemisphere. Columbus **founded** towns on the island of Hispaniola. Many local people died of **smallpox** and other diseases brought from Europe. In 1519, Hernando Cortés invaded Mexico. Cortés's soldiers remained in Mexico as colonists. Francisco Pizarro defeated the Incan Empire in Peru.

The **Spanish borderlands** lay north of Mexico. They formed a **barrier** between the Spanish **empire** and the French and English colonies. In the late 1500s, Spanish officials began to colonize this region. They built a fort and the town of St. Augustine in Florida. Spanish farmers also settled in present-day New Mexico. Colonial governors **imposed** Spanish rule over local Native Americans. Spanish priests built **missions** in present-day Arizona and California.

France and the Netherlands were latecomers in colonizing America. France's first colony was Quebec. Like most colonies in **New France**, Quebec was a mission and fur trading post. The Dutch also wanted a share of the fur trade. They set up trading posts along the Hudson River. The largest was **New Amsterdam**. The Dutch called their colony **New Netherland**. They attracted farmers by giving large estates to **patroons** who brought other farmers to New Netherland.

Chapter Review

1 Write the first draft of a paragraph that summarizes what you have learned about the Spanish, French, and Dutch colonies. Include all the chapter's vocabulary words. Compare your draft with that of your partner. Then write a final draft.

2 Design banners to fly over the Spanish, French, and Dutch colonies. What key words would each banner have? What symbols best represent those colonies? What colors would you choose? Explain your reasons for each choice.

3 Write a description of Spanish colonization from a Native American's point of view.

Skill Builder

Working with a Timeline

Chronology, the arrangement of events in time, is essential to understanding history. It tells when events took place and tells the sequence or order in which they happened. Knowing the sequence of events can also help us understand how they are related. Some events are caused by an earlier event.

A timeline is an easy way to show chronology. It is a visual tool that gives the dates of events and the sequence or order in which they happened. To show how events are related over time, timelines are divided into regular segments. The dates when events happened within each segment are clearly shown.

The timeline below shows major events in the European colonization of the Americas. Use the timeline to answer these questions:

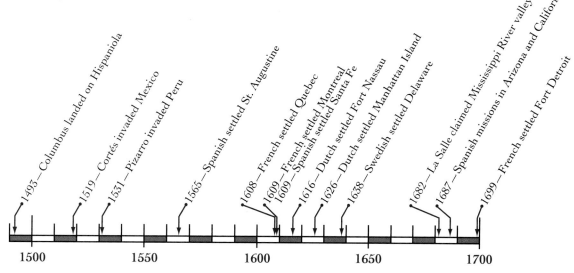

1   When was Santa Fe settled?

2   What was the first French settlement in Canada?

3   Which European nation took the lead in colonizing?

4   How much time passed between the first Spanish and French settlements?

5   Are any of the events on the timeline related to other events?

Chapter 4

THE ENGLISH COLONIES

Getting Focused

Skim this chapter to predict what you will be learning.

- Read the lesson titles and subheadings.
- Look at the illustrations and read the captions.
- Examine the maps.
- Review the vocabulary words and terms.

The English colonists were strangers in a strange land. Think about a time when you were a stranger. How did you feel? How did those feelings affect your actions? Describe that situation in your notebook.

LESSON 1 The Southern Colonies

Thinking on Your Own

Read the Focus Your Reading questions. Then make two columns in your notebook. Label the first column "What England Wanted." As you read, fill in that column with what England wanted to get from the colonies. Label the second column "What the Colonies Produced." Fill it in with what products the colonies provided.

Why were there no English colonies in 1582, wondered Richard Hakluyt, an English geographer? Hakluyt believed that colonies would give England access to America's gold, slaves, fish, timber, furs, and sugar cane. Colonies would also provide a market for English goods. He urged the people of England to "advance the honor of our country" by "the possessing of those lands" not yet controlled by Spain.

focus your reading

Why did England want colonies in North America?

Why did the Roanoke Colony fail?

What did the English colonies export to England?

vocabulary

Spanish Armada

defeated

joint-stock company

indigo

The Roanoke Colony

Queen Elizabeth I followed Richard Hakluyt's advice. In 1584, she asked Sir Walter Raleigh to set up a colony in North America. Three years later, he sent 113 colonists to Roanoke Island. Roanoke Island is off the coast of present-day North Carolina. The ship that brought them went back to England for supplies. Before the ship could return, a war broke out.

The Roanoke Colony was a victim of bad timing. In 1588, the **Spanish Armada**, a fleet of 130 ships, attacked England. The queen outfitted every available ship for war. England **defeated** the armada, but it took Raleigh two years to find another supply ship. By the time the supply ship finally reached Roanoke in 1590, the settlers had vanished.

The word "Croatoah" was all that remained of the Roanoke colonists.

Success in Virginia

Nearly twenty years later, King James I gave the Virginia Company the right to establish a colony in North America. This **joint-stock company** expected to make a profit from the colony. The company was jointly owned by people who bought shares, or parts, of the company. They were known as shareholders.

In May 1607, the company sent three ships with 104 men and boys to Virginia. There they founded the settlement of Jamestown. The company forced the settlers to look for gold and silver instead of planting crops. That summer, almost half of the people died from malaria. The rest nearly starved.

The colony was saved by Captain John Smith. He asked the Powhatan People for food. They captured him and threatened to kill him. The chief's daughter, Pocahontas,

Pocahontas visited England.

Tobacco was a major crop of the Southern Colonies.

persuaded her father to save Smith's life. The remaining colonists survived by trading with the Powhatan for food.

In the end, it was tobacco and not gold that made Virginia a profitable colony. A colonist named John Rolfe learned how to grow this plant. Tobacco became the colony's main export. John Rolfe later married Pocahontas.

Cecilius Calvert

ANNO Dm 1647
Ætatis 99

Other Southern Colonies

Other English colonies were established in what is now the southern part of the United States. In 1634, Cecilius Calvert, an English Catholic, founded the Maryland Colony. The town of St. Mary's was its first settlement. This colony allowed settlers to have Catholic Church services, a practice that was outlawed in England.

James Oglethorpe landing in Georgia

In 1670, more colonists settled in Carolina. They settled Charles Town—later Charleston. They traded with the native peoples for furs and grew rice and **indigo**. Indigo is a plant used for making dye.

The last Southern colony was Georgia. James Oglethorpe founded Georgia in 1733 to give poor people in England a new start in life. The colony also served to protect the colonies from Spanish settlements in Florida.

Putting It All Together

The Roanoke Colony vanished, but the Jamestown Colony survived. Create a Venn diagram with two overlapping circles. Label one circle "The Roanoke Colony" and the other "The Jamestown Colony." Discuss with a partner the similarities and differences between the two colonies. List the differences in the outer circles and list the similarities in the overlapping area.

L. Superior

FRENCH TERRITORY

L. Huron

L. Michigan

L. Erie

L. Ontario

St. Lawrence R.

Mississippi R.

Ohio R.

Cumberland R.

Tennessee R.

Appalachian Mountains

NH

MA

Boston 1630
Plymouth 1620
Providence 1636
CT   RI

NY

PA

NJ   New York 1664

Philadelphia 1682

MD

Wilmington 1664

DE

St. Mary's 1634

Chesapeake Bay

VA

Jamestown 1607

Edenton 1685

Roanoke 1587

New Bern 1710

NC

GA   SC

Charles Town 1670

Port Royal 1562

Savannah 1733

SPANISH

N
W   E
S

Settlements of the English Colonies

New England Colonies

Middle Colonies

Southern Colonies

Proclamation Line of 1763

0   250 miles

Biography

John Smith (1580–1631)

In September 1607, the young colony at Jamestown was in trouble. Huddled inside a small fort, the settlers lived in constant fear of a Native American attack. No houses were built, no fields planted. Half the 104 settlers already had died of malaria. The survivors were giving up hope. Then John Smith took charge.

John Smith was at his best in difficult times. He had been shipwrecked at sea, robbed by Frenchmen, and captured by Turks. In 1602, Smith had joined a Christian army that tried to drive the Muslim Turks out of Europe. He killed three men in hand-to-hand combat, or so he claimed. When the Turks defeated the Christians, they captured Smith and sold him into slavery. He escaped by killing his Muslim overseer and fleeing to Christian Russia. From there he made his way back to England.

To rescue the colony, Smith made contact with the Powhatan. He began by trading hatchets and beads for food, which the colonists desperately needed. Then the Powhatan turned against the colonists, perhaps because they, too, were running out of food. They captured Smith and took him to the Powhatan chief. As the chief prepared to kill him, Smith was saved by Pocahontas, the chief's daughter. She went to Jamestown to live and later married a colonist, John Rolfe. Her friendship probably saved Jamestown.

In 1609, John Smith returned to England, but not for long. In March 1614, he again set sail for America, this time as an explorer. That summer, he explored the coastline north of Virginia and traded furs with the locals. He returned to England with the best map yet of that region, which he named New England.

John Smith spent the rest of his life promoting the settlement of New England. He hoped to found his own colony there, but he failed to get financial support. To advertise the region, he published his map as well as a book entitled *Description of New England.* He also published *General History of Virginia* and *True Travels,* an account of his early travels. He died in 1631, still yearning to return to New England.

Read a Primary Source

A Letter from Jamestown

In 1623, Richard Frethorne was a servant on a plantation near Jamestown. He described conditions there in this letter to his parents.

reading for understanding

What does Richard probably mean by being "in a most heavy case"?

What food does Richard's master allow him?

How well did the colonists get along with the Native Americans?

"Loving and kind father and mother . . . This is to let you understand that I, your child, am in a most heavy case, by reason of the nature of the country. . . . For since I came out of the ship, I never ate anything but peas, and loblollie (that is water gruel) [flour mixed with water]. As for deer or venison, I never saw any since I came into this land; there is indeed some fowl, but we are not allowed to go and get it, but must work hard both early and late for a mess of water gruel, and a mouthful of bread, and beef. . . . We live in fear of the enemy [Indians] every hour, yet we have had a combat with them . . . and took two alive and make slaves of them."

Richard Frethorne, "Letter to His Father and Mother, March 20, April 2 and 3, 1623," in Susan M. Kingsbury, ed., *The Records of the Virginia Company of London* (Vol. IV, Washington, D. C. Government Printing Office, 1935).

New England Colonies

Thinking on Your Own

Make a list of the vocabulary words. With a partner, guess what each word means and write your definition next to the word. Check the Glossary to see how close you came. As you read each word in the lesson, write a sentence that summarizes what the word tells you about the founding of the New England colonies.

In 1534, King Henry VIII broke away from the Roman Catholic Church. He set up a Protestant church called the Church of England. Some English Protestants thought the English Church was still too Catholic. The **Puritans** wanted to purify it by simplifying its ceremonies and teachings. **Separatists** wanted to separate from it altogether. Both groups looked to North America to achieve their goals.

focus your reading

What was the Mayflower Compact?

Why did colonists settle in Massachusetts?

Why were other colonies founded in New England?

vocabulary

Puritans

Separatists

Pilgrims

Puritan commonwealth

The Plymouth Colony

In 1620, William Bradford and a group of Separatists sailed on the *Mayflower* from England. They wanted to get as far away as possible from the Church of England. While on the ship, the **Pilgrims** signed the Mayflower Compact. Pilgrims are people who take a journey for a religious purpose. The Mayflower Compact is a written agreement that set out the rules by which the Pilgrims would govern themselves.

Replica of the *Mayflower*

Pilgrims landing at Plymouth Rock

The Separatists founded the town of Plymouth along the coast of Massachusetts. The first winter was difficult. The colonists ran out of food. The next spring, a Pawtucket named Squanto showed them how to plant corn and where to fish. Despite its early hardships, the Plymouth settlement survived.

The Massachusetts Bay Colony

In 1630, English Puritans sailed into Massachusetts Bay with seventeen ships and more than 1,000 people. They founded seven towns. The largest was the seaport of Boston. They had decided that the best way to purify the Church of England was to set up a church in New England to serve as a model. "We shall be as a city upon a hill," said John Winthrop, the colony's leader. "The eyes of the people are upon us."

The signing of the Mayflower Compact

John Winthrop and Puritans arrive in Massachusetts.

The Massachusetts Bay Colony grew rapidly, attracting thousands of English Puritans. It was a **Puritan commonwealth**, a community in which the government enforced the Puritans' religious beliefs. Only church members could vote. The Puritan leaders expelled, or sent away, anyone who disagreed with them.

stop and think

The Pilgrims made a compact with each other promising to live according to certain rules. Discuss with a partner a compact that you have made to follow rules.

Roger Williams

Rhode Island, Connecticut, and New Hampshire

Among those expelled by the Puritans was Roger Williams. Williams was a Separatist minister. He insisted that church and state should be separate. In 1636, he founded Providence, the first settlement in the colony of Rhode Island. It allowed freedom of religion. The Puritans also expelled Anne Hutchinson for her religious views. She, too, settled in Rhode Island.

Anne Hutchinson was expelled from Massachusetts Bay Colony.

Puritans who needed more farmland founded other New England colonies. In 1635, people from the Massachusetts Bay Colony began to settle in the Connecticut River valley. The settlements joined together to become the colony of Connecticut in 1662. Farmers who moved north from Massachusetts settled in New Hampshire in 1638. It became a separate colony in 1680.

Minister Hooker established Hartford on the Connecticut River in 1636.

Putting It All Together

Imagine that you are a dissatisfied Massachusetts Bay colonist. Write a letter to John Winthrop telling him why you are unhappy with life in Massachusetts Bay Colony. Explain alternatives to staying in the colony.

The Middle Colonies

Thinking on Your Own

Think back to a time when you were not free to express yourself. As you read, write specific ways in which colonists in New York, New Jersey, and Pennsylvania were more free than people in the Massachusetts Bay Colony.

In 1624, the Netherlands claimed what is now New York, New Jersey, and Pennsylvania. In 1638, they added the present-day state of Delaware by expelling the Swedish settlers who lived there. Many of the 8,000 people who lived in New Netherland were unhappy with Dutch rule. The government was unable to protect them from repeated Native American attacks. Besides that, Governor Peter Stuyvesant was a harsh governor.

focus your reading

How did New Netherland become New York?

Why were New York and New Jersey successful colonies?

Why did William Penn want a colony in North America?

vocabulary

proprietor   Quakers

New York and New Jersey

On August 29, 1664, a fleet of English ships sailed into the harbor at New Amsterdam. Its commander, Colonel Richard Nichols, demanded that the Dutch surrender. Governor Stuyvesant handed over the city without a fight. He had little choice, as many of the settlers were glad to see the British arrive.

The English take control of New Netherland.

As the new governor, Nichols changed the name of New Netherland to New York, in honor of the duke of York. The duke, King Charles II's brother, was the new **proprietor**, or owner, of the colony. The colony's main city of New Amsterdam became New York City.

The duke sold part of the area south of New York to two friends, Lord John Berkeley and Sir George Carteret. They became the proprietors of East and West Jersey, which later became the colony of New Jersey.

stop and think

Imagine when Colonel Richard Nichols was sailing into New Amsterdam's harbor. From what you have read, how do you think the people reacted to Nichols? Why did they react that way? Describe the scene in your notebook. Include dialogue between the residents.

The colonies of New York and New Jersey did well and grew under English control. Both colonies were well governed. To avoid religious fights, the colonial governors granted freedom of religion to everyone. The rich soil of the region attracted settlers. New York City served as the seaport for both colonies.

Pennsylvania and Delaware

King Charles II gave William Penn part of what had been New Netherland. Penn was the son of an English admiral to whom the king owed money. He also was a member of a religious sect called the Society of Friends. The **Quakers**, as

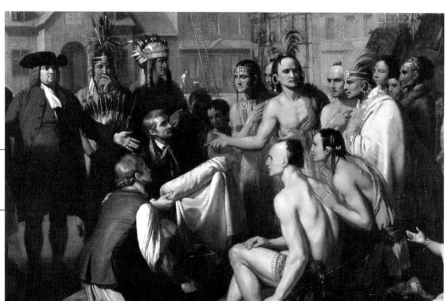

William Penn paying Native Americans for the land used to found Pennsylvania

they were called, refused to swear loyalty to the government or serve in the army. Thousands of Quakers had been thrown in jail because of their beliefs. Penn wanted to set up a colony where Quakers could practice their religion freely. By giving Penn land, the king paid off his debt and found a way to move the Quakers out of England. Later, he also gave Penn the area taken from the Dutch that became the colony of Delaware.

In 1681, William Penn founded the colony of Pennsylvania. The king named it in honor of Penn's father. The colony was a great success from the beginning. Penn avoided problems with the Native Americans by paying them for their land. He offered settlers farmland at prices they could afford. Since the colony tolerated all Christian beliefs, settlers began to arrive from throughout Europe. Philadelphia, established in 1682, became a prosperous seaport city.

The early settlement of Philadelphia

Putting It All Together

The Middle Colonies prospered and grew quickly. Make a two-column chart with "Problems" and "Solutions" as the headings. List the problems these colonies faced and the solutions the colonists used to address them.

Chapter Summary

In 1587, Sir Walter Raleigh sent colonists to Roanoke Island. Although England **defeated** the **Spanish Armada**, a lack of supplies doomed the Roanoke Colony. Virginia was England's first successful colony. A **joint-stock company** expected to make a profit from the colony. Maryland, Carolina, and Georgia were other English colonies. The Southern Colonies prospered by exporting tobacco, rice, and **indigo**.

The New England Colonies were founded by **Separatists** and **Puritans**. In 1620, Separatists, also known as the **Pilgrims**, began the Plymouth Colony. The Puritans in 1630 founded the Massachusetts Bay Colony. That colony was a **Puritan commonwealth**, a community in which the settlers used the government to enforce their religious beliefs. They expelled people who disagreed with them.

In August 1664, England took over the Dutch colony of New Netherland. The English governor changed the name to New York. The colony's new **proprietor** sold part of the area to people who founded the colony of New Jersey. King Charles gave another part of New Netherland to William Penn, a **Quaker** who wanted to establish a colony where Quakers were free to practice their religion.

Chapter Review

1   Design a logo that represents the struggles and accomplishments of the English colonists. Review the vocabulary in this chapter for ideas.

2   Choose an event, person, or place that you found most interesting. Write a bulleted list of facts about your choice.

3   Create a three-column chart with the labels "Southern Colonies," "New England Colonies," and "Middle Colonies." Fill the columns with words or phrases that best describe each. Use the information to write a short paragraph about the English colonies.

Skill Builder

Reading a Table

Tables present different kinds of information in a small space. The information most often is presented in columns and rows.

The table below presents information about the English colonies in North America. It includes the names of the colonies organized by region (New England, Middle, Southern), when they were founded, and why they were founded.

Use the table to answer these questions:

1 In which region was the first colony founded?

2 In which region were the colonies most often founded for religious reasons?

3 What was the most common reason for English settlement?

4 Which region did England take the longest period of time to settle?

The Founding of the English Colonies

	Colonies	Date Founded or Claimed by England	Reason for Founding

New England	Massachusetts
	    Plymouth
	    Massachusetts Bay
	Connecticut
	Rhode Island
	New Hampshire
		
		1620
		1630
		1635
		1636
		1638
			
			Religious freedom, farming, trade
			Puritan commonwealth, farming, trade
			Farming, trade
			Religious freedom, farming, trade
			Farming, trade

Middle	New York New Jersey Pennsylvania Delaware	1664 (Dutch 1624) 1664 (Dutch 1629) 1681 1701 (Dutch 1638)	Trade, farming Farming, trade Farming, trade Farming, trade
Southern	Virginia Maryland Carolina* Georgia	1607 1634 1670 1733	Search for gold, farming Religious freedom, farming, trade Trade, farming Refuge for poor, farming, buffer from Spanish Florida

*Divided into North Carolina and South Carolina by King George II in 1729

3 UNIT

COLONIAL SOCIETIES

By 1700, the English settlements in North America were solidly established. They had survived their first struggling years. Most of the 250,000 English colonists lived in villages and farms close to the Atlantic coast. They had stronger ties to England than to their neighbors north or south.

The English colonies expanded rapidly during the next fifty years. By 1750, the population had increased to nearly two million. Three distinct societies emerged. The people of New England, the Middle Colonies, and the South had very different ways of life. They also had less in common with their cousins overseas.

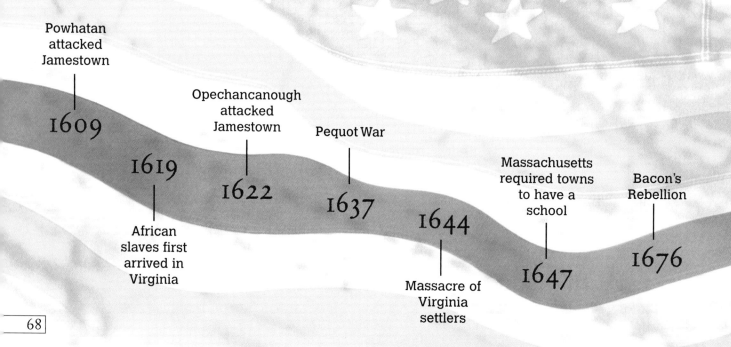

Powhatan attacked Jamestown

1609

1619
African slaves first arrived in Virginia

Opechancanough attacked Jamestown

1622

Pequot War

1637

1644
Massacre of Virginia settlers

Massachusetts required towns to have a school

1647

Bacon's Rebellion

1676

Why did the
South use
slave labor?

Why were the Middle Colonies
called the breadbasket?

How did religion
shape life in New
England?

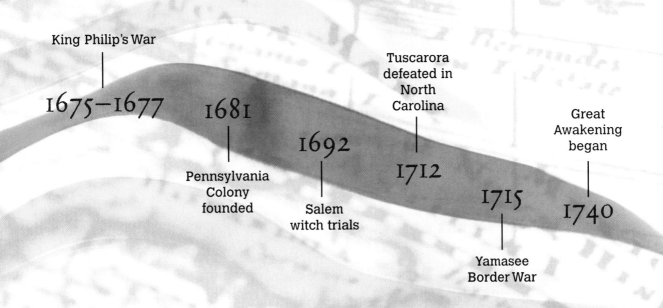

King Philip's War

1675–1677

1681

Pennsylvania
Colony
founded

1692

Salem
witch trials

Tuscarora
defeated in
North
Carolina

1712

1715

Yamasee
Border War

Great
Awakening
began

1740

Chapter 5

LIFE IN THE SOUTHERN COLONIES

Getting Focused

Skim this chapter to predict what you will be learning.

- Read the lesson titles and subheadings.
- Look at the illustrations and read the captions.
- Examine the maps.
- Review the vocabulary words and terms.

In your notebook write a statement predicting what you will learn about life in the Southern colonies. Explain why you think so to a partner. Then copy the vocabulary words into your notebook. As you read each vocabulary word in the lesson, write a sentence using the word.

Settling the South

Thinking on Your Own

Read the Focus Your Reading questions. As you read, write answers in your notebook.

By 1630, the future of the Virginia Colony looked bright. It had survived the early years when three out of four colonists died of disease, starvation, or Native American attacks. The colony had a **cash crop** that provided a steady income. John Rolfe learned how to grow and cure a mild variety of West Indian tobacco. It sold very well in London. A single crop, it was said, could pay for a Virginia plantation.

focus your reading

Why did tobacco growers want large plantations?

Where were small farms located?

Why did few people live in cities?

vocabulary

cash crop   frontier

plantations   homespun

Southern Plantations

Englishmen with money to invest went to Virginia or Maryland in large numbers. Later, many people went to North Carolina and Georgia. They laid out **plantations**, or large farms, along the rivers. Tobacco planters needed more land than they could use in any year, because the plants robbed the soil of its nutrients. New fields had to be cleared every two or three years. Planters settled along the river

Many plantations were located along rivers.

so that oceangoing ships could come to pick up their tobacco. The colonists in South Carolina grew rice and indigo.

In the Southern Colonies, the planters were the upper class. They built large frame or brick houses with columns in front. The planters could afford to import fine furniture and beautiful clothes from England.

Plantations consisted of many buildings and fields for planting.

Colonial Farms

The majority of settlers in the Southern Colonies owned small farms. Arriving with little or no money, they worked as servants or rented land. In time, many of them bought a few acres inland from the rivers. Some settled on the **frontier**—the western edge of settlement. Land was cheap on the frontier.

Tenant farms included small houses and plots of land for growing crops.

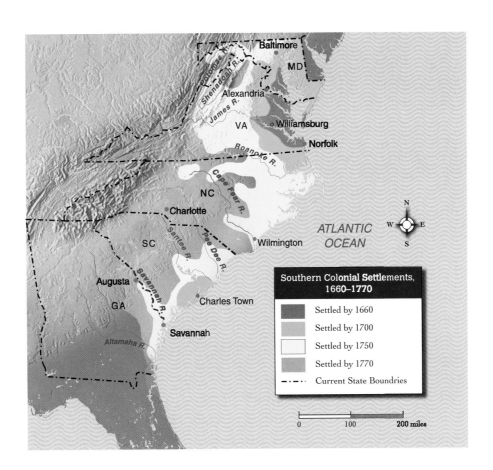

Southern Colonial Settlements, 1660–1770

	Settled by 1660
	Settled by 1700
	Settled by 1750
	Settled by 1770
-·-·-	Current State Boundries

0   100   200 miles

They raised, grew, or made most of what they needed. A small patch of tobacco provided cash to buy what they could not make for themselves.

Small farmers made up the middle class in the Southern Colonies. They lived in frame houses of three or four rooms. Frontier farmers often lived in log cabins. Most farmers wore clothes made of **homespun**, or homemade, cloth. They could not afford luxuries.

Towns and Cities

Few people settled in towns or cities, as hardly any towns existed. In the Southern Colonies, plantations served many of the purposes of towns. The planters acted as merchants. They shipped their tobacco, as well as crops grown by their poorer neighbors, from their wharves. They ordered manufactured goods directly from England. The planters did not need townspeople

stop and think

In your notebook, write three facts about where and how people lived in the Southern Colonies.

Slave labor was used for growing, drying, and packing tobacco.

such as carpenters, wagon-makers, and blacksmiths. They had skilled slaves to do that work.

Most of the towns and small cities that did exist were centers of colonial government. These included Annapolis, the capital of the Maryland Colony. In 1699, Williamsburg replaced the little village of Jamestown as Virginia's capital. Savannah was both the capital and main port city of Georgia. The largest city was Charles Town, South Carolina, which had a population of 7,000 people by 1750.

Many of the wealthier rice and indigo planters kept homes in seacoast cities. These homes were used to escape the heat and humidity of the interior. While in the city, wealthy planters socialized and established themselves as community leaders.

Large port cities provided access to ships.

Putting It All Together

Discuss your Focus Your Reading answers with a partner. Then work together to create a table labeled "Plantation Owners" and "Small Farmers." Compare their ways of life.

Biography

Eliza Lucas Pinckney (1722 –1793)

Early in 1740, Colonel George Lucas wrote a letter to his eighteen-year-old daughter, Eliza. Lucas was on duty with the British army in the Caribbean. Eliza was at home in South Carolina. Colonel Lucas suggested that it was time for Eliza to think about marriage. He proposed two men as suitable husbands, one an elderly gentleman with money. "I beg leave to say to you," she quickly replied, "that the riches of Peru and Chile, if he had them put together, could not purchase a sufficient esteem for him to make him my husband." Her father said nothing more on that subject.

Eliza Lucas was a determined young woman. In 1738, she moved from England with her family to South Carolina, where her father had bought three plantations. In his absence, and with her mother in ill health, she managed one plantation by herself. She supervised the overseers at the other two. She also read for two hours each day, practiced music two hours, did needlework for an hour, and helped her younger sister learn to read and write.

Eliza Lucas also experimented with indigo, a plant used to make blue dye. Her father sent her indigo seeds, convinced that this Caribbean plant could be a moneymaker for South Carolina. Frost killed the first crop. The plants came up the next year, but the dye maker ruined the dye. The next crop was a complete failure. Finally, in 1744, Eliza Lucas's patience paid off. She grew the colony's first successful crop of indigo. Three years later, South Carolina exported 135,000 pounds of the blue dye. Production increased thereafter.

In 1744, Eliza married Charles Pinckney, a husband of her own choosing. They had four children. The eldest, Charles Cotesworth Pinckney, was a general in the Revolutionary War. Their youngest son, Thomas, became governor of South Carolina. Eliza Lucas Pinckney died of cancer in 1793 at age seventy. President George Washington asked to be a pallbearer at her funeral.

Servants and Slaves

Thinking on Your Own

Read the Focus Your Reading questions and vocabulary. What do they tell you about who did most of the work in the Southern Colonies? Talk about your ideas with a partner. Then write a short paragraph summarizing your main points.

The Southern Colonies always needed farm workers. Tobacco, rice, and indigo were **labor-intensive** crops. Growing, harvesting, and shipping these crops to market required long hours of manual labor. The servants and slaves who did this work made up the lower classes in the Southern Colonies.

Unfree Servants

In the early years of colonization, planters solved the labor problem by importing unfree white workers. Some were convicts shipped to the colonies to work out their prison terms. Others were **redemptioners**, people in the colonies who sold their labor. The buyer owned the person's services for a fixed period in return for food, clothing, and shelter. Most unfree workers came to the colonies as **indentured servants**.

At least half of the white settlers in the English colonies were indentured servants. These workers signed a labor contract before leaving England. The contractor paid their passage to America and provided them with food and clothing. In return, the servant agreed to work in the colonies for a period of four to seven years. At the end of the time period, most servants received a few acres of farmland as freedom dues.

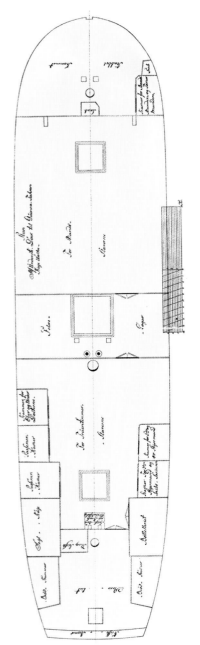

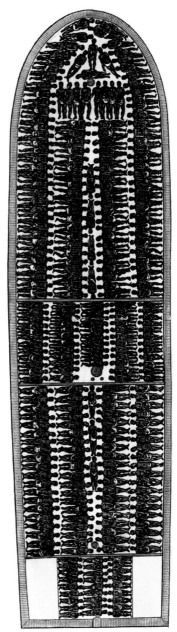

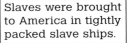

Slaves were brought to America in tightly packed slave ships.

Being a servant was a hard life. Most worked in the fields or cleared new farmland. They could not leave the farm or plantation without permission. Single people needed permission to marry. Servants had to make up any time that was lost due to illness or absence. Many tried to run away, often successfully.

stop and think

Think about how owning land and social class relate to each other. Write two or three sentences that explain the relationship. Discuss your answer with a partner or the class.

African Slaves

In 1619, a Dutch slave trader sold the first African slaves in Virginia. The number of slaves grew slowly. It was cheaper for a planter to import a servant than to buy a slave. However, servants who ran away were difficult to recover. They blended into the white population. Every five years or so, planters had to train new workers. In time, they decided that slaves cost less in the long run.

Many of the slave traders followed a route that became known as the **triangle trade**. This is because the routes formed the

> **TO BE SOLD,**
> A Likely negro Man, his Wife and Child; the negro Man capable of doing all forts of Plantation Work, and a good Miller: The Woman exceeding fit for a Farmer, being capable of doing any Work, belonging to a Houfe in the Country, at reafonable Rates, inquire of the Printer hereof.

shape of a triangle. On one leg, traders brought sugar and molasses from the West Indies to the colonies. These products were used to make rum, which was shipped to Africa and traded for slaves. The slaves were then shipped to the West Indies and the colonies. Many other goods were also shipped across the Atlantic, such as indigo, wood, and iron.

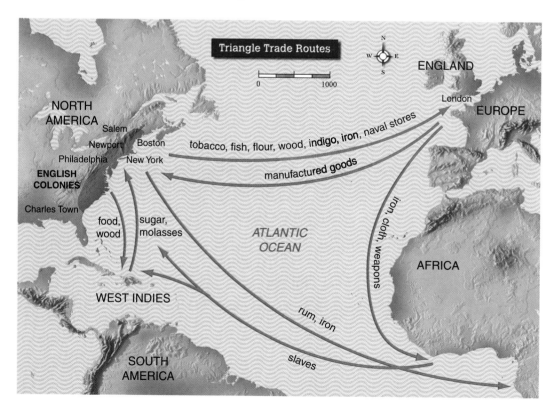

Conditions on the slave ship were terrible.

By 1700, African slaves were common throughout the Southern Colonies. Virginia had approximately 10,000 African slaves by that time. At first, African slaves and English servants were treated in a similar way. As the number of slaves increased, that changed. The colonies enacted **slave codes**. These laws enslaved Africans and their descendants for as long as they lived. The slave codes also controlled every aspect of a slave's life.

Slaves arriving at Jamestown

Putting It All Together

Create a two-column chart in your notebook. Label the first column "Unfree Servants" and the second "Slaves." Using information from the chapter, describe each type of labor in the appropriate column.

Read a Primary Source

A Tightly Packed Slave Ship

Slave ship captains disagreed on how tightly to pack their human cargo. The "loose-packers" argued that slaves arrived in better condition and brought higher prices if allowed some additional space. The "tight-packers" replied that the larger the cargo, the greater the profits, even if more slaves died on the voyage. The following is a firsthand description of a tightly packed ship.

"The cargo of a vessel of a hundred tons or a little more is calculated to purchase from 220 to 250 slaves. Their lodging rooms below the deck which are three (for the men, the boys and the women) besides a place for the sick, are sometimes more than five feet high and sometimes less; and this height is divided toward the middle for the slaves to lie in two rows, one above the other, on each side of the ship, close to each other like books upon a shelf. I have known them so close that the shelf would not easily contain one more.

The poor creatures, thus cramped, are likewise in irons for the most part which makes it difficult for them to turn or move or attempt to rise or to lie down without hurting themselves or each other. Every morning, perhaps, more instances than one are found of the living and the dead fastened together."

Quoted in Daniel P. Mannix in collaboration with Malcolm Cowley, *Black Cargoes: A History of the Atlantic Slave Trade, 1518–1865.*

Settlers and Native Americans

Thinking on Your Own

Read the Focus Your Reading questions with a partner. Together, discuss possible answers. Write a possible answer for each question in your notebook.

The growing number of farms and plantations caused serious problems for the native people. Entire villages died from diseases brought by explorers and settlers. By clearing fields in the forests, the settlers destroyed native hunting grounds. Settlers' dogs also chased the deer away. The colonial settlements succeeded, but only at the expense of the Native Americans.

focus your reading

How did the Powhatan chiefs react to the English settlement of Virginia?

Why did angry frontier settlers attack and burn Jamestown?

What did white settlers in the Carolinas do to the Native Americans besides taking their land?

vocabulary

Bacon's Rebellion

Yamasee Border War

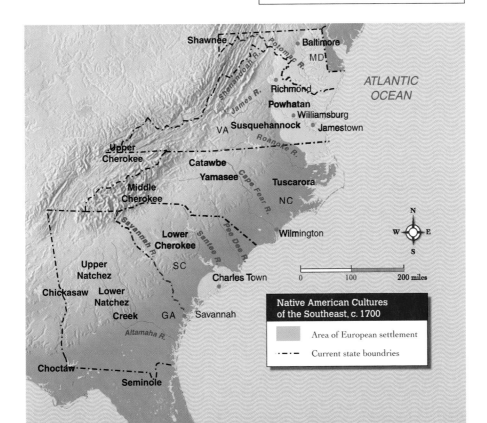

Native American Cultures of the Southeast, c. 1700

▨ Area of European settlement

-·-·- Current state boundries

Uprisings in Virginia

Powhatan, the chief of the Powhatan Confederation, kept waiting for the English to leave Jamestown. He did not want them to stay forever. Instead of leaving, however, the settlers kept coming. In 1609, Powhatan declared war against the settlers. Fighting continued for the next four years. Opechancanough, the next chief, tried to drive the colonists out once and for all. A surprise attack in 1622 killed at least 347 settlers. In 1664, another 500 colonists died in a second

stop and think

Make a Venn diagram to describe what happened to Native Americans in the Southern Colonies. Label one circle "Virginia" and the other "The Carolinas." In the overlapping area, write words that describe what they experienced in common. In the other circles describe how they were treated differently.

Jamestown was burned during Bacon's Rebellion.

uprising. Each time, the colonists hit back, destroying every native village they could find. In the end, the colonists drove the native people out of eastern Virginia.

Bacon's Rebellion

The conflict then shifted to the Virginia frontier. In 1676, fighting broke out between settlers and the Susquehannock. Led by Nathaniel Bacon, the settlers asked Governor William Berkeley to send troops. Berkeley refused because he wanted to protect his business of trading furs with the locals. Bacon led 400 armed men to Jamestown. The farmers burned the town because they were angry at Berkeley. This uprising, known as **Bacon's Rebellion**, ended when Bacon fell ill and died. His followers either surrendered or were captured. Twenty-three participants in the uprising were convicted and hanged. Conflict on the frontier continued until the settlers drove the native population completely out of Virginia.

Conflict in the Carolinas

Fighting between settlers and native people broke out next in North and South Carolina. The colonists not only took land, but they also enslaved the local people. In 1712, the Tuscarora of North Carolina attacked and killed 130 slave traders. The survivors burned a Tuscarora fort, killing over 150 Native

Americans. The **Yamasee Border War** broke out in 1715 in South Carolina. The Yamasee killed more than 400 settlers. Most of the Yamasee were tracked down and killed or sold as slaves. The violence continued until 1718, when the remaining Native Americans left the Carolinas.

Some colonists found themselves in conflict with Native American groups.

Putting It All Together

Return to the answers you wrote earlier for the Focus Your Reading questions. Revise or expand your answers based on what you have read. Share your answers with a partner or the class.

Chapter Summary

Tobacco provided Virginia and its neighboring colonies with a **cash crop**. The tobacco planters had large **plantations**. They needed a great deal of land because tobacco drained the soil of nutrients. Families who owned small farms made up the middle class. They settled inland from the rivers, or on the **frontier**. They grew, raised, or made most of what they needed, including **homespun** clothing.

Tobacco, rice, and indigo were **labor-intensive** crops. Planters tried to solve their labor problem by hiring white servants called **redemptioners** and **indentured servants**. Both sold their labor for a period of four to seven years.

By 1700, African slaves were common throughout the Southern Colonies. The **triangle trade** routes brought many slaves to the colonies. At first, they were treated much like white servants, but that did not last long. As their number increased, the colonies enacted **slave codes**. These laws enslaved Africans and their children forever.

As colonial settlement grew, Native Americans were pushed off their land. The Powhatan fought with the Virginia colonists many times. In 1676, **Bacon's Rebellion** increased tension with native groups. Later, in 1715, the **Yamasee Border War** resulted in the deaths of more than 400 colonists.

Chapter Review

1. Create a poster that describes plantation, farm, and city life in the Southern Colonies.

2. Imagine a conversation between a white indentured servant and an African slave about their lives. Write their pretend dialogue.

3. Write an article for a London newspaper about life in colonial Virginia. Include information about and possible quotes from Chief Powhatan and John Rolfe.

4. Read over the vocabulary. Choose five words that are the least familiar to you and invent a way to remember their definitions. Use symbols, word games, pictures, or rhymes.

Skill Builder

Comparing Tables

Tables present different kinds of information. Both tables below contain information about the growth of slavery in England's North American colonies. But the information is not the same. The first step in using a table is to see what kind of information it contains. It also is important to compare tables if more than one is available. A second table may provide valuable information that the first does not include.

Use the two tables to answer the following questions:

1   Both tables have a "Total" column. How are they different?

2   Which table tells you the number of slaves in the New England and Middle Colonies in 1700? What is the answer?

3   Which table would you use to find out what percentage of slaves lived in the South in 1740? What was the percentage?

4   In what year did the slave population exceed 10 percent of the total population? Which table includes that information?

5   In what decade—a period of ten years—did the total colonial population grow the fastest? In what decade did the slave population grow the fastest?

Slave Population, 1650–1760

Year	North	South	Total
1650	880	720	1,600
1660	1,162	1,758	2,920
1670	1,125	3,410	4,535
1680	1,895	5,076	6,971
1690	3,340	13,389	16,729
1700	5,206	22,611	27,817
1710	8,303	36,563	44,866
1720	14,091	54,748	68,839
1730	17,323	73,698	91,021
1740	23,958	126,066	150,024
1750	30,222	206,198	236,420
1760	40,033	285,773	325,806

Colonial Population, 1650–1760

Year	Total population	% Black
1650	50,368	3%
1660	75,058	3%
1670	111,935	4%
1680	151,507	5%
1690	210,372	7%
1700	250,888	11%
1710	331,711	13%
1720	466,185	14%
1730	629,445	14%
1740	905,563	16%
1750	1,170,760	20%
1760	1,593,625	20%

Chapter

6 LIFE IN THE NEW ENGLAND AND MIDDLE COLONIES

Getting Focused

Skim this chapter to predict what you will be learning.

- Read the lesson titles and subheadings.
- Look at the illustrations and read the captions.
- Examine the maps.
- Review the vocabulary words and terms.

Compare the topics covered in Chapter 5 with those in Chapter 6 by examining the vocabulary words in each chapter. Write three predictions in your notebook about what you will learn in Chapter 6.

The Expansion of New England

Thinking on Your Own

Make a three-column chart in your notebook. Label the columns "Reasons for Villages," "Reasons for Native American Conflict," and "Reasons for Schools." As you read, make notes in each column concerning these topics.

During the 1600s, the New England Colonies attracted thousands of Puritan **immigrants**. The eight towns that existed in 1630 increased to thirty-three by 1647. Fifty years later, Puritan settlements lined the coast from Maine to Rhode Island. They extended west into central Massachusetts and Connecticut.

focus your reading

Why did New England colonists settle in villages?

What caused King Philip's War?

What was the Great Awakening?

vocabulary

immigrants

meetinghouse

Great Awakening

grammar schools

Latin schools

Farm and Fishing Villages

Most New England colonists settled in farm villages. They cleared fields in the forest and divided the land for planting. The first homes of the settlement were built close together in the village. The houses were clustered around the **meetinghouse.** This central location made it easy to attend religious services and other events.

The fireplace was the center of life in the New England home.

The farmers walked out to their fields each day to tend their crops. Later settlers lived on farms that were located farther away from the central meetinghouse.

Settlers along the coast lived in fishing villages. Men sailed out to catch codfish off the coast of Newfoundland. After salting or drying their catch, they shipped the best fish to Europe. The less tasty fish were sent to Virginia or to the West Indies to feed the slaves. Fish was New England's most valuable export.

New England towns were built around a central meetinghouse.

Relations with Native Cultures

The expanding Puritan settlements caused conflict with the native people. The colonists wanted more land for farming and settlement. The settlers continued to clear land, ruining Native American hunting grounds. The settlers' pigs uprooted the unfenced cornfields of the local people. Trying to preserve their way of life, angry Pequot attacked a Connecticut village in 1637. In response, the colony formed an army made up of settlers and attacked the natives. The colonists slaughtered most of the Pequot.

stop and think

Imagine that you are planning a new settlement in New England. Create a flyer that describes the settlement to attract new settlers.

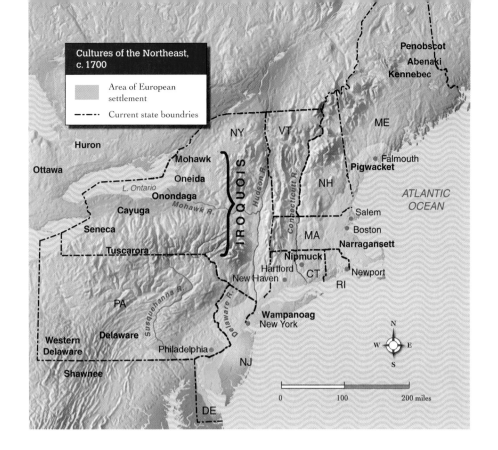

Cultures of the Northeast, c. 1700

Area of European settlement

Current state boundries

Huron

Ottawa

Mohawk
Oneida
Onondaga
Cayuga
Seneca
Tuscarora

IROQUOIS

NY

VT

ME

Penobscot
Abenaki
Kennebec

Falmouth
Pigwacket

NH

Salem
Boston

MA

Narragansett

Nipmuck

Hartford
New Haven

CT

Newport

RI

ATLANTIC
OCEAN

L. Ontario

Mohawk R.

Hudson R.

Connecticut R.

PA

Susquehanna R.

Delaware R.

Delaware

Western
Delaware

Philadelphia

Wampanoag
New York

NJ

Shawnee

DE

N
W E
S

0   100   200 miles

In 1675, the Wampanoag attacked Puritan towns in Massachusetts. Their leader was Chief Metacomet. The Puritans called him King Philip. The colony declared war against the Wampanoag and their native allies. An army of colonists attacked the Native Americans. They killed Chief Metacomet and most of his warriors. King Philip's War, as the colonists called it, virtually wiped out the native people of eastern Massachusetts.

Tensions between the Wampanoag and the Puritan settlers resulted in King Philip's War.

Life in the New England and Middle Colonies 89

Accusations of witchcraft led to the Salem witch trials.

Religion and Education

Religion was a strong force in Puritan life. In Salem Village in 1692, several people began acting strangely. The bizarre behavior was thought to be the work of the devil. A court tried and executed twenty people for practicing witchcraft and being possessed by the devil.

New England's increasing wealth also alarmed Puritan ministers. In the 1740s, Jonathan Edwards and George Whitefield helped bring about a revival of religious enthusiasm known as the **Great Awakening**. They warned people at revival meetings that they would burn in hell if they neglected religion.

Reading and writing were required in Massachusetts Bay Colony.

The Puritans also placed great emphasis on education. Everyone, they believed, should be able to read the Bible. In 1647, the Massachusetts Bay Colony required each town of fifty families or more to open a school. **Grammar schools** taught reading and writing. **Latin schools** prepared boys for college. The Puritans established Harvard and other colleges to prepare young men to become ministers.

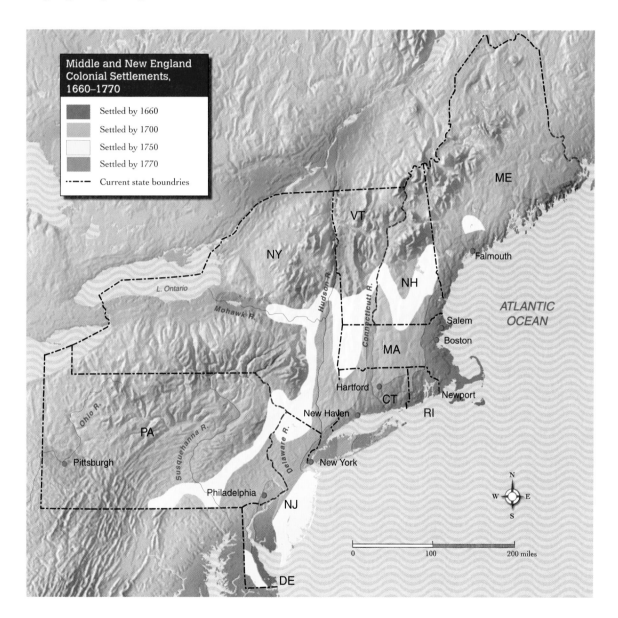

Middle and New England Colonial Settlements, 1660–1770

- Settled by 1660
- Settled by 1700
- Settled by 1750
- Settled by 1770
- ·—·— Current state boundries

Putting It All Together

Go back to the three-column chart that you created. Use the information from your chart to write a short paragraph about the expansion of New England.

Read a Primary Source

The Pequot Massacre

In his last will and testament, John Underhill described the 1637 massacre of Pequot at Mystic River. The account also helps to explain the mindset of the Puritans who killed about 500 Pequot that day.

reading for understanding

At what time of day did the attack take place?

What reasons did the writer give for the attack?

Why was Underhill convinced the Puritans were in the right?

"Drawing near to the fort, we yielded up ourselves to God and entreated His assistance in so weighty an enterprise. . . .

"We could not but admire at the providence of God in it, that soldiers so unexpert in the use of their arms, should give so complete a volley, as though the finger of God had touched both match and flint. Which volley being given at break of day, and themselves fast asleep for the most part, bred in them such a terror, that they brake forth into a most doleful cry; so as if God had not fitted the hearts of men for the service, it would have bred in them a commiseration toward them. But every man being bereaved of pity, fell upon the work without compassion, considering the blood they [the Pequots] had shed of our native countrymen, and how barbarously they had dealt with them, and slain, first and last, about thirty persons. . . .

"It may be demanded, Why should you be so furious (as some have said)? Should not Christians have more mercy and compassion? But I would refer you to [King] David's war. . . . Sometimes the Scripture declareth women and children must perish with their parents. Sometimes the case alters; but we will not dispute it now. We have sufficient light from the Word of God for our proceedings."

From Charles M. Segal and David C. Stineback, *Puritans, Indians, and Manifest Destiny* (New York: Putnam's, 1977).

Growth of the Middle Colonies

Thinking on Your Own

Imagine you live in a region that people call a "breadbasket." What characteristics do you think give the region this name? Write three characteristics in your notebook.

The Middle Colonies grew more rapidly than England's other colonies. The fertile soil of New York, New Jersey, Pennsylvania, and Delaware attracted tens of thousands of settlers. These colonies also welcomed people of all religious beliefs, so long as they were Christians. As the most **tolerant**, or open-minded, of England's colonies, they attracted the most diverse group of settlers.

focus your reading

Who did farmers depend upon for farm labor?

Why were the Middle Colonies more diverse than New England?

How did William Penn treat the native people of Pennsylvania?

vocabulary

tolerant

breadbasket

haven

Pennsylvania Dutch

Scots-Irish

Farming in the Middle Colonies

By founding Pennsylvania in 1682, William Penn opened a floodgate of immigration. Four thousand immigrants arrived the first year. Immigrants kept coming to the colonies. Some settled in Philadelphia. Most went inland to buy farms. The farms were larger than those in New England but smaller than Virginia plantations. Immigrants also settled on farms in New York, New Jersey, and Delaware.

The Middle Colonies were England's **breadbasket** colonies. Wheat was the main cash crop. From the wheat came flour and bread. The colonies also produced corn, vegetables, and livestock.

The Middle Colonies became known as the breadbasket because of the rich soil.

These colonies had relatively few slaves. Farmers mainly depended on their families for labor. For extra help, they hired farm laborers or bought the time of indentured servants. About half of North America's indentured servants lived in Pennsylvania.

Social Diversity

The Middle Colonies had the most diverse population in colonial America. Under the rule of both the Dutch and the English, New York tolerated most religious groups. Pennsylvania was a **haven** for religious minorities, including Quakers and Mennonites. About one-third of the settlers were German Lutherans, also known as the **Pennsylvania Dutch**. The term *Dutch* comes from the German word *deutsch*, which simply means *German*. Cheap land on the frontier attracted large numbers of poor **Scots-Irish** immigrants from Northern Ireland.

Folk art designs, such as the one painted on this pie dish, became popular among the Pennsylvania Dutch.

Colonists and Native People

The settlers of the Middle Colonies had fewer conflicts with the Native Americans than most colonists. English officials in New York made peace with the powerful Iroquois Confederation. The English colonists wanted to profit from the fur trade, which the Iroquois controlled. In Pennsylvania, William Penn won the friendship of the Delaware People. He insisted on paying them a fair price for their land.

stop and think

Create a concept web for the Middle Colonies with "Keys to Success" in the middle. On lines extending out from the center, write words or terms that help explain the success of these colonies.

William Penn's sons, Thomas and John Penn, did not continue that policy. After inheriting the colony, they signed a new treaty that cheated the Delaware out of much of the land that remained. The Penns called on the Iroquois, the Delaware's enemy, to help enforce the treaty. Together, they pushed the Delaware out of Pennsylvania.

William Penn treated the native cultures fairly, which helped to ease tensions.

Putting It All Together

In your notebook, summarize in one paragraph why the Middle Colonies attracted more settlers than other colonies during the 1700s.

Biography

Phillis Wheatley (1753?–1784)

In March 1776, George Washington wrote Phillis Wheatley a letter. He thanked her for a poem she had written. Her poem praised him for taking command of the colonial army.

"If you should ever come to Cambridge, or near headquarters," he replied, "I shall be happy to see a person so favored by the muses." The man who became the father of his country wrote this compliment to an African-born slave.

Phillis Wheatley was born about 1753 in Africa. At age seven, she was captured by slave traders. A frail, little girl, Phillis barely survived the voyage to Boston.

Susanna Wheatley, the wife of a Boston merchant, bought Phillis. She needed a girl to train as a maid. She placed her daughter, Mary, in charge of Phillis's education. Before she could explain the household duties, Mary had to teach Phillis to speak English. A quick learner, Phillis also mastered the alphabet. Within two years, Phyllis could read the Bible. Then she learned how to write. Most of all, she liked to read and write poetry.

Phillis published her first poem at age fourteen. Among her best-known poetry was the elegy or funeral poem that she wrote at age seventeen for the preacher George Whitefield.

When the poem was published in 1770, Phillis was in poor health. She was only able to do light housework and to write poems.

In 1773, Phillis sailed for London. The Wheatleys' doctor thought the sea air would do her good. She became very popular in England, where people called her the "African poetess." That year, she published a book of poems, and the Wheatleys gave Phillis her freedom.

Susanna Wheatley died shortly after Phillis returned from England. Phillis left the Wheatley household in 1778 upon the death of John Wheatley. That year, she married John Peters, also a free African American. Her health grew steadily worse. Phillis Wheatley Peters, the first African American to publish a book of poetry, died in December 1784 at age thirty-one.

"May Whitefield's Virtues flourish with his Fame,

And Ages yet unborn record his Name.

All Praise and Glory be to God on High,

Whose dread Command is, That we all must die.

To live to Life eternal, may we emulate

The worthy Man that's gone, e'er tis too late."

Cities of the Northeast

Thinking on Your Own

Create two columns in your notebook titled "Ship Owners, Merchants, and Shopkeepers" and "Craftspeople and Laborers." As you read, fill in the columns with key information about each group.

Towns and cities played an important role in the New England and Middle Colonies. They provided a market for the products of colonial farms and forests. Their workshops and stores sold goods that the colonists could not make themselves. They also provided education, entertainment, and music.

focus your reading

Why did the New England and Middle Colonies need cities?

What items did city merchants import?

What products did colonial cities export?

vocabulary

farm produce

forest products

craftspeople

Ship Owners, Merchants, and Shopkeepers

The largest cities of the Northeast were seaports. Merchants imported cloth, hardware, books, tea, and other items from England. They exported grain, meat, and other **farm produce**. They also exported **forest products** such as ships' masts and roof shingles.

The ship owners of New England were involved in a three-sided, or triangular, trade. That is, they shipped rum to Africa to exchange for slaves. They sold the slaves in the West Indies, where they bought sugar. They sold the sugar in Boston to distillers who made the rum.

Wealthy merchants and ship owners were the cities' upper class. These families lived in big houses in the center of town and wore fine clothes. Below them in status were shopkeepers, whose homes were smaller and less well furnished. They also dressed more plainly.

New York skyline during the early eighteenth century

Craftspeople and Laborers

Cities were also places for work. Boston's meatpackers slaughtered cattle and pigs, pickled the meat, and packed it in barrels. Millers in New York and Philadelphia ground wheat into flour. Every large city had a printer, such as Benjamin Franklin in Philadelphia. **Craftspeople**, or skilled workers, made shoes, silverware, and clothing. Unskilled laborers loaded and unloaded ships and kept the streets in repair.

Skilled workers and their families occupied the bottom half of society. The craftspeople usually worked at home. They often turned the front room of their home into a shop. Unskilled workers were the poorest of all. They lived in shacks on the edge of the city.

stop and think

Create a movie in your mind about a day in a colonial city. Illustrate three scenes in the movie. Use a bulleted list to make notes of details for each scene.

Printers contributed to the economic development of the colonies.

Centers of Culture

City people were more likely than others to write books, open libraries, hold concerts, and put on plays. Most books, especially in New England, had religious themes. Boston produced two widely read women poets—Phillis Wheatley and Anne Bradstreet. Wheatley, a slave, was the first African American woman to have her work published.

In Philadelphia in 1731, Benjamin Franklin set up the colonies' first lending library. Music lovers in Boston and New York City could attend classical music concerts by the 1750s. By then, every colonial city had a theater. People especially liked to watch plays by William Shakespeare.

The wealthy often gathered to listen to classical music.

Putting It All Together

Look through Lesson 3. Find three kinds of connections with what you have read: 1) how it relates to something else you have read; 2) how it relates to something in your own life; and 3) how it relates to something you know about. Choose the strongest connection and write a paragraph about it in your notebook.

Chapter Summary

During the 1600s, the New England Colonies attracted thousands of **immigrants**. Most New England colonists settled in farm villages with homes clustered around the **meetinghouse**. The expanding settlements caused conflict with the native people.

In the 1740s, New England Puritan ministers led a religious revival called the **Great Awakening**. Education was also important. The Puritans set up **grammar schools** to teach reading and writing and **Latin schools** to prepare boys for college.

The Middle Colonies also grew rapidly. The fertile soil of New York, New Jersey, Pennsylvania, and Delaware attracted tens of thousands of settlers. Because wheat was their main cash crop, these colonies were called England's **breadbasket**.

Pennsylvania was a **haven** for religious minorities. Because the colony was **tolerant**, it attracted **Pennsylvania Dutch** and **Scots-Irish** immigrants. These settlers had fewer conflicts with native people than other colonies had.

Towns and cities played an important role in the New England and Middle Colonies. Wealthy merchants imported goods from England, and exported **farm produce** and **forest products**. **Craftspeople** made shoes, silverware, and clothing. Laborers worked on the docks.

Chapter Review

1   Imagine that you are a newspaper reporter interviewing colonists from the New England and Middle Colonies about life in those regions. Write questions that could be asked of a city resident and a village resident. Then write answers that explain the benefits of each region.

2   Use each vocabulary word in a sentence. Relate each word to life in the colonies.

3   Write a paragraph describing English colonization in the New England and Middle Colonies from the point of view of the native people of those areas.

Skill Builder

Reading a Bar Graph

Information presented in graph form is easy to visualize. The bars or lines on a graph also make it easy to compare information. Bar graphs present information in vertical or horizontal bars, as on the population graph below. That graph compares the populations of five colonial cities at three periods in time.

Use the population bar graph to answer the following questions:

1 Which was the largest city in 1730?

2 Which city experienced the most rapid growth between 1730 and 1760?

3 In what year did the population of New York City exceed that of Boston?

4 Which city grew at the slowest rate between 1700 and 1760?

5 What is the difference in population between the largest and smallest city in 1700? in 1730? in 1760?

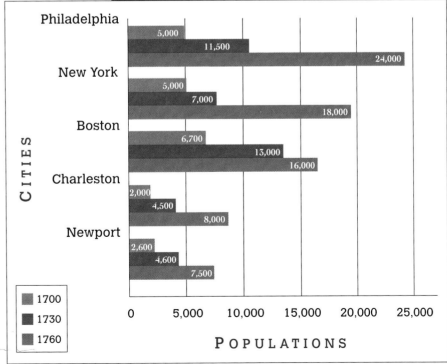

Colonial Populations, 1700–1760

Philadelphia: 5,000 / 11,500 / 24,000
New York: 5,000 / 7,000 / 18,000
Boston: 6,700 / 13,000 / 16,000
Charleston: 2,000 / 4,500 / 8,000
Newport: 2,600 / 4,600 / 7,500

CITIES

POPULATIONS: 0, 5,000, 10,000, 15,000, 20,000, 25,000

Legend: 1700, 1730, 1760

UNIT 4
THE AMERICAN REVOLUTION

The American Revolution was a process that required twenty years to complete. At the end of the French and Indian War in 1763, American colonists were loyal subjects of Great Britain. By 1783, they were free and independent citizens of the United States of America.

The War for Independence began as a change in the hearts and minds of the people. Laws passed by Parliament and regulations approved by the king threatened liberties they had long enjoyed. Bonds of affection turned into chains meant to enslave them. The revolution in the colonists' feelings led to the Declaration of Independence. The War for Independence established the United States of America.

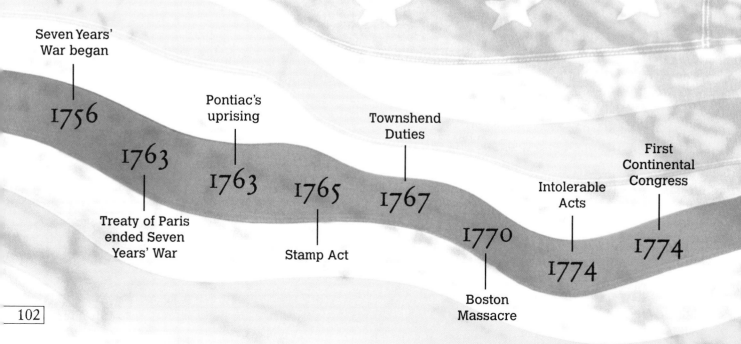

Seven Years'
War began

1756

Pontiac's
uprising

1763

Treaty of Paris
ended Seven
Years' War

1763

Stamp Act

1765

Townshend
Duties

1767

Boston
Massacre

1770

Intolerable
Acts

1774

First
Continental
Congress

1774

How did the United States of America win its independence?

Why does the Declaration of Independence still inspire people in their search for freedom, liberty, and dignity?

What traditional freedoms did Parliament and King George III threaten?

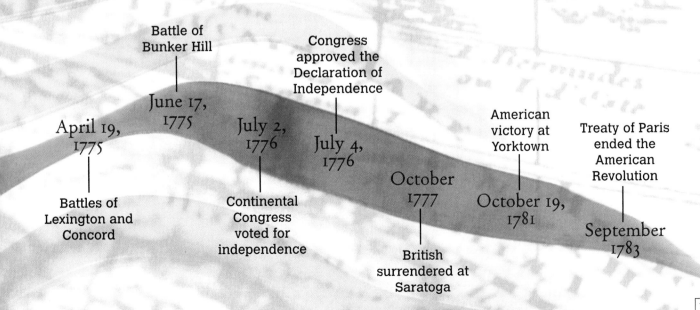

April 19, 1775

Battles of Lexington and Concord

Battle of Bunker Hill

June 17, 1775

July 2, 1776

Continental Congress voted for independence

Congress approved the Declaration of Independence

July 4, 1776

October 1777

British surrendered at Saratoga

American victory at Yorktown

October 19, 1781

Treaty of Paris ended the American Revolution

September 1783

Chapter 7 · CONFLICT WITH BRITAIN

Getting Focused

Skim this chapter to predict what you will be learning.

- Read the lesson titles and subheadings.
- Look at the illustrations and read the captions.
- Examine the maps.
- Review the vocabulary words and terms.

Sometimes disputes over property and rights cause people to set strict limits: This is mine, and that is yours. As you read, look for signs of limits that led to conflict and how the conflicts were resolved. Take notes in your notebook.

The Expanding Empire

Thinking on Your Own

Read the Focus Your Reading questions and discuss possible answers with a partner. Skim through this lesson looking for clues. In your notebook, predict answers for each question.

In the 1750s, **Great Britain** and France clashed over control of the Ohio Valley. The Virginia Colony granted land there to companies. Farmers wanted to buy farms and settle there. The French were determined to keep control of the Ohio Valley because of its valuable fur trade. French officials in Canada and their Native American allies tried to stop British settlement.

focus your reading

How did the French try to block British expansion?

How did the Treaty of Paris change the map of North America?

Why did Parliament pass the Stamp Act?

vocabulary

Great Britain   proclamation

militia   Parliament

Frontier Fighting

To block British expansion, the French built Fort Duquesne on the Ohio River. In 1754, the governor of Virginia sent Colonel George Washington and forty **militia**, or volunteer, soldiers to destroy the fort. A much larger force of French troops and their Native American allies attacked Washington's small army. The Virginians surrendered and returned home.

George Washington in the Ohio Valley

When news of Washington's defeat reached Britain, the government sent General Edward Braddock with a larger army to Virginia. Joined by Virginia militiamen, Braddock's troops set out early in 1755 for Fort Duquesne. They were attacked by surprise. Shooting from behind trees and boulders, the French and Native American fighters nearly wiped out the British. General Braddock died on the battlefield.

General Braddock's troops were ambushed in 1755.

The French and Indian War

Braddock's defeat triggered a full-scale war between England and France. They fought in Europe as well as in the colonies. Determined to drive their rival out of North America, the British attacked the French in Canada. They captured Quebec in 1758. That year, British and colonial forces also seized control of Fort Duquesne, which they renamed Fort Pitt—present-day Pittsburgh. In 1760, the British captured Montreal, Canada's second major city. That brought the fighting in North America to an end.

The British captured Quebec in 1758.

In Europe, the war was known as the Seven Years' War (1756–1763). Fighting there ended three years later. In the peace treaty signed in Paris, France gave up its claim to Canada.

The Treaty of Paris also turned over to Britain all of France's territory east of the Mississippi, except the town of New Orleans.

Defending the British Empire

The war with France greatly increased Britain's territory in North America. It also created problems. The war nearly doubled Britain's national debt. Although nearly broke, Britain had to pay for additional soldiers to defend the new territory. The Native Americans also were of concern. In 1763, Pontiac, an Ottawa chief, led an uprising of native groups in the West. They burned British forts and attacked colonists who settled on Native American land.

stop and think

Turn over the book and discuss with a partner what you have learned about 1) events that led to the Treaty of Paris, and 2) how the treaty changed the map of North America. Write a three-sentence summary of your discussion in your notebook.

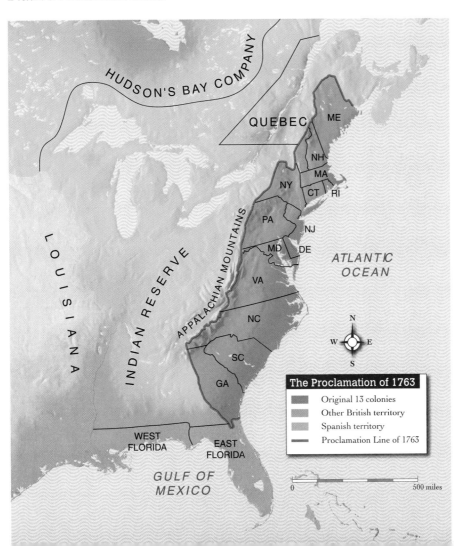

The Proclamation of 1763
- Original 13 colonies
- Other British territory
- Spanish territory
- Proclamation Line of 1763

Chief Pontiac met with British Major Gladwyn in 1763 to discuss peace.

The British government acted quickly. To restore peace with the native people, King George III issued the **Proclamation** of 1763. It prohibited colonists from settling on Native American land west of the Appalachian Mountains. The British government insisted that the colonists should help keep the peace and pay part of the cost of defense. The colonists were forced to pay the salaries of soldiers, feed them, and provide them with housing. In 1764, the British **Parliament**, or legislature, passed the Sugar Act. It placed import duties, or fees, on sugar and other products shipped into the colonies. The Stamp Act of 1765 taxed legal documents and other printed matter.

Stamps were required on many taxed items.

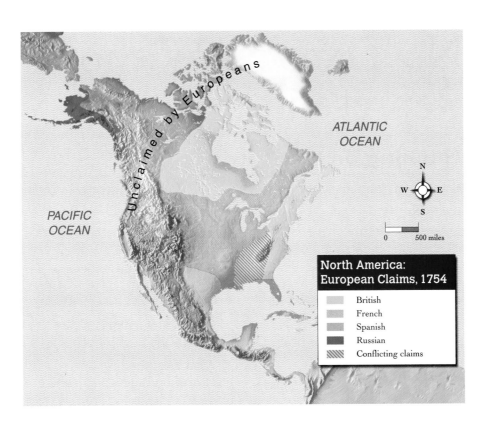

ATLANTIC
OCEAN

PACIFIC
OCEAN

Unclaimed by Europeans

N
W—E
S

0   500 miles

**North America:
European Claims, 1754**

British
French
Spanish
Russian
Conflicting claims

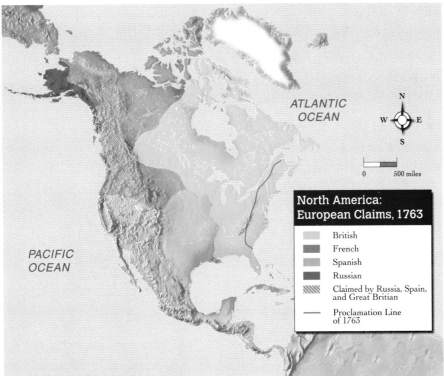

ATLANTIC
OCEAN

PACIFIC
OCEAN

N
W—E
S

0   500 miles

**North America:
European Claims, 1763**

British
French
Spanish
Russian
Claimed by Russia, Spain,
and Great Britian
Proclamation Line
of 1763

Putting It All Together

Review the predictions you made for the Focus Your Reading
questions. Make changes, if needed, based on what you now
know. Write your answers in your notebook.

No Taxation Without Representation

Thinking on Your Own

Read the vocabulary words. As you read this lesson, use each word in a sentence of your own. Make sure that your sentences show the meaning of each word. Write your sentences in your notebook.

Policies that seemed reasonable to the king and Parliament outraged the colonists. The Proclamation of 1763 angered those who wanted land in the Ohio Valley. Parliament had required importers to pay duties before, but the laws were seldom enforced. This time Parliament intended to collect the duties. It cracked down on **smuggling**—importing goods without paying duties. That reduced the profits of certain merchants. Most troubling of all was the Stamp Act.

The Stamp Act Crisis

The tax imposed by the Parliament in the Stamp Act threatened a basic right. Until then, the colonists were taxed only by representatives they elected to their colonial **assemblies**, or legislatures. This time, they were taxed by Parliament, where they had no representatives.

> **focus your reading**
>
> Why did the colonists oppose the Stamp Act?
>
> What was Charles Townshend's new tax plan?
>
> How did Britain try to restore order in Boston?
>
> **vocabulary**
>
> smuggling   boycott
>
> assemblies   repeal

Resistance to the Stamp Act was strong among merchants.

The colonists protested against the Stamp Act. "No taxation without representation," they insisted. In Boston, a mob ruined the house of the lieutenant governor, who supported the act. Nine colonies sent delegates to a Stamp Act Congress in New York City. The Stamp Act Congress sent a declaration to Parliament defending the colonists' right to tax themselves. The colonists also agreed to **boycott**, or refuse to buy, English goods.

Stamp Act protestors in Boston wrecked the lieutenant governor's house.

Under pressure from British merchants, Parliament decided to **repeal** the Stamp Act in March 1766. However, it still insisted that it had the right to tax the colonies. The issue was far from settled.

The Townshend Duties

In 1767, Charles Townshend, the British finance minister, came up with a new tax plan. He noticed that the colonists did not object to duties collected at the port. They opposed only direct, or internal, taxes. Townshend asked Parliament to place import duties on more goods being shipped to the colonies. The new Townshend Revenue Act included duties on glass, lead, paint, paper, and tea.

The colonists saw this as just another attempt to tax them. This time they objected to any kind of taxes by Parliament. Once again the colonists stopped buying British goods. Instead, they bought smuggled goods. British officials accused John Hancock, a Boston merchant, of smuggling. They seized one of his ships. In protest, people in Boston rioted in the streets.

stop and think

Imagine that you hear an argument over the Stamp Act between a British member of Parliament and an American colonist. Write four or five lines of dialogue that you overheard.

Crispus Attucks was killed in the Boston Massacre.

The Boston Massacre

To restore law and order, the British government sent troops to Boston. By late 1769, approximately 4,000 troops had arrived in a city that had only 15,000 residents. That created tension. Off-duty soldiers competed with citizens for jobs. Fights broke out. On March 5, 1770, a Boston mob attacked a detachment of troops with clubs and snowballs.

In the confusion, the troops fired into the crowd. Five rioters were killed, including Crispus Attucks, a former African American slave. Although little is known about Crispus Attucks, many people believe that he was the first death of the Revolutionary War.

Colonists rushed to Boston from nearby towns to protest the Boston Massacre, as it was called. Colonial officials restored order by arresting the soldiers accused of firing the shots. They were promised a fair trial in Boston. Britain withdrew the remainder of the troops from the city.

Putting It All Together

At the beginning of this chapter, you looked for the strict limits, or boundaries, set by the colonists and Parliament as signs of conflict. Write a paragraph describing the limits set by each side over taxes and import duties.

Read a Primary Source

The Boston Massacre: An American Account

On the night of March 5, 1770, British troops fired into a Boston crowd, killing five people and wounding others. The following is an account of what happened. It was published in Boston shortly after the event. The author was not present, however, he interviewed people who were there that night.

reading for understanding

According to this writer, who began the fight?

How did the crowd respond?

What orders did Preston give the soldiers?

" . . . the ringing of the meetinghouse bell brought out a number of the inhabitants, who . . . were naturally led to King Street . . . [where they joined] a number of boys, round the sentry at the Custom House. . . . There was much foul language between them, and some of them, in consequence of his pushing at them with his bayonet, threw snowballs at him. . . .

"The officer on guard was Captain Preston, who with seven or eight soldiers, with firearms and charged bayonets, issued from the guardhouse, and in great haste posted himself and his soldiers in front of the Custom House. . . . In passing to this station the soldiers pushed several persons with their bayonets. . . . This occasioned some snowballs to be thrown at them, which seems to have been the only provocation that was given. . . .

"Captain Preston is said to have ordered them to fire, and to have repeated that order. One gun was first; then others in succession, and with deliberation, till ten or a dozen guns were fired. . . . By which means eleven persons were killed or wounded. . . . "

From *A Short Narrative of the Horrid Massacre in Boston,* (Boston, 1770).

In Defense of Liberty

Thinking on Your Own

Divide one page in your notebook into top, middle, and bottom sections. Entitle the sections "Tea Act," "Intolerable Acts," and "Continental Congress." As you read this lesson, write two questions that you have about each topic.

A period of calm followed the violence in Boston. Parliament repealed the Townshend Duties, except for the tax on tea. It softened the Proclamation of 1763, allowing settlers to move into eastern Tennessee and Kentucky. For many colonists, this was too little, too late. They refused to pay the tax on English tea, smuggling in Dutch tea instead. Leaders in each colony set up Committees of Correspondence to keep in touch with other colonies. One misstep by Parliament could start a new round of protest.

focus your reading

Why did the colonists oppose the Tea Act?

What were the Intolerable Acts?

How did the colonists respond to those acts?

vocabulary

Intolerable Acts

delegates

Samuel Adams founded the Committees of Correspondence.

The Tea Act

A misstep came in 1773, when Parliament passed the Tea Act. This act helped the East India Company, a British trading company in India, cut its costs. The act allowed the company to sell directly to the colonies. It no longer had to ship the tea to London, where merchants charged a handling fee. The company could undersell smugglers, even after the colonists had paid the tea tax.

Dressed as Native Americans, protestors dumped tea into Boston Harbor.

Many colonists believed the Tea Act was Parliament's way of tricking them into paying that tax. When the company's ships arrived, they refused to unload the tea. In Boston, the protestors took more direct action. On December 16, 1773, they boarded the ship and dumped the tea into the harbor. They called it the Boston Tea Party.

The Intolerable Acts

For Parliament, dumping the tea was the last straw. It moved quickly to punish Boston and the Massachusetts Colony. It wanted to set an example that would keep other colonies in line. Parliament passed a set of laws that the colonists called the **Intolerable Acts**. These laws

- closed the port of Boston until the tea was paid for
- allowed Boston to hold only one town meeting each year
- permitted any British official accused of a crime to be sent to England for trial
- required Massachusetts to house British troops in empty houses, barns, or buildings at the colony's expense

stop and think

Do you agree or disagree with the patriots that the term "Intolerable Acts" is a good description of those acts of Parliament? Why? Discuss your reason with a partner.

At the same time, Parliament passed the Quebec Act. This law shifted control of land in the Ohio Valley to Britain's new colony in Quebec. That angered colonists in Pennsylvania and Virginia, who wanted that land for farms.

The Continental Congress

The punishment of Massachusetts did not have the effect that Parliament wanted. The other colonies rallied behind Massachusetts. Each colony agreed to send **delegates**, or representatives, to a Continental Congress to decide what to do next. Patrick Henry, a delegate from Virginia, said he went to the meeting "not as a Virginian, but as an American."

Patrick Henry represented Virginia at the First Continental Congress.

Meeting in Philadelphia in 1774, the Continental Congress drew up a list of rights that Parliament should respect. The delegates also agreed to a new boycott against British-made goods. But they were not ready to cut their ties to Britain. They declared their loyalty to the king, but they refused to obey Parliament. They also agreed to defend themselves from any future attack by the British army.

Putting It All Together

With a partner, compare the questions you wrote about the Tea Act, the Intolerable Acts, and the Continental Congress. Together write possible answers to each question.

Biography

Patrick Henry (1736–1799)

On March 23, 1775, Patrick Henry addressed the Virginia Assembly. He urged the reluctant delegates to prepare for war against Britain. "Gentlemen may cry, peace, peace—but there is no peace. The war is actually begun. . . . Is life so dear, or peace so sweet, as to be purchased at the price of chains and slavery? Forbid it, Almighty God! I know not what course others may take; but as for me, give me liberty or give me death!" His motion to create a Virginia militia won by a solid majority.

Patrick Henry was born in western Virginia in 1736. He received little formal education and barely passed his law exam. He learned about the power of the human voice by listening to revival preachers. His magic with words made him a very successful trial lawyer and a vote-getting politician. Elected to the Virginia Assembly in 1764, he represented the common people of western Virginia. In the assembly, he became a thorn in the side of Virginia's aristocratic planters.

Patrick Henry realized earlier than most Virginians that Parliament posed a serious threat to the colonies. In 1765, he led the opposition to the Stamp Act. He persuaded the Virginia Assembly to defy the law. He stepped forward again in 1774 to protest against the Intolerable Acts. He went to Philadelphia with George Washington and other Virginian delegates to serve in the Continental Congress. There he became good friends with Sam and John Adams, who shared his views about the likelihood of war. He returned from Philadelphia to give his famous "Liberty or Death" speech.

Patrick Henry spent the remainder of his life serving Virginia. He commanded the Virginia militia in 1775, and in 1776 was elected the first governor of the State of Virginia. In 1787, he opposed the U.S. Constitution on the grounds that it took too much power away from Virginia and other states. He died on June 6, 1799, active in Virginia politics to the end.

Chapter Summary

In the 1750s, **Great Britain** and France clashed over control of the Ohio Valley. France defeated a Virginia **militia** led by Colonel George Washington. This led to the French and Indian War. The Treaty of Paris gave Canada and most of France's territory east of the Mississippi to the British. The **Proclamation** of 1763 prohibited colonists from settling west of the Appalachian Mountains. To raise money, the British **Parliament** taxed the colonists.

The colonists insisted that only their elected **assemblies** had the right to tax them. In protest, they agreed to **boycott** British goods. Under pressure from British merchants, Parliament chose to **repeal** the Stamp Act. To raise money, it placed new import duties on goods shipped to the colonies. It also cracked down on **smuggling** in Boston.

In 1773, many colonists saw the Tea Act as Parliament's way to trick them into paying a tax. When tea arrived in Boston, protestors held the Boston Tea Party. Parliament passed the **Intolerable Acts** to punish the people of Massachusetts. To protest these acts, the colonies sent **delegates** to a Continental Congress in Philadelphia. The colonists boycotted British goods.

Chapter Review

1 Go back to the argument over the Stamp Act that you overheard in Stop and Think for Lesson 2. Knowing what happened in the years following that act, write a paragraph defending one of the positions.

2 The Proclamation of 1763 set limits on where colonists could live. Write an editorial arguing against this law.

3 Describe at least three times when Britain and the colonies set limits with each other between 1763 and 1774.

4 Do any of your questions from Putting It All Together for Lesson 3 remain unanswered? If so, work with a partner to compile a list of possible resources that you can use to answer these questions. Find the answers to the questions.

Skill Builder

Identifying Propaganda

Information presented in a way to win people over to a point of view is called propaganda. Propaganda may include untrue or biased statements. It may also present the truth, but not the whole truth. When looking at words or images, keep in mind the following questions:

- What is the intent of the author?
- Is the author presenting opinion as fact?
- Does the article, book, or picture present both sides of the issue?
- Does the style appeal more to emotions than to reason?

Paul Revere made this engraving of the clash in Boston on March 5, 1770, between British soldiers and townspeople. The engraving is entitled *The Bloody Massacre*. It shows a British officer ordering his troops to fire into the crowd. The poem printed at the bottom of the engraving begins:

Analyze Revere's print for its propaganda value by answering the following questions:

1 What was Revere trying to accomplish with this engraving?

2 Does the engraving appeal primarily to emotion or reason?

3 How is Crispus Attuchs portrayed in this image? How does this differ from the image on page 112? How is this propoganda?

4 Do the title and poem try to win over the reader to a particular point of view? Which view?

Unhappy Boston! See thy sons deplore,

Thy hallowe'd Walks besmear'd with guiltless Gore;

While faithless P[resto]n, and his savage Bands

With murd'rous Rancour stretch their bloody hands;

Like fierce Babarians grinning o'er their Prey,

Approve the Carnage, and enjoy the Day.

Chapter 8

THE WAR FOR INDEPENDENCE

Getting Focused

Skim this chapter to predict what you will be learning.

- Read the lesson titles and subheadings.
- Look at the illustrations and read the captions.
- Examine the maps.
- Review the vocabulary words and terms.

Think about the consequences of not being able to resolve a conflict peacefully. In your notebook write three questions that you have about the War for Independence.

From Peaceful Protest to Violence

Thinking on Your Own

Create a two-column chart in your notebook. On one side write the three Focus Your Reading questions. As you read, fill in the other side with the answers. Use the vocabulary in your answers.

In their struggle with Parliament, the colonists looked to King George III for help. The king, however, chose to side with Parliament. He considered the colonists to be in rebellion. "Blows must decide whether they are to be subject to the Country or Independent," he told a British official. The king demanded that rebel leaders in Massachusetts be arrested. He appointed General Thomas Gage as the colony's new governor.

focus your reading

Why did British troops march to Concord?

Who did the Continental Congress ask for help?

Why did the British leave Boston?

vocabulary

patriots

minutemen

redcoats

Olive Branch Petition

Continental army

Paul Revere raised the alarm of approaching British troops.

British soldiers fired at the militia lined up on Lexington Green.

Lexington and Concord

In Boston, General Gage ordered British troops to capture the leaders of the **patriots**, those who favored independence, and to destroy their military supplies. Gage believed that the patriots were hiding supplies in the town of Concord. The soldiers set out for Concord on the morning of April 19, 1775. Paul Revere, who learned of their plans, rode ahead with Dr. Samuel Prescott and William Dawes to warn the patriots.

A monument recalls the words of Captain John Parker at the Battle of Lexington.

At Lexington, the British troops fired on the **minutemen**, or colonial militia, gathered there. They killed eight men. At Concord, they burned the supplies the colonists had not managed to remove. By then, hundreds of militia armed with muskets had set out for Concord. They killed seventy-three **redcoats**—the nickname given the British soldiers—and wounded dozens more as the patriots marched back to Boston.

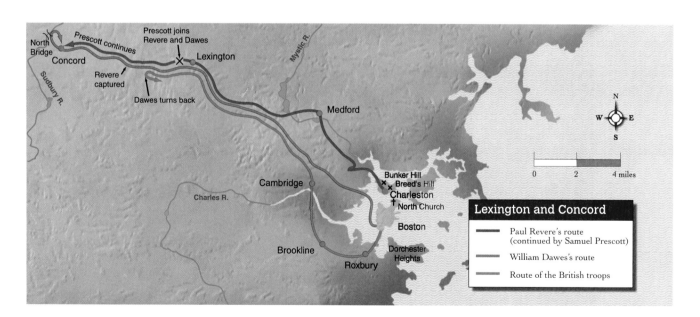

Patriots and British troops skirmished at Concord's North Bridge.

The Olive Branch Petition

In May 1775, delegates met again in Philadelphia. This Second Continental Congress sent George III an **Olive Branch Petition**, or peace petition. It again declared the colonies' loyalty to the king and asked for his help in their struggle against Parliament. The majority of colonists still hoped for a peaceful settlement. Nevertheless, Congress created a **Continental army**, made George Washington its commander, and printed money to support the troops. Unlike each colony's militia, the Continental army enlisted soldiers from several colonies.

stop and think

Discuss with a partner the arguments the Second Continental Congress probably made in the Olive Branch Petition. Write two or three sentences in your notebook that summarize your discussion. If needed, find more information in the library or the Internet.

Battle of Bunker Hill

After Lexington and Concord, militia soldiers gathered on the hills around Boston. They surrounded the British army in the city. On June 17, 1775, General Gage led an attack against Breed's Hill. The British finally captured the hill, but at a terrible price. At the Battle of Bunker Hill—actually Breed's Hill—the British suffered 1,000 casualties. Patriot losses were less than half of British losses. The minutemen proved they had the courage to stand and fight.

Scene from Battle of Bunker Hill

General Washington arrived two weeks later. He took command of the militia and enlisted them into the Continental army. That winter, he had cannons brought down from a fort captured from the British on Lake Champlain. With cannons mounted on the hills above them, the British army was forced to withdraw from Boston. They sailed to Nova Scotia in March 1776, taking 1,000 Loyalists with them.

Militiamen fire on British troops.

Putting It All Together

On a page in your notebook, write the heading "Successful Moves by the Minutemen." Under the heading, list at least three of those successes.

Read a Primary Source

Who Shot First?

On the morning of April 19, 1775, British troops killed eight minutemen at Lexington, Massachusetts. Their deaths became a rallying cry for the patriots who wanted independence from Great Britain. Who was responsible for firing the first shots in the War for Independence? The following are three eyewitness accounts of the "shot heard around the world."

---

reading for understanding

What was the American version of what happened?

How did the British commander's view differ?

Considering Lieutenant Gould's account, can we really know what happened that morning?

John Parker, Militia Commander

66Upon their [British soldiers] sudden approach, I immediately ordered our Militia to disperse and not to fire. Immediately said Troops made their appearance, and rushed furiously, fired upon and killed eight of our party, without receiving any provocation therefore from us.99

What Happened on Lexington Green?
(Menlo Park, 1970).

Major John Pitcairn, British Commander

66When I came within about One Hundred Yards of them [the militia], they began to File off towards some stone Walls. . . . I instantly called to the Soldiers not to fire, but to surround them and disarm them. . . . Some of the Rebels who had jumped over the Wall, Fired Four or Five Shott at the soldiers. . . . Upon this the Light Infantry began a scattered Fire . . . contrary to the repeated orders both of me and the officers that were present.99

What Happened on Lexington Green?
(Menlo Park, 1970).

Lieutenant Edward Gould, Captured British Officer

66On our arrival at that place, we saw a body of Provincial Troops armed, to the number of about sixty or seventy men; on our approach they dispersed, and soon after firing began; but which party fired first, I cannot exactly say, as our Troops rushed on shouting and huzzaing [cheering] previous to the firing.99

What Happened on Lexington Green?
(Menlo Park, 1970).

Moving Toward Independence

Thinking on Your Own

Read the Focus Your Reading questions. With a partner, discuss what you know about the Declaration of Independence. In your notebook, write one sentence summarizing what you know.

In November 1775, the delegates at Philadelphia learned that the king had rejected the Olive Branch Petition and declared the colonists "open and avowed enemies." They soon learned that he had also blocked all trade with the colonies. A British fleet was on its way to enforce the **blockade**. The members of the Continental Congress had to choose between submitting to the king and Parliament or declaring independence.

King George III

focus your reading

Why did the delegates conclude that they could not rely on the king?

How are the pamphlet *Common Sense* and the Declaration of Independence related?

How did Jefferson make the Declaration of Independence a statement about human rights?

vocabulary

blockade   human rights

tyranny

Common Sense

The publication of *Common Sense* in January 1776, made that choice easier. Offering "simple facts, plain arguments, and common sense," this pamphlet was a slashing attack against King George III. Its author, Thomas Paine, called the king "a royal brute" who ruled by force. He insisted that the king had lost any claim to the colonists' loyalty. Paine urged the colonists to declare independence from Britain.

COMMON SENSE;
INHABITANTS
OF
AMERICA,

Common Sense was published in 1776.

Thomas Paine put into words what many colonists were thinking. Few dared to say it so bluntly. *Common Sense* became a bestseller. It sold 120,000 copies in three months. Paine's message also had a political impact. One by one, the colonies instructed their delegates at Philadelphia to vote for independence.

stop and think

Imagine that you are listening to a discussion among colonists who have just read *Common Sense*. In your notebook, write four or five lines of dialogue from that conversation.

Congress Votes for Independence

In June 1776, the Second Continental Congress created a committee to write a draft for a declaration of independence. The committee asked Thomas Jefferson, one of its members, to write a draft. After making a few changes, the committee sent Jefferson's document to Congress.

On July 2, the Continental Congress voted in favor of independence. "Yesterday," John Adams wrote on July 3, "the greatest question was decided, which ever was debated in America." On July 4, Congress voted to approve Jefferson's Declaration of Independence. It announced to the world that the thirteen former British colonies had become the free and independent United States of America.

Thomas Jefferson drafted the Declaration of Independence in 1776.

The Declaration of Independence was signed on July 4, 1776.

The Declaration of Independence

In the Declaration, Jefferson took care to explain why the colonists cut their ties with Great Britain. People, he wrote, "are endowed by their Creator with certain unalienable Rights." Among them are the right to "Life, Liberty, and the pursuit of Happiness." All people, he said, are justified in getting rid of any government that abuses those rights. He then included a long list of abuses by King George III, who tried to establish "an absolute **Tyranny** over these States." Tyranny is a government in which one person has absolute power.

By basing the Declaration on broad principles that apply to all people, Jefferson made the document a declaration of **human rights**. He defended everyone's right to get rid of an oppressive government. This has made the Declaration a timeless, living document. It continues to inspire people in their search for freedom, liberty, and dignity.

The Declaration was publicly read to soldiers.

Putting It All Together

Create a concept map with "Declaration of Independence" in the middle circle. Then read the copy of the Declaration of Independence included in this book. As you read, list on lines extending out from the circle the major points made in the Declaration.

Biography

Abigail Smith Adams (1744–1818)

In March 1776, Abigail Adams wrote to her husband, John Adams, who was attending the Continental Congress. She hoped that Congress would soon declare independence and create a "Code of Laws" for the new nation. When that time came, she added, "I desire you would Remember the Ladies, and be more generous and favourable to them than your ancestors. Do not put such unlimited power into the hands of the Husbands."

Abigail Adams was ahead of her time. The delegates who gathered in Philadelphia in 1776 were not there to grant rights to women. Their wives had no legal rights and could not vote, hold office, or take part in town meetings. That was fine with John Adams and his friends. Even Abigail Adams did not expect to see much change in her lifetime. But she could not resist reminding her husband that King George III was not the world's only tyrant.

Abigail Adams was subordinate to her husband in every way but one. John always admitted that his wife was intellectually his equal. He fell in love with his "Miss Adorable" partly because of her "habit of Reading, Writing, and Thinking." She loved poetry and memorized page after page of William Shakespeare and Alexander Pope. They married in 1764 when John, a rising young lawyer, was twenty-nine and she was almost twenty.

During the coming years, Abigail became more independent than most women of her time. She raised four children largely by herself. One of their children—John Quincy Adams—became the sixth president of the United States. She managed the family farm when John Adams served as a delegate to the Continental Congress and as a diplomat in Europe. She called herself "Mrs. Delegate" because he had left so much work for her at home.

In time, Abigail shared John Adams's public life. In 1785, she joined her husband in London, where he was the first United States minister to Great Britain. She helped him represent the United States at diplomatic events. As wife of the first vice president of the United States (1789–1797) and as first lady during her husband's administration (1797–1801), she entertained official guests at the nation's capital. In 1801, Abigail and John Adams returned to Massachusetts. She died there in 1818.

Winning Independence

Thinking on Your Own

Read the Focus Your Reading questions. Divide a page in your notebook into two columns, one headed "Militia/Continental Army," the other "British Army." As you read, list the battles won by each side in the conflict.

A colonial soldier

Britain focused on putting down the rebellion in the New England and Middle Colonies. The patriots there seemed to be the biggest troublemakers. In August 1776, British General William Howe landed 32,000 **troops** near New York City. Facing him was General Washington's Continental army of 13,000 men. Howe won battles at Brooklyn Heights and White Plains, but failed to destroy Washington's army. Washington won victories that winter in New Jersey at Trenton and Princeton. These victories lifted the patriots' spirits.

focus your reading

What did the British try to accomplish in the North?

Who were the Tories?

Why did the British expect to do better in the South?

How did France help the Americans win their independence?

vocabulary

troops   ally

Tories

The War in the North

The winter at Valley Forge was brutal, and the troops suffered greatly.

In 1777, the British unleashed a major attack from Canada. They hoped to isolate and occupy New England. Instead, American militia troops defeated the British at the Battles of Saratoga and Oriskany in New York.

That summer, General Howe attacked the Continental army in Pennsylvania. Washington lost battles at Brandywine Creek and Germantown, but again saved his army. The army spent the winter camped at Valley Forge. Howe occupied Philadelphia, but withdrew the next summer. The British accomplished little from their attacks in the north.

The War on the Frontier

On the frontier, the results were no better. There the British fought American militia soldiers for control of the frontier. In 1777, the Americans defeated the British and their Iroquois allies in western New York. The British and the Shawnee then

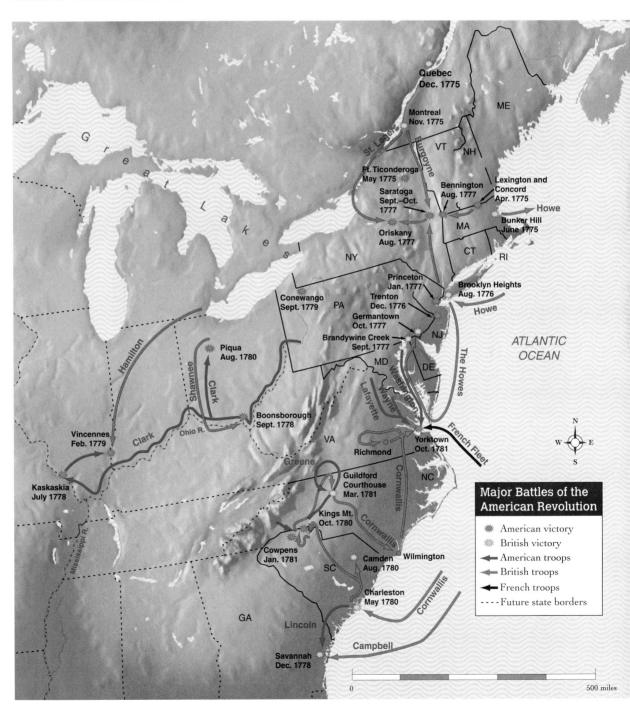

Major Battles of the American Revolution

* American victory
* British victory
← American troops
← British troops
← French troops
---- Future state borders

attacked American settlers in Kentucky. George Rogers Clark led Virginia militia troops to drive the British out of the Ohio Valley. They captured British forts at Kaskaskia and Vincennes. These Battles of the Old Northwest gave the United States a strong claim to the Ohio Valley at the end of the war.

Tories were harrassed in the colonies.

stop and think

During most of the war, General George Washington lost more battles than he won. What did he do that caused people to consider him a great military leader? Write a brief answer to this question in your notebook and compare it with that of a partner.

Tories and Traitors

The patriots' most hated enemies were Americans who were loyal to Britain. Some 20 percent of the population was made up of **Tories**, or Loyalists. Patriots forced suspected Loyalists to sign oaths of loyalty to the United States. Many Tories lost their homes and property. In fact, not all patriots could be trusted. American General Benedict Arnold tried to turn over the fort at West Point to the British.

The War in the South

In 1780, the British decided to concentrate their efforts in the South, which had more Loyalists. They captured Charleston, South Carolina. With Loyalist help, an army under Lord Cornwallis also defeated the Americans at Camden. Then the tide turned. The patriots defeated Tory armies at Kings Mountain and at Cowpens. Losing Tory support, the British army withdrew to Yorktown, Virginia, in 1781.

Molly Pitcher and other women fought for independence from Britain.

Daniel Morgan at the Battle of Cowpens

The British move to Yorktown was a mistake. Yorktown placed the British within striking distance of Washington's army. By then, the United States had a powerful **ally**—or partner. France agreed to provide the United States with military supplies. It also sent an army and a fleet to help the Americans. The combined armies surrounded Yorktown by land. The French fleet prevented the British from escaping by sea and provided the support needed to achieve victory.

The fighting ended when General Cornwallis surrendered on October 19, 1781. The Treaty of Paris officially ended the war in November 1783. The treaty recognized American independence and made the Mississippi River the western boundary of the United States.

North America, 1783

- British
- French
- Spanish
- Russian
- United States
- Conflicting claims

Unclaimed by Europeans

RUSSIAN AMERICA

RUPERT'S LAND (Hudson's Bay Company)

CANADA

0   500 miles

N
W   E
S

SPANISH LOUSIANA

UNITED STATES

ATLANTIC OCEAN

NEW SPAIN

PACIFIC OCEAN

Florida

St. Domingue (Fr.)

Cuba

Puerto Rico

Jamaica   Santo Domingo

New Granada

Putting It All Together

Why did the Americans win the War for Independence? List three reasons in your notebook. Rank these in order of importance. Compare your reasons with those of other students.

Chapter Summary

In the colonists' struggle with Parliament, King George III sided with Parliament. He demanded that the **patriot** leaders be arrested. On April 19, 1775, British soldiers killed eight **minutemen** at Lexington. The colonial militia killed seventy-three **redcoats** as the troops marched back to Boston. In May, delegates meeting in Philadelphia sent the **Olive Branch Petition** to the king. They also appointed George Washington as commander of the **Continental army**.

In November 1775, the delegates at Philadelphia learned that the king had rejected their Olive Branch Petition. He also established a **blockade** of the colonies. On July 4, 1776, Congress approved the Declaration of Independence. It accused King George of trying to establish a **tyranny** over the colonies. It also was a declaration of **human rights**.

Britain tried to put down the rebellion. General Washington, outnumbered by British **troops**, moved his army to New Jersey. In 1777, British General Howe captured Philadelphia, but again failed to destroy Washington's army.

In 1780, the British concentrated their efforts in the South—a region with more **Tories**. The next year, the Americans and their French **ally** won a major victory at the Battle of Yorktown. The Treaty of Paris recognized the United States as an independent nation and ended the war in 1783.

Chapter Review

1 Review the vocabulary words. Write a sentence related to this chapter for each word.

2 Create a flag for the new United States of America of 1776 that does not include stars and stripes. Research other flags and think of symbols that represent the United States and what it stood for. Write a paragraph explaining why you chose those symbols for your flag.

3 Return to the questions that you wrote at the beginning of the chapter. Write answers for them based on your reading.

Skill Builder

Historical Works of Art

Paintings, portraits, and other works of art can be useful tools for learning history. They help us visualize what events, people, or everyday life was like in the past. However, like other historical source materials, they must be used critically. To view a historical work of art critically means asking at least the following questions:

- Is the artist biased?
- Does the piece of art favor one person or point of view?
- Does it take sides in a controversy?
- Is it faithful to known historical facts?
- How far removed was the artist from the subject or time period?

The painting below is one artist's interpretation of the Battle of Lexington on April 19, 1775. Look at the painting critically by answering the following questions:

1 Does the artist show a bias toward the colonists or the British soldiers?

2 Is the painting faithful to the known facts about the Battle of Lexington?

3 How does this artist's view of the battle compare with the illustration on page 122?

Use the information presented in this chapter, including primary sources and illustrations, to answer the above questions. Then write a critical review of the painting in your notebook.

5

THE NEW NATION

The newly independent United States needed a new government. The thirteen former British colonies quickly created state governments. Most government decisions were made at that level. A central government was needed to take actions that affected all the states. For a time, the nation relied on the Continental Congress for this purpose. But something more permanent was needed.

The United States created a new national government by trial and error. The first attempt—the Articles of Confederation—proved too weak. In 1787, delegates gathered in Philadelphia to try again. Pooling their wisdom and experience, they created the Constitution of the United States. The new nation finally had a government that would last for generations to come.

States begin to adopt new constitutions

1776

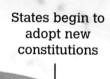

1777

Articles of Confederation written

1781

Articles of Confederation approved

1783

Treaty of Paris ended Revolutionary War

Land Ordinance of 1785

1785

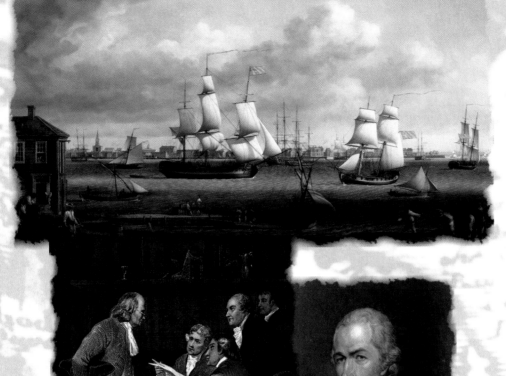

Why did the
Articles of
Confederation
fail?

Why did the
Constitution succeed?

What kind of governments
did the states create?

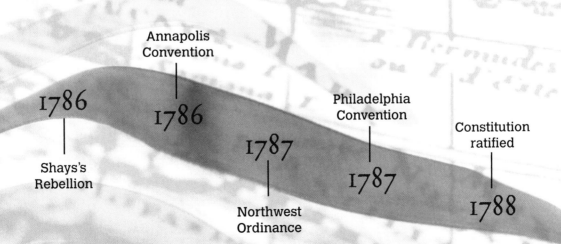

Shays's
Rebellion
1786

Annapolis
Convention
1786

Northwest
Ordinance
1787

Philadelphia
Convention
1787

Constitution
ratified
1788

Chapter 9 THE CONFEDERATION PERIOD

Getting Focused

Skim this chapter to predict what you will be learning.

- Read the lesson titles and subheadings.
- Look at the illustrations and read the captions.
- Examine the maps.
- Review the vocabulary words and terms.

There are many different styles of government around the world. Make a list of the words and phrases that come to mind when you hear the word *government*. After reviewing the lesson, add more words to the list in your notebook.

Governing the New Nation

Thinking on Your Own

Read the Focus Your Reading questions and the vocabulary words. Write the vocabulary words in your notebook. Discuss the possible meanings of the words with a partner.

During the War for Independence, Americans set up new governments. They replaced their old colonial charters with new state **constitutions**. A constitution is a document that outlines a plan of government. The old charters gave the colonists only limited power. This power came from the king. The Declaration of Independence swept that aside. The nation also created a new government to replace the Continental Congress.

focus your reading

How were the state constitutions and the colonial charters different?

Why was the first central government called a confederation?

What did the Confederation Congress accomplish?

vocabulary

constitutions

republic

bill of rights

confederation

Northwest Territory

State Governments

Early in 1776, the Continental Congress asked the individual colonies to form new governments. Most quickly adopted written constitutions. After July 4, 1776, these constitutions provided the basis for new state governments.

The Virginia state legislature met in the House of Burgess's capitol building.

The new governments had much in common. Each was a **republic**, or a government that derives its power from the people. Within the republics, people elected representatives to make and enforce the laws. The new constitutions placed most of the power in the elected assemblies. Because of this, the states had weak governors.

Most of the constitutions included a **bill of rights**. These were "natural rights" that no government should be allowed to violate. They included the right to hold property, to a trial by jury, freedom of the press, and freedom of speech and assembly.

The Articles of Confederation

The Continental Congress also created a plan for a central government. Called the Articles of Confederation, it created a **confederation**, or a loose alliance, of states. A dispute over western lands delayed the states' approval of the Articles. Some states claimed land in the Ohio Valley. Landless states opposed these claims. The states finally agreed to turn over all western land claims to Congress. The states approved the Articles of Confederation in 1781.

The Articles of Confederation provided for a congress similar to the Continental Congress. There was no president or national system of courts. Congress had the power to declare war, make peace, coin and borrow money, and regulate Native American affairs. The states retained many important powers of government. They alone had the power to enforce laws, regulate trade, and impose taxes. Each state had one vote in Congress, and nine votes were required to pass a law. The Articles reflected the American people's fear of a strong central government.

The Articles of Confederation were adopted in 1781.

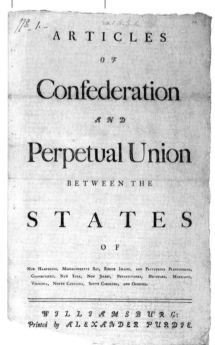

stop and think

Make sentences of the vocabulary words that you have found so far. For each word, write a sentence in your notebook using the word in context.

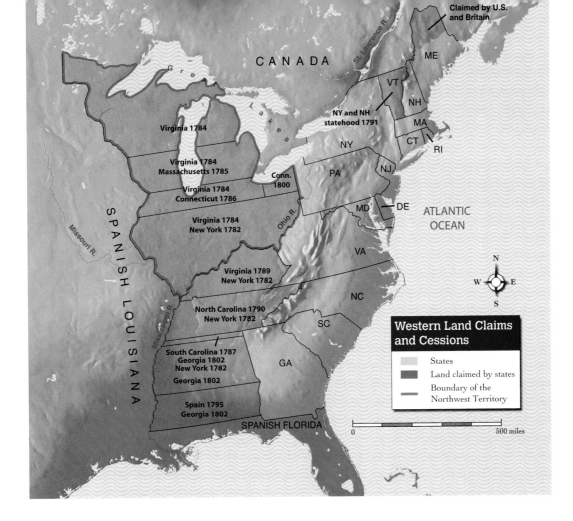

Virginia 1784

Virginia 1784
Massachusetts 1785

Virginia 1784
Connecticut 1786

Conn.
1800

Virginia 1784
New York 1782

Virginia 1789
New York 1782

North Carolina 1790
New York 1782

South Carolina 1787
Georgia 1802
New York 1782

Georgia 1802

Spain 1795
Georgia 1802

Claimed by U.S.
and Britain

NY and NH
statehood 1791

CANADA

SPANISH LOUISIANA

SPANISH FLORIDA

ATLANTIC
OCEAN

ME

VT

NH

MA

CT

RI

NY

NJ

PA

MD

DE

VA

NC

SC

GA

Western Land Claims and Cessions

- States
- Land claimed by states
- Boundary of the Northwest Territory

0   500 miles

Successes of Congress

Although its power was limited, the Confederation Congress did accomplish important things. It negotiated the peace treaty that ended the war with Britain. The Treaty of Paris (1783) was more favorable to the United States than most people had expected. The boundaries to which Britain agreed created a nation ten times the size of Great Britain and four times larger than France.

Benjamin West's unfinished portrait of the American representatives drafting the Treaty of Paris. The British delegates refused to sit for the painting.

Congress also opened the **Northwest Territory** to settlement. The Northwest Territory was the western land located north of the Ohio River. The Land Ordinance of 1785 put this land for sale in sections of 640 acres for one dollar per acre.

The Northwest Ordinance of 1787 created a way to admit new states into the confederation. It allowed settlers to create territorial governments. The ordinance also outlawed slavery in these future territories.

Once a region had 5,000 adult white males, it could elect a legislature and send a nonvoting member to Congress. When the region reached 60,000 people, it could draft a constitution and become a state. Five states emerged from the Northwest Territory.

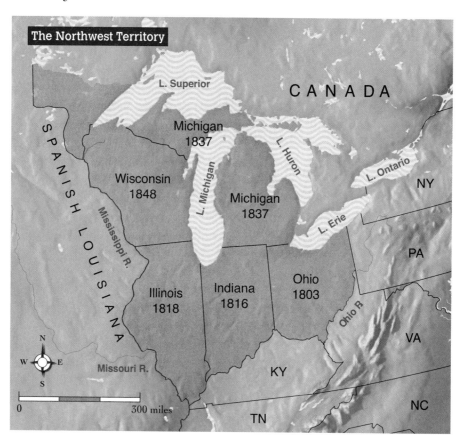

The Northwest Territory

Putting It All Together

In your notebook write "State Governments" in the middle of a concept web. Go back and gather notes from the paragraphs related to the states. On lines coming from the circle, add words that describe the responsibilities of the state governments.

Problems of the Confederation

Thinking on Your Own

Read the Focus Your Reading questions. Create a chart in your notebook labeled "The Nation's Problems." List the major problems as you read about them. Include the vocabulary words that are related to the problems.

The confederation period (1781–1789) was a difficult time for the new nation. Congress faced many problems that it could not solve. It could not pay the nation's debts because it had no power to tax. It could not remove British troops from western forts. It failed to persuade Spain to let Americans trade at New Orleans. To make matters worse, the new nation faced economic hard times. Congress could do even less about that.

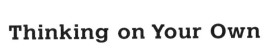

focus your reading

What problems did the nation face during the confederation period?

Why did some members of Congress want to change the Articles of Confederation?

How are Shays's Rebellion and the Philadelphia Convention related?

vocabulary

national debt

convention

Shays's Rebellion

Difficult Times

During the war, the Continental Congress had borrowed millions of dollars from foreign governments and banks. This debt had to be paid. Britain demanded payment of prewar debts owed to its merchants. It refused to withdraw its troops from western forts until these debts were paid. Exports had slumped because Britain closed its ports to American ships. Crop prices were down, and workmen were out of work. Yet the states kept raising taxes to pay their debts.

During the 1780s, American ships were prohibited from entering British ports.

Congress could do little to solve these problems. Lacking the power to tax, it could not pay off the **national debt**. It lacked an army to drive British troops out of western forts. It could not make new trade agreements, as only states could regulate, or control, trade. The states further restricted trade by placing import duties on goods made in other states.

Calls for Change

Several leaders in Congress wanted a stronger central government. Among them were James Madison of Virginia and Alexander Hamilton of New York. In 1781, they tried to change the Articles of Confederation to give Congress the power to tax. Twelve states agreed, but Rhode Island voted against the proposed change. To change the Articles, all thirteen states had to agree. On two occasions Congress asked the states to give it the power to regulate trade. Each time they refused.

Robert Morris proposed the Capitol National Bank in 1781, which helped to stabilize the economy.

In 1786, Virginia invited other states to a **convention**—or a meeting of delegates—at Annapolis, Maryland, to consider ways to regulate trade. Because representatives from only

stop and think

In your notebook, list three powers that Congress lacked that would have helped the nation solve its problems. Next to each power, write an example.

five states came, the meeting accomplished little. Before they left for home, the delegates asked Congress to call another convention to meet in Philadelphia in 1787.

Shays's Rebellion

In 1786, an armed uprising in western Massachusetts shocked the nation. Angry farmers attacked the county courts. The courts were seizing, or taking, their farms for nonpayment of debts and taxes. Leading a mob of 1,000 farmers, Daniel Shays tried to capture muskets from a state arsenal. The Confederation Congress was powerless. It could create an army only in case of Native American attack. Massachusetts finally put down the rebellion by creating a private army of 4,000 men.

Shays's Rebellion touched off attacks against courts and tax collectors in other states. This frightened many Americans. "We are fast verging on anarchy and confusion," George Washington wrote. Fearing more lawlessness, Congress agreed to call a convention to revise the Articles of Confederation.

Shays's Rebellion helped Congress realize the weaknesses in the Articles of Confederation.

Putting It All Together

Compare and contrast the powers of the state governments and those of Congress. Compare your ideas with a partner and write a brief paragraph about this topic.

Read a Primary Source

Abigail Adams and Thomas Jefferson on Shays's Rebellion

Thomas Jefferson, the United States minister to France, asked Abigail Adams for information about Shays's Rebellion. In her response, Abigail Adams told Jefferson what she thought about the riots. She was living in London, where her husband, John Adams, was the United States minister to Great Britain. Jefferson then shared his thoughts about the rebellion with his friend James Madison.

reading for understanding

What did Abigail Adams think of the leaders of the rebellion?

What does Jefferson see as the major disadvantage of republican government?

What benefits does this disadvantage produce?

"With regard to the tumults in my native state which you inquire about, I wish I could say that report had exaggerated them. It is too true, sir, that they have been carried to so alarming a height as to stop the courts of justice in several counties. Ignorant, restless desperadoes, without conscience or principles, have led a deluded multitude to follow their standard, under pretense of grievances which have no existence but in their imaginations."

Abigail Adams to Thomas Jefferson, January 2, 1787; Julian P. Boyd, ed., *Jefferson Papers* (Princeton, 1955).

"I am impatient to learn your sentiments on the late troubles in the Eastern states. . . . This uneasiness has produced [violent] acts absolutely unjustifiable: but I hope they will provoke no severities from their governments. . . . [Republican government] has its evils too: the principal of which is the turbulence to which it is subject. . . . Even this evil is productive of good. It prevents the degeneracy of government and nourishes a general attention to the public affairs. I hold that a little rebellion now and then is a good thing, and as necessary in the political world as storms in the physical. . . . An observation of this truth should render honest republican governors so mild in their punishments of rebellions, as not to discourage them too much. It is a medicine necessary for the sound health of government."

Thomas Jefferson to James Madison, January 30, 1787; Paul L. Ford, ed., *The Writings of Thomas Jefferson* (New York, 1894).

Making the Constitution

Thinking on Your Own

Write the Focus Your Reading questions in your notebook. As you read, write answers for each question. Compare your answers with those of a partner and rewrite if necessary.

In May 1787, fifty-five delegates arrived in Philadelphia. They came from every state but Rhode Island, which refused to participate. The delegates agreed that the United States needed a stronger central government. The question was whether the Articles should be revised or replaced with something new.

Independence Hall, Philadelphia

Opening Moves

The Virginia delegates arrived with a bold proposal for a new national government. Prepared by James Madison, it included a two-house **legislature**, or assembly. The Virginia Plan also called for an **executive**, or president, and a **judiciary**, or court system. The number of representatives in the legislature would be determined by a state's population. Delegates from the larger states liked this plan.

Those who wanted to revise, but not replace, the Articles of Confederation introduced an alternative plan. The New Jersey Plan was introduced by William

focus your reading

How were the Virginia and New Jersey Plans different?

What role did compromise play in creating the Constitution of the United States?

Why did many Americans oppose the Constitution?

vocabulary

legislature

executive

judiciary

Great Compromise

ratify

Federalists

Anti-Federalists

Patterson of New Jersey. The plan gave Congress the power to tax and to regulate trade. It kept the Articles of Confederation's one-house legislature. It would have a weak executive branch appointed by Congress. This plan appealed to delegates from the smaller states, as each state would have only one vote in Congress.

A Product of Compromise

The delegates voted to use the Virginia Plan as the basis for a new constitution. However, the small-state delegates insisted on changes. The result was a set of compromises.

The Constitutional Convention met in 1787 to revise the Articles of Confederation.

A Connecticut delegate, Roger Sherman, proposed that representation in one house of the legislature should be determined by population. States should be equally represented in the other. The convention delegates adopted this Connecticut Compromise, also known as the **Great Compromise**.

Slavery was another issue at the convention. The delegates from the South wanted to count slaves when determining a state's representation, but not when

> **stop and think**
>
> Make a two-column chart with the titles "Virginia Plan" and "New Jersey Plan." List the main characteristics of each.

determining its share of taxes. Northern delegates took the opposite view. The Three-Fifths Compromise ended this deadlock. The South was allowed to count three-fifths of the slaves for both purposes.

The convention appointed a committee to prepare a final draft of the Constitution. The result was a document limited to "essential principles only," as one member described it. This framework allowed each generation to interpret and apply the document to changing times.

Ratification

The Confederation Congress sent the Constitution to the states to be **ratified**, or formally approved. In most states, ratification was a hard-fought contest. In Virginia, George Washington and James Madison led the **Federalists** who supported the Constitution. Patrick Henry, Sam Adams, and other **Anti-Federalists** opposed it. They thought the Constitution gave too much power to the central government.

New York City celebrated ratification of the Constitution in 1788.

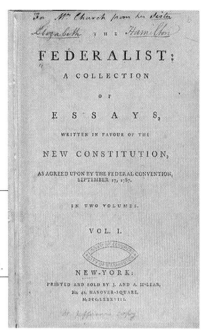

The Federalist Papers were published to support the ratification of the Constitution.

The Federalists won over some opponents by promising to add a bill of rights to the Constitution as soon as the new Congress met. James Madison, Alexander Hamilton, and John Jay helped persuade voters by writing a series of essays known today as *The Federalist Papers*.

The eighty-five *Federalist Papers* were written between 1787 and 1788. It is believed that Hamilton wrote fifty-two papers, Madison wrote twenty-eight papers, and Jay wrote the remaining five papers. The papers were published in New York. Each of the authors went on to become an important figure in the new government. James Madison became president, John Jay became the first chief justice of the Supreme Court, and Alexander Hamilton served in the cabinet.

John Jay

By August 1788, eleven states had ratified the Constitution. During the next two years, North Carolina and Rhode Island also gave their approval.

Putting It all Together

In your notebook write the heading "The Constitution as a Product of Compromise." Using bulleted notes, make a list of the major compromises that led to ratification of the Constitution.

Dates of Ratification of the Constitution

State	Date
Delaware	December 7, 1787
Pennsylvania	December 12, 1787
New Jersey	December 18, 1787
Georgia	January 2, 1788
Connecticut	January 9, 1788
Massachusetts	February 6, 1788
Maryland	April 28, 1788
South Carolina	May 23, 1788
New Hampshire	June 21, 1788
Virginia	June 25, 1788
New York	July 26, 1788
North Carolina	November 21, 1789
Rhode Island	May 29, 1790

Biography

Benjamin Franklin (1706–1790)

Carved into the back of the president's chair at the Philadelphia Convention was half of a sun. Benjamin Franklin, a delegate from Pennsylvania, worried about the meaning of that sun. Was the sun setting on the American republic? As the delegates lined up on September 17, 1787, to sign the Constitution, he knew the answer. "Now at length, I have the happiness to know it is a rising and not a setting sun."

Franklin had contributed much to the rise of the American republic. In 1757, he went to England as the agent of the colony of Pennsylvania. He spent most of the next fifteen years there. As the conflict with Parliament heated up, Franklin began to speak for all of the colonies. He was the first American diplomat.

Franklin returned from England in May 1775, the month the Second Continental Congress met in Philadelphia. He joined the Pennsylvania delegation. There Franklin spoke for the radical patriots, arguing for full independence. He helped draft the Declaration of Independence and wrote Pennsylvania's state constitution.

In October 1776, Congress sent Franklin overseas to help negotiate an alliance with France. He helped prod the French government into signing a treaty of alliance with the United States. It was America's first and perhaps greatest diplomatic victory.

In 1781, at age seventy-five, Franklin wanted to come home. Instead, Congress asked him to help negotiate a peace treaty with Britain. In 1783, Franklin, John Adams, John Jay, and Henry Laurens signed the Treaty of Paris, which ended the Revolutionary war.

In 1787, Franklin served as a delegate to the Constitutional Convention. He played a major role in the convention as a voice for reason and compromise. He had reservations about the final document, but signed it and helped get it ratified.

Benjamin Franklin was the only person to sign all four major documents that established American independence: the Declaration of Independence, the treaty of alliance with France, the Treaty of Paris with Britain, and the Constitution.

Chapter Summary

During the Revolutionary War, new state **constitutions** replaced old colonial charters. The new state governments were **republics**. Most of the constitutions included a **bill of rights**. The Articles of Confederation created a **confederation** of states. Although weak, the Confederation Congress opened the **Northwest Territory** to settlement.

The Confederation period was difficult as Congress could not pay off the **national debt**. It lacked the power to tax. Several leaders in Congress wanted a stronger central government. When the states refused, Congress invited delegates to a **convention** to revise the Articles of Confederation.

In 1786, Daniel Shays led an uprising in Massachusetts. Congress lacked the power to restore order. **Shays's Rebellion** showed that the United States government needed to be stronger.

In May 1787, delegates from twelve states met to review the Virginia Plan that included a **legislature**, an **executive**, and a **judiciary**. A state's population would determine the number of its representatives in Congress. It gave Congress more power, but each state had an equal vote.

The **Great Compromise** made population the basis of representation in the House of Representatives. It gave each state an equal vote in the Senate. The convention submitted the new Constitution of the United States to the states to be **ratified**. The **Federalists** supported the new constitution. The **Anti-Federalists** opposed it. By August 1788, the necessary nine states had ratified the Constitution.

Chapter Review

1 Imagine that you are a friend of Patrick Henry and that you favor the new Constitution. Write a letter to him explaining why he should change his mind and support the Constitution.

2 Revise your list of the words and phrases that are associated with the word *government*. Use them in a paragraph that describes the new nation's struggle to organize an effective government.

Skill Builder

Recognizing Persuasive Writing

People use persuasion to win other people over to their point of view. Persuasion is neither good nor bad in itself, but it is a special kind of speech or writing. It typically presents only one point of view. It tends to appeal to the reader or listener's emotions. A critical reader or listener must be able to recognize persuasion.

In 1788, James Madison, Alexander Hamilton, and John Jay wrote a series of persuasive essays entitled *The Federalist Papers*. They were trying to persuade delegates to state conventions to ratify the Constitution. The following is an excerpt from one of Alexander Hamilton's *Federalist* essays (No. 15).

As you read, answer the following questions:

1 How does Hamilton appeal to patriotism in his argument for a stronger government?

2 How does he try to make his readers feel ashamed, weak, or defenseless due to the lack of a strong government?

3 What evidence is Hamilton not presenting about the present state of affairs?

"We may indeed . . . be said to have reached almost the last stage of national humiliation. There is scarcely any thing that can wound the pride or degrade the character of an independent nation which we do not experience. . . . Do we owe debts to foreigners and to our own citizens? . . . These remain without any proper or satisfactory provision for their discharge. Have we valuable territories and important posts in the possession of a foreign power which . . . ought long since to have been surrendered? These are still retained. . . . Are we in a condition to resent or to repel the aggression? We have neither troops, nor treasury, nor government."

Chapter 10

THE CONSTITUTION

Getting Focused

Skim this chapter to predict what you will be learning.

- Read the lesson titles and subheadings.
- Look at the illustrations and read the captions.
- Examine the maps.
- Review the vocabulary words and terms.

The Constitution of the United States places limits on the power of government. Look over the major headings, tables, and charts for clues about how this was accomplished. List these clues in your notebook.

The Federal Government

Thinking on Your Own

Read the Focus Your Reading questions and the vocabulary words. Create a two-column chart in your notebook. Write the vocabulary words on one side. As you read, define the words on the other side.

The Constitution of the United States created a **federal government**. That means that the national and state governments share power. The new central government was stronger than the Confederation Congress that it replaced. But it was not all-powerful. Some powers are shared with the states; others belong only to the states.

focus your reading

Why do we call the United States government a federal government?

What is the difference between Congress's enumerated and implied powers?

What powers are reserved for the states?

vocabulary

federal government

enumerated powers

implied powers

concurrent powers

Powers of the National Government

The Constitution created a central, or national, government with three branches, or divisions. Article I of the Constitution describes and lists the powers of the legislative branch. The Congress—or legislature—consists of the Senate and the House of Representatives. Its **enumerated powers**, or stated powers, include the power to tax, regulate trade, and declare war.

Congress maintains the nation's armed forces, can coin and borrow money, and can make immigrants citizens. The Constitution also allows Congress to pass any law "necessary and proper" to carrying out its powers. This "elastic clause" gives the Congress **implied powers** not specifically stated in the Constitution.

The powers of the executive branch—the presidency—are listed in Article II. The president acts as commander-in-chief of the armed forces, makes treaties, and appoints ambassadors, judges, and other officials. Article III set up the judicial branch, which consists of the Supreme Court and other federal courts.

Comparison of the Articles of Confederation with the Constitution	
The Articles	**The Constitution**
The Executive Branch	
• Congress has exclusive power to govern • Executive Committee acts for Congress when it is not in session • No executive branch to enforce legislation	• President administers and enforces federal laws • President chosen by electors who have been chosen by the states
The Legislative Branch	
• A one-house legislature • Each state has one vote • Nine votes needed to pass legislation	• A two-house legislature • Each state has equal number of representatives in the Senate • Representation in the House determined by state population • Simple majority required to enact legislation
The Judicial Branch	
• No national court system • Congress can establish temporary courts to hear cases of piracy	• National court system directed by the Supreme Court • Courts hear cases related to national laws, treaties, the Constitution; cases between states, between citizens of different states, or between a state and citizens of another state
Other Provisions	
• Admission to the confederation requires nine votes • Amendment of the Articles must be unanimous	• Congress to admit new states • All states must have a republican form of government • Amendment of the Constitution by two-thirds vote of both houses of Congress, or by a national convention, and ratified by three-fourths of the states

State Governments' Powers

The Constitution places limits on the power of the national government. Powers not specifically granted to Congress, or implied under the necessary and proper clause, are reserved to the states. The Tenth Amendment states this clearly. States alone can set up town, city, or county governments. State legislatures have the power to set up business corporations and regulate trade within the state. Only states can create a police force, establish schools, and pass marriage laws. The Constitution also places limits on the powers of the states (Article IV) and places federal law above state law (Article VI).

Concurrent Powers

The Constitution allows the federal government and the states to exercise some nearly identical powers. Both governments can make and enforce similar laws. For example, states make laws regulating state elections, while the federal government controls congressional and presidential elections. Both state legislatures and Congress can levy taxes, charter banks, and borrow money.

States have court systems to administer justice, including a supreme court. So does the national government. Powers that exist at both levels of government are called **concurrent powers**.

The Federal System: Division of Powers

Powers Delegated to the Federal Government	Powers Shared by the Federal and State Governments	Powers Reserved to the States
• Declare war • Regulate interstate and foreign trade • Coin money • Establish post offices • Set standards for weights and measurements • Admit new states • Establish foreign policy • Establish laws for citizenship • Regulate patents and copyrights • Pass laws necessary for carrying out its powers	• Enforce laws • Borrow money • Levy taxes • Charter banks • Establish courts • Provide for general welfare	• Establish local governments • Regulate commerce within a state • Provide for public safety • Create corporation laws • Establish schools • Make marriage laws • Assume all the powers not granted to the federal government or prohibited by the Constitution

Putting It All Together

Draw three boxes. Label them "National Government Powers," "State Government Powers," and "Concurrent Powers." Write at least three powers of government in each box.

Separation of Powers

Thinking on Your Own

The major concept in this lesson is "checks and balances." As you read, make notes that describe the checks and balances built into the Constitution.

The men who created the Constitution of the United States did not trust governments with unlimited power. As colonists, they had experienced the abuse of power by Parliament and King George III. The delegates wanted a stronger central government, but not one that would become tyrannical.

focus your reading

Why does the Constitution divide the government into three branches?

What purpose do checks and balances serve?

Why is the veto power a good example of checks and balances?

vocabulary

checks and balances

impeach

veto

A Division of Power

The writers of the Constitution took care to divide power within the central government. The "accumulation of all powers, legislative, executive, and judiciary in the same hands," wrote James Madison, is "the very definition of tyranny." The delegates at Philadelphia divided the powers of the new government among three branches of government.

They gave the legislative branch—or Congress—the power to make laws and do certain other things. They divided those powers, in turn, between the House of Representatives and the Senate. The House has the sole power to initiate and write tax bills and budgets. Only the Senate can ratify treaties and approve the appointment of top officials.

The Constitution created an executive branch to enforce the laws passed by Congress. It consists of the president, vice

Division of Powers		
Executive Branch	Legislative Branch	Judicial Branch
President • Enforces the laws • Acts as commander-in-chief of the armed forces • Appoints ambassadors, judges, and other officials • Makes treaties with other nations	**Congress** • Writes the laws • Raises troops for armed forces • Decides how much money may be spent on government programs	**Supreme Court** • Interprets the laws • Reviews court decisions

president, and officials in the executive departments. The president's cabinet is part of the executive branch. The executive branch also has the power to conduct war, sign treaties, and nominate people for federal office.

The judiciary is the third branch of the government. The Constitution gives it the power to decide conflicts between states and between individuals in different states. It includes the Supreme Court and any other federal courts that Congress deems necessary.

stop and think

Think about what you have just read concerning the separation of powers. Write three sentences in your notebook to explain this concept.

Checks and Balances

The delegates in Philadelphia created **checks and balances** to prevent any branch of the government from gaining too much power. The Constitution requires treaties signed by the executive branch to be ratified, or approved, by the Senate. The Senate also must approve top-level appointments made by the president, including justices of the Supreme Court. Congress also has the power to **impeach** the president or judges. Impeachment means to bring a public official to trial for misconduct.

Congress can pass legislation by a simple majority. The Constitution gives the president power to **veto**—or refuse to approve—this act of Congress. However, it also limits this power by allowing Congress to override a veto. A vetoed bill can become law if passed again in both houses by a two-thirds majority. This allows the two branches to check and balance each other. The president checks the judiciary by having the power to appoint federal judges and to pardon persons convicted in federal courts.

The Supreme Court plays a major role in the system of checks and balances. It can overturn acts of Congress and actions of the president if it finds that they violate the Constitution. The Supreme Court first exerted these powers in its decisions in the cases of *Marbury v. Madison* (1803) and *Ex parte Milligan* (1866). The only check given the Court in the Constitution is the power of the chief justice to preside over the impeachment trial of the president.

System of Checks and Balances

can
- propose legislation
- veto legislation
- call special legislative sessions
- recommend appointments

can
- appoint federal judges
- grant pardons and reprieves to federal offenders

can
- pass legislation
- override a presidential veto
- confirm executive appointments
- ratify treaties
- impeach and remove a president

Executive Branch

can
- declare executive actions and laws unconstitutional

Legislative Branch

Judicial Branch

can
- create lower federal courts and judgeships
- impeach judges
- propose constitutional amendments to overrule judicial decisions
- approve appointments of federal judges

can
- declare legislation unconstitutional

Putting It All Together

Using your notes about checks and balances, write a paragraph about the concept. Include information about each of the three branches.

Biography

Roger Sherman (1721–1793)

Roger Sherman attended the Constitutional Convention in 1787 as a delegate from Connecticut. He was the most awkward person John Adams had ever seen. "When he moves a hand . . . it is stiffness and awkwardness itself, rigid as starched linen." Adams and his college-educated friends could barely keep from laughing at Sherman's back-country language. A delegate from Georgia called him "unaccountably strange in his manner."

Roger Sherman was an odd but honest man. The people of Connecticut trusted him. They trusted him as a young man to make a good pair of shoes at an honest price. When he was twenty-four, they chose the young cobbler to be county surveyor. They could depend on him to settle boundary disputes fairly. They elected him to Connecticut's colonial assembly ten years later. By then, the honest surveyor had become a large landowner and successful merchant.

Like most colonial merchants, Roger Sherman opposed Parliament's taxes on imports. In 1774, the Connecticut assembly sent him to the Continental Congress to protest against parliamentary taxation. Sherman spent the next eight years as a member of Congress. There he took charge of military supplies, planning, and finance. War contractors dreaded doing business with the tight-fisted Sherman. He kept trying to cut costs.

Despite his odd ways and rough manners, Roger Sherman was a good politician. He knew when to stand firm and when to compromise. At the Constitutional Convention, Sherman put this ability to good use. He favored the New Jersey Plan, which gave each state an equal vote in Congress. Most delegates wanted representation based on population. Sherman proposed a compromise—give the states equal representation in the Senate, but base representation in the House of Representatives on population.

The Connecticut Compromise—known as the Great Compomise—was Sherman's greatest contribution to the new republic. It saved the Philadelphia Convention, which almost broke up over this issue. Roger Sherman died in New Haven, Connecticut, on July 23, 1793, at the age of seventy-two.

The Bill of Rights

Thinking on Your Own

Read the Focus Your Reading questions and the vocabulary words. In your notebook, write two questions that you have about the Bill of Rights.

In 1787, many Americans opposed the Constitution despite its separation of powers and system of checks and balances. They worried that Congress or the president would misuse the power and abuse the rights of the people. To win support for ratification, the Federalists agreed to add a **bill of rights**, or list of rights.

focus your reading

Why did many Americans demand a bill of rights?

Why did the delegates in Philadelphia allow amendments to the Constitution?

What basic rights were protected by the Bill of Rights?

vocabulary

bill of rights   amendments

Amending the Constitution

The delegates in Philadelphia tried to make the Constitution a timeless document. With that in mind, they made it possible to add **amendments**, or make changes. "In framing a system which we wish to last for all ages," James Madison said, "we should not lose sight of the changes which ages will produce."

According to Article V, Congress or the state legislatures, by

How the Constitution Is Amended

STEP 1 Amendment Proposed by:

A two-thirds vote of both houses of Congress

OR

A constitutional convention called by Congress on petition of two-thirds of the 50 states

STEP 2 Amendment Ratified by:

Three-fourths of the 50 state legislatures

OR

Three-fourths of special constitutional conventions called by the 50 states

New Amendment to the Constitution

a two-thirds vote, can propose an amendment. It can be ratified by a vote of three-fourths of the legislatures or conventions called by the states for that purpose. To date, twenty-seven amendments have been added to the Constitution.

stop and think

Discuss with a partner how the men who wrote the Constitution planned to make it last "for all ages." Write two sentences in your notebook summarizing your points.

Adding the Bill of Rights

During its first session, Congress took up the question of a bill of rights. The states had submitted dozens of proposals. James Madison organized them into nineteen amendments. Congress approved twelve and sent them to the states for ratification. The states, in turn, ratified ten of them. An amendment related to representation in Congress was never approved. The other amendment, concerning congressional pay, was ratified in 1992 as the Twenty-Seventh Amendment.

The Bill of Rights

The Bill of Rights addresses several of the American people's most important concerns. The first four amendments protect basic rights that Britain violated during the protest over taxes and tea. These include freedom of speech, press, assembly and religion; the right of people's militias to keep and bear arms; the right not to have troops quartered, or live, in a person's house; and freedom from unreasonable searches and seizures of property. The next four amendments protect Americans against unfair court procedures, trials, and convictions. The Ninth Amendment protects rights not

The Bill of Rights	
1	Guarantees freedom of religion, speech, assembly, and press, and the right of people to petition the government
2	Protects the rights of states to maintain a militia and of citizens to bear arms
3	Restricts quartering of troops in private homes
4	Protects against unreasonable searches and seizures
5	Assures the right not to be deprived of life, liberty, or property without due process of law
6	Guarantees the right to a speedy and public trial by an impartial jury
7	Assures the right to a jury trial in cases involving the common law—the law established by previous court decisions
8	Protects against excessive bail, or cruel and unusual punishment
9	Provides that people's rights are not restricted to those specified in the first eight Amendments
10	Restates the Constitution's principle of federalism by providing that powers not granted to the national government nor prohibited to the states are reserved to the states and to the people

specifically mentioned in the Constitution. The Tenth Amendment is another "catchall" amendment. It reserves to the states any powers not delegated to the central government or prohibited by the Constitution.

Putting It All Together

Review the questions that you had before reading this lesson. Did you find the answers? What other questions do you have now? In your notebook, make a list of places where you can find more information about the Bill of Rights.

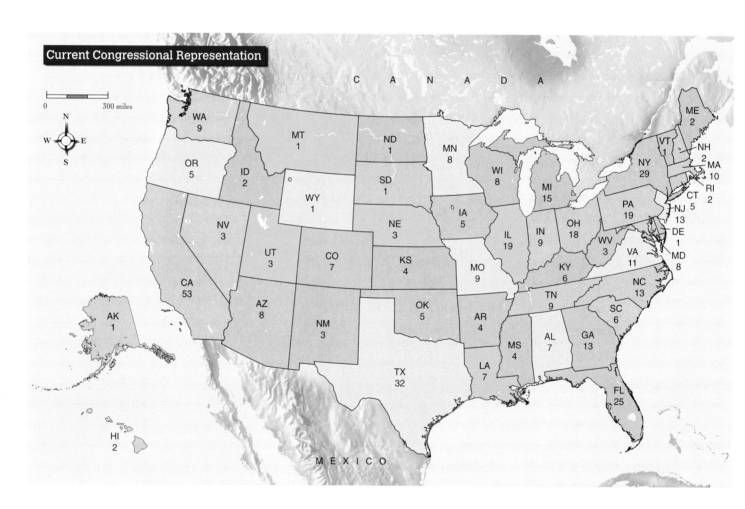

Current Congressional Representation

0   300 miles

CANADA

MEXICO

WA 9
MT 1
ND 1
MN 8
ME 2
VT 1
NH 2
OR 5
ID 2
SD 1
WI 8
NY 29
MA 10
RI 2
WY 1
IA 5
MI 15
PA 19
CT 5
NJ 13
NV 3
NE 3
IL 19
IN 9
OH 18
WV 3
DE 1
MD 8
UT 3
CO 7
KS 4
MO 9
KY 6
VA 11
CA 53
NC 13
AK 1
AZ 8
NM 3
OK 5
AR 4
TN 9
SC 6
MS 4
AL 7
GA 13
TX 32
LA 7
FL 25
HI 2

Read a Primary Source

Sam Adams Against the Constitution

At first, Sam Adams opposed ratifying the Constitution. He eventually supported it after the Federalists promised to add a bill of rights.

reading for understanding

Why did Adams describe the Constitution as a "national" government?

What problem did he foresee from such a government?

Why did he prefer a confederation of sovereign states?

"I [find the Constitution to be] a national government, instead of a federal union of sovereign states. I am not able to conceive why the wisdom of the Convention led them to give the preference to the former before the latter. If the several states in the union are to become one entire nation, under one legislature, the powers of which shall extend to every subject of legislation . . . can this national legislature be competent to make laws for the free internal government of one people, living in climates so remote and whose 'Habits & particular Interests' are and probably always will be so different?

Should we continue distinct sovereign states, confederated for the purposes of mutual safety and happiness . . . the people would govern themselves more easily, the laws of each state being well adapted to its own genius and circumstances, and the liberties of the United States would be more secure than they can be, as I humbly conceive, under the proposed new constitution."

Letter from Sam Adams to Richard Henry Lee, December 3, 1787; in William V. Wells, *The Life and Public Services of Samuel Adams*, III (Boston, 1866).

Chapter Summary

The Constitution of the United States created a **federal government**. Congress has **enumerated powers**, which include the power to tax, regulate trade, and declare war. The Constitution also gives Congress **implied powers** not mentioned in the Constitution. The Constitution leaves to the states all powers not granted to Congress or implied under the necessary and proper clause. The national and state governments share some powers, such as the power to tax and borrow money. These are called **concurrent powers**.

The Constitution divides power within the national government. The legislative branch has the power to make laws. The executive branch enforces the laws. The judicial branch interprets the laws. To prevent any branch from gaining too much power, the Constitution includes **checks and balances**. For example, the president has the power to **veto** an act of Congress, but Congress can override his veto. Congress can **impeach** the president, but the Supreme Court oversees the trial.

To win support for ratification, the Federalists promised to add a **bill of rights**. This was possible by adding **amendments**. During its first session, Congress approved the first ten amendments—the Bill of Rights. They protected basic rights and guarded against unfair trials and court proceedings.

Chapter Review

1 Design a poster about the Bill of Rights. Include logos that would match the different rights that it protects.

2 Look over the vocabulary words. Work with a partner to organize the words into categories. Write the categories in your notebook. Then explain in writing why you chose these categories.

3 Imagine that you are a newspaper reporter in 1788 writing an article about the Constitution's system of checks and balances. What major points would you include in your article?

Skill Builder

Reading a Historical Document: The Constitution of the United States

Historical documents from early periods can pose problems for modern readers. They often use words that are no longer in everyday use. Words may be arranged in ways that now sound odd. The document may be divided into sections or parts for reasons that are not obvious. The following are useful guidelines for reading historical documents:

- Find out who wrote the document.
- Check when it was written.
- Read the introduction to learn what the document is about.
- Read the subtitles to determine how the document is organized.
- Read the document one section at a time.
- Try to define unknown words by using context clues.

Apply the above guidelines to the Constitution of the United States by answering the following questions. The Constitution can be found at the back of this book.

1. Where are the names of the delegates to the Philadelphia Convention listed?

2. On what date did these men sign the Constitution?

3. What does the Preamble—Introduction—indicate this document is about?

4. Into how many articles—subsections—is the Constitution divided, and what is each about?

5. Why are some articles divided into sections?

6. Read one article carefully. In your own words, explain what it is about.

7. What unfamiliar words did you learn the meaning of by using context clues?

UNIT 6

THE YOUNG REPUBLIC

In 1789, the Federalists created a new government under the Constitution of the United States. At first, everything went smoothly. Congress created new executive departments. President Washington appointed executive department heads and judges. Then the quarreling began. The two factions or groups that emerged became the nation's first political parties.

In 1800, the Republicans elected Thomas Jefferson. His presidency was a period of growth and expansion. The Louisiana Purchase nearly doubled the size of the United States. Then Britain and France caused problems on the high seas. To protect American rights, James Madison led the country to war. This was a difficult time for the young republic.

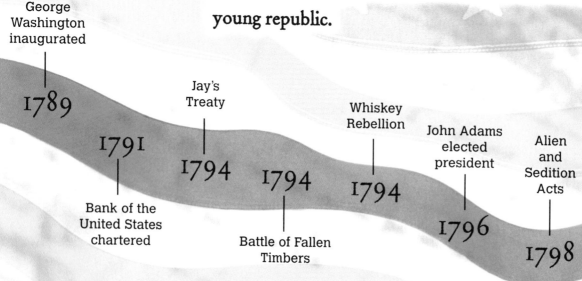

President George Washington inaugurated
1789

Bank of the United States chartered
1791

Jay's Treaty
1794

Battle of Fallen Timbers
1794

Whiskey Rebellion
1794

John Adams elected president
1796

Alien and Sedition Acts
1798

Why did the
United States go
to war in 1812?

What issues divided
the Federalists?

What did the Republicans
hope to achieve?

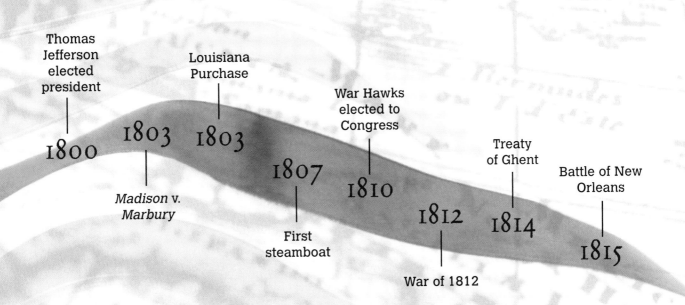

Thomas
Jefferson
elected
president

Louisiana
Purchase

War Hawks
elected to
Congress

Treaty
of Ghent

Battle of New
Orleans

1800

1803

1803

1807

1810

1812

1814

1815

Madison v.
Marbury

First
steamboat

War of 1812

Chapter 11

THE FEDERALISTS IN POWER

Getting Focused

Skim this chapter to predict what you will be learning.

- Read the lesson titles and subheadings.
- Look at the illustrations and read the captions.
- Examine the maps.
- Review the vocabulary words and terms.

As you review the chapter, look for the basic features of the new government. Create questions that you expect the chapter to answer.

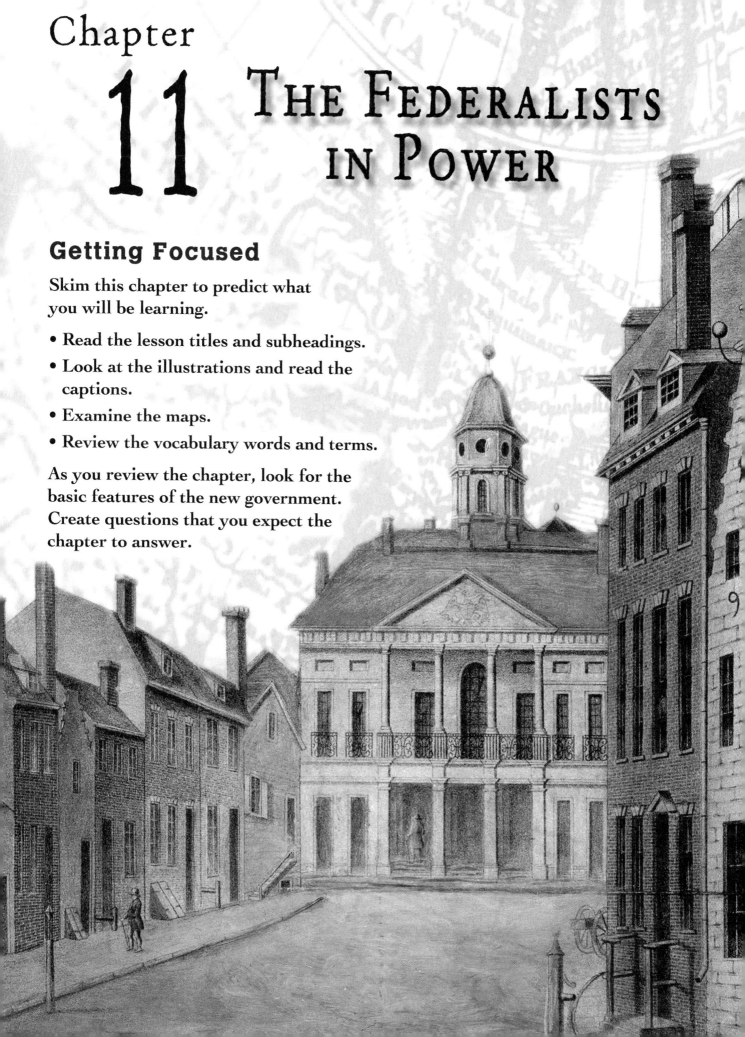

Creating a New Government

Thinking on Your Own

Read the Focus Your Reading questions. Create a two-column chart in your notebook. Label the first column "Important Facts" and the second column "Connections." As you read, note the important facts in the first column. In the other column, write connections between these facts and the people or events in the chapter.

In 1789, the United States faced a major task. It had to fill in the details for the new government created by the outline in the Constitution. The American people had to elect a new president. The president had to appoint executive officials and federal judges. The new Congress had to solve a variety of problems.

focus your reading

What executive departments did Congress create?

Whom did President Washington appoint to these offices?

What was Alexander Hamilton's financial plan?

vocabulary

inauguration   bonds
tariff duties

The New Government Takes Shape

In early April 1789, Congress met in New York City, then the nation's capital. After counting the electoral votes, the Senate declared George Washington president. The new vice president was John Adams. He had received the second highest number of votes.

George Washington decided not to wear his military uniform to his **inauguration**, or swearing in ceremony. He wore a plain, brown suit instead. He wanted people to see the president as an ordinary citizen. Some proposed that the president be called "His Excellency" or "His Highness." Washington asked to be called simply "Mr. President."

George Washington was inaugurated for a second term on March 4, 1793.

Congress created the first three executive departments. It set up the Department of State to deal with other nations. Congress created the Treasury Department to look after finances and the War Department to defend the nation. It also set up the offices of attorney general and postmaster general.

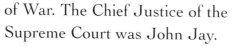
Thomas Jefferson

With the Senate's approval, President Washington appointed the heads of the departments and the justices of the Supreme Court. He appointed Thomas Jefferson as Secretary of State. Alexander Hamilton became the first Secretary of the Treasury. Henry Knox was the new Secretary of War. The Chief Justice of the Supreme Court was John Jay.

To provide money to operate the government, Congress passed the Tariff Act of 1789. Thereafter, **tariff duties**, or taxes collected on imports, paid most of the government's expenses. Congress

stop and think

Create a four-level concept graph with "Executive Departments" on the top. On the second level, create three circles each with one of the executive departments in them. Underneath the circles, write a brief description of the departments. On the fourth level, write the names of the heads of the departments under each description.

also passed the Judiciary Act of 1801, which created a new system of federal courts. It also sent the Bill of Rights to the states for ratification.

George Washington with his cabinet

Hamilton's Financial Plan

In 1790, Secretary of the Treasury Hamilton turned his attention to the nation's finances. During the war, Congress had borrowed about $42 million from the American people. It gave the lenders loan certificates, or IOUs, that it promised someday to repay in hard cash. Hamilton asked Congress to exchange these IOUs for **bonds,** or certificates, that earned interest. He also proposed that Congress pay the $25 million in loans owed by the states. Finally, Hamilton asked Congress to create a Bank of the United States. He said that a bank was needed to collect taxes and circulate money.

Putting It All Together

Discuss with a partner the significant points of Hamilton's financial plan. Write them in your notebook. Then write a paragraph explaining his plan.

Read a Primary Source

Alexander Hamilton on the Importance of Manufacturing

In his *Report on Manufacturers*, Alexander Hamilton explained the benefits of manufacturing for the United States. He also called upon Congress to pass laws to support manufacturing.

reading for understanding

What kind of occupations did Hamilton think a nation needed?

What kind of country did he think would have the most trade?

How is manufacturing related to national security?

"The spirit of enterprise . . . must necessarily be . . . less in a nation of mere cultivators than in a nation of cultivators and merchants; less in a nation of cultivators and merchants than in a nation of cultivators, [skilled workers], and merchants. . . .

"There seems to be a moral certainty that the trade of a country which is both manufacturing and agricultural will be more lucrative and prosperous than that of a country which is merely agricultural.

"Not only the wealth, but the independence and security of a country . . . connected with the prosperity of manufacturers. Every nation . . . ought to endeavor to possess within itself all the essentials of national supply. These comprise the means of subsistence, habitation, clothing, and defense. . . ."

Reports of the Secretary of the Treasury of the United States (Washington, D. C., 1897).

Federalists Disagree

Thinking on Your Own

Read the Focus Your Reading questions and the vocabulary. Write the vocabulary words in your notebook. As you read their definitions, write a sentence for each word that includes the definition.

In 1789, the Federalists were united in support of the Constitution. They all wanted a national government stronger than the one provided by the Articles of Confederation. But once in office, the Federalists began to disagree among themselves.

Debate over Hamilton's Plan

Several congressmen opposed Hamilton's financial plan. The group's leader was Congressman James Madison of Virginia. Madison thought the plan favored **speculators**, or men who hoped to profit from the wartime loan certificates. Many of the original lenders had sold these IOUs for as little as 25 cents on the dollar. Under Hamilton's plan, the people who bought them could exchange the certificates for bonds at face value.

Madison also opposed having the federal government take over the states' debts. Virginia and several southern states had already paid off their wartime loans. They did not want to have to pay the debts of other states.

focus your reading

Why did some congressmen oppose Hamilton's financial plan?

Why did Thomas Jefferson oppose the Bank of the United States?

What problems did the United States have with other nations?

vocabulary

speculators

excise tax

Whiskey Rebellion

strict interpretation

broad interpretation

Congressman James Madison

Hamilton's friends in Congress argued that his plan would make the government stronger. It would create a wealthy and powerful class of bondholders who would be loyal to the national government. Taking over the states' debts would do that as well.

Hamilton finally won enough southern votes in Congress to get his plan approved. He did this by promising northern support for a bill the South wanted. That bill would move the nation's capital from New York City to a new federal city on the banks of the Potomac River. Both bills passed in July 1790.

To pay the interest on the new bonds, Congress placed an **excise tax** on whiskey. This tax hurt many western farmers. Distilling their corn into whiskey was the cheapest way for them to ship it to market. In 1794, farmers in western Pennsylvania refused to pay the tax. President Washington sent 13,000 militia troops to Pennsylvania to put down the **Whiskey Rebellion**.

The Whiskey Rebellion focused attention on new taxes passed by Congress.

The Bank of the United States in Philadelphia remains the oldest bank building in the country.

The Bank of the United States

Federalists also disagreed about Hamilton's plan for a Bank of the United States. Secretary of State Thomas Jefferson led the opposition. He believed that a federal bank was unnecessary. It would only benefit the rich people who owned stock in the bank. Using a **strict interpretation** of the Constitution, he insisted that Congress lacked the power to charter a bank. Hamilton argued that the "necessary and proper" clause gave Congress that power. This was a loose interpretation, or **broad interpretation**, of the Constitution. In 1791, Congress passed the bank bill.

Jay's Treaty of 1794 was not popular and he was burned in effigy.

European and Native American Problems

Issues concerning relations with Europe also divided the Federalists. In 1793, France and Britain went to war. The South mainly supported France, the United States' old ally. Southerners accused Britain of taking sailors off American ships. The British also had not withdrawn their soldiers from frontier forts. Northern merchants favored Britain. They wanted closer relations and expanded trade with the British.

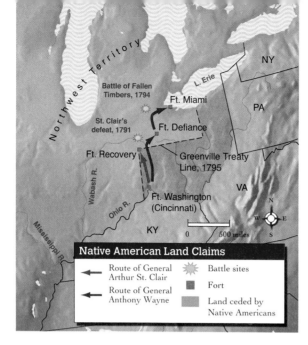

President Washington managed to ease relations with Britain. He sent John Jay to London to negotiate a treaty. In Jay's Treaty (1794), Britain agreed to remove its soldiers from American forts.

The Republicans attacked the treaty, which failed to settle other issues. Spain was concerned about Jay's Treaty and how it would impact Spanish territory in North America. Thomas Pinckney's treaty with Spain (1795) settled the issue by opening the Mississippi River and New Orleans to American trade.

Tecumseh

The government also faced a Native American crisis. Tecumseh, a Shawnee leader, tried to unite the Ohio Valley tribes against the settlers there. The United States army put down this uprising at the Battle of Fallen Timbers (1794). Defeated, the Native Americans signed the Treaty of Greenville (1795), in which they agreed to leave the Ohio Valley.

General Anthony Wayne led the victory at the Battle of Fallen Timbers.

Putting It All Together

In your notebook, write the following statement: "Hamilton's financial plan was good for the United States." Under the statement write "True" on one side and "False" on the other. Choose a position on this issue. Find facts from the lesson to support your position and list them under one of the above columns. Discuss your position with a partner.

Biography

Alexander Hamilton (1755–1804)

In December 1791, Secretary of the Treasury Alexander Hamilton sent his *Report on Manufacturers* to Congress. It presented his vision of a powerful nation bound together by a strong economy. The rural South and Middle Atlantic states would provide the nation with food and raw materials. The Northeast would produce its manufactured goods. Hamilton looked forward to an America of cities, factories, and workshops as well as plantations, farms, and villages. More than most Americans of his time, he had a national perspective.

A broad, national view came easily for Hamilton. As a recent immigrant, he had few local or regional loyalties. Born in the British West Indies in 1755, he grew up on the Dutch island of St. Croix. He arrived in New York City in 1772, at age seventeen. When the War for Independence began, Hamilton joined the patriots as captain of a New York artillery company.

In 1776, Hamilton's company joined George Washington's army in its retreat through New Jersey. Washington liked the young man and appointed him to his headquarters staff. Hamilton spent the war years as a lieutenant-colonel in the Continental Army. That also helped give him a national point of view.

After the war, Hamilton served in Congress. There he saw firsthand the need for a stronger national government. Unable to raise money, Congress could not pay its debts. In 1786, Hamilton, James Madison, and others called for a Constitutional Convention. He attended the Philadelphia convention as a New York delegate. With Madison and John Jay, he wrote the *Federalist* essays to win support for the new constitution.

In 1789, President Washington appointed his former aide-de-camp as secretary of the treasury. That gave Hamilton an opportunity to develop national policies. Congress approved his plans to pay off the nation's debts and to create the Bank of the United States. It also passed laws to support manufacturing, as he had called for in his *Report* in 1791. He returned to private life in 1795, having helped create a new national government and a stronger nation.

Alexander Hamilton was killed in a duel with former vice president Aaron Burr. He died on July 11, 1804, at age forty-nine.

Federalists vs. Republicans

Thinking on Your Own

Read the Focus Your Reading questions and the vocabulary words. In your notebook, write "America's Difficulties with France." As you read, write a bulleted note of any fact that relates to that statement.

In his farewell address in 1796, President Washington warned Americans against the danger of **factions**. Factions are opposing groups within a political party. Washington saw the factions that had developed among the Federalists as a threat to national unity.

focus your reading

Why did the United States almost go to war with France?

How did the Federalists try to silence their opponents?

What did the Republicans stand for in 1800?

vocabulary

factions   sedition

XYZ Affair   nullify

alien

Adams Elected President

In 1796, each faction had its own candidate for president. The Federalists nominated John Adams. The Republicans supported Thomas Jefferson. Adams won the election. The new president faced a crisis in foreign affairs. France had stepped up attacks against American shipping. It had captured 300 American ships by the time Adams took office. Hamilton and other Federalists called for war against France. The Republicans opposed going to war.

President Adams sent diplomats to talk with the French government. The French foreign

President John Adams

minister announced that he would not meet with them until they paid him $250,000. News of this insult, called the **XYZ Affair**, produced still louder cries for war.

The Alien and Sedition Acts

stop and think

In your notebook, write a bulleted list of issues that faced President Adams. Then work with a partner and write how Adams solved each issue.

President Adams was concerned about the tension with France. He thought that French citizens living in the United States might side with France if a conflict began. The Federalists in Congress used this crisis to crack down on their Republican opponents. In 1798, they passed laws known as the **Alien** and **Sedition** Acts. These acts gave the president the power to expel or jail any alien, or non-citizen. They also gave the government the power to charge people with sedition, or rebellious acts.

A fight in Congress, and later a letter to the editor, led to sedition charges against Matthew Lyons.

One of the Alien Acts increased the time a foreigner had to live in the United States before he could become a citizen. The time increased from five to fourteen years. Another of the Alien Acts allowed the president to deport any foreigner he thought was "dangerous to the peace and safety of the United States." At the time, new immigrants were usually Republicans.

The goal of the Sedition Act was to prevent people from speaking out against the government. The act also made it a crime to "impede the operation of any law." It provided fines and jail terms for anyone guilty of sedition, or stirring up of discontent. The Federalists used the law against Republican newspapers. The law banned articles that could damage the reputation of a government official. Twenty-five Republican editors and printers were jailed under this act.

The Kentucky and Virginia Resolutions

The Republicans fought back. Jefferson and Madison wrote resolutions declaring that the Alien and Sedition Acts violated the Constitution. The Kentucky and Virginia legislatures adopted these resolutions. Kentucky even claimed that states had a right to **nullify**, or strike down, an act of Congress.

In the meantime, President Adams sent a new set of delegates to France. They signed an agreement in which the French government agreed to protect American rights. This prevented a war with France, which was President Adams's greatest achievement. It displeased many Federalists, who wanted a war with France.

In 1800, the Republicans nominated Thomas Jefferson and Aaron Burr for president and vice president. They ran against the Federalists John Adams and Charles C. Pinckney. The Republicans

Thomas Jefferson was often criticized by the Federalists for his foreign policy.

THE PROVIDENTIAL DETECTION

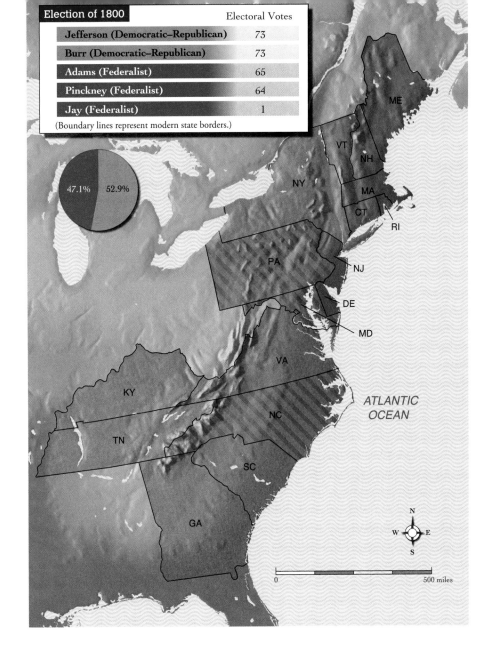

Election of 1800	Electoral Votes
Jefferson (Democratic–Republican)	73
Burr (Democratic–Republican)	73
Adams (Federalist)	65
Pinckney (Federalist)	64
Jay (Federalist)	1

(Boundary lines represent modern state borders.)

47.1% 52.9%

ME

VT

NH

NY

MA

CT

RI

PA

NJ

DE

MD

VA

KY

NC

TN

SC

GA

ATLANTIC OCEAN

N
W   E
S

0   500 miles

campaigned against the unpopular Alien and Sedition Acts. Jefferson and Burr won, but both received the same number of votes. This electoral tie threw the election into the Federalist House of Representatives. After 36 ballots, the House finally elected Jefferson president. This led to the Twelfth Amendment, which prevented such ties in the future.

Putting It All Together

List the major events that led to Thomas Jefferson's election as president. Write them in your notebook. Then write a short paragraph about the events.

Chapter Summary

In 1789, George Washington was **inaugurated** as president of the United States. Congress passed several laws, including the Tariff Act of 1789. Thereafter, **tariff duties** paid most of the government's expenses. In 1790, Secretary Hamilton proposed that Congress pay its debts with **bonds**.

After 1789, the Federalists began to disagree. Several congressmen opposed Hamilton's plan. They thought it favored **speculators**. Hamilton's friends in Congress enacted the plan into law. To pay the interest on the new bonds, Congress placed an **excise tax** on whiskey. This produced a **Whiskey Rebellion** in Pennsylvania. Using a **strict interpretation** of the Constitution, Jefferson argued that Congress lacked the power to create a bank. Hamilton, using a **broad interpretation**, said that the Constitution's phrase "necessary and proper" gave Congress the right to start the Bank of the United States.

President Washington warned Americans against the danger of **factions**. President Adams almost got involved in a war with France. The French government had insulted the United States in the **XYZ Affair**. The Federalists in Congress passed **alien** and **sedition** acts that banned newspaper articles critical of the Federalists. The Republicans passed the Kentucky and Virginia Resolutions, which threatened to **nullify** these acts of Congress.

Chapter Review

1 Write a letter either to Hamilton or Madison asking for a job as his public relations person. Include in your letter the viewpoints you share with the person you choose.

2 Use this chapter's vocabulary words in a first-draft paragraph to summarize what you have learned about the Federalists in power. Compare your paragraph with that of a partner. Then write a final draft.

3 Create a war brochure that a Federalist may have written calling for war against France. Include the reasons for wanting a war.

Skill Builder

Understanding Cause and Effect

Looking for cause and effect is one way to answer "why" questions.

1. Why were you late to school? Because you overslept.
2. Why did you oversleep? Because you forgot to set the alarm.
3. Why did you forget to set the alarm? Because you had other things on your mind.

Think of each of the above questions as an effect. Each effect had at least one cause. As you can see, some events also can be both effects and causes.

Looking for cause and effect helps us understand history. We can better understand why something happened in the past (effect) if we know what other people, conditions, or events helped make it happen (cause). George Washington's service to the nation during the American Revolution (cause) helps to explain his being elected president in 1789 (effect).

By 1796, the Federalists had divided into two factions. The majority of Federalists looked to John Adams and Alexander Hamilton for leadership. A group that called themselves Republicans rallied around Thomas Jefferson and James Madison.

In your notebook, make a "Cause and Effect Chart" like the one below. Reread Lesson 2 and identify at least three causes that help explain the emergence of factions. Then reread Lesson 3. Examine how those factions acted as a cause that had at least three other effects. Write the causes and effects in your chart.

Chapter 12

THE REPUBLICAN ERA

Treaty

Between the United States of America and the French Republic

Getting Focused

Skim this chapter to predict what you will be learning.

- Read the lesson titles and subheadings.
- Look at the illustrations and read the captions.
- Examine the maps.
- Review the vocabulary words and terms.

Many changes took place in the United States during the early 1800s. After reviewing the chapter, make a bulleted list of changes. Add to your list as you read.

The Republicans in Power

Thinking on Your Own

Write the Focus Your Reading questions in your notebook on the left side of a two-column chart. When you come to the answers to the questions, write them in the right column of the chart.

Thomas Jefferson saw his election as the beginning of a new era. He looked forward to a time of "**republican** simplicity" in American life. He wanted to bring republican, or more democratic, values to public life. Presidents Washington and Adams rode to their inaugurations in carriages. Jefferson, the first president to be inaugurated at the capitol in Washington, D.C., walked to the ceremony. He spent the next eight years trying to simplify and reduce the size of government.

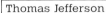

focus your reading

How did Jefferson cut back the role of government?

What power did the *Marbury v. Madison* decision give the Supreme Court?

Why did Jefferson think twice about purchasing Louisiana?

vocabulary

republican

midnight appointees

Louisiana Purchase

Lewis and Clark Expedition

Republican Government

Jefferson and the Republicans in Congress moved quickly to cut back the role of the federal government. Congress let the hated Alien and Sedition Acts expire. It repealed the Naturalization Act. Jefferson persuaded Congress to cut military spending. It also shrank the size of the navy from 25 to 7 ships. Jefferson closed nearly half of the American embassies in Europe.

These savings allowed Congress to remove all excise taxes. With no taxes to collect, it abolished the internal

Thomas Jefferson

revenue department. That cut another 500 federal jobs. The cutbacks allowed Jefferson to pay off the national debt more quickly than Hamilton had intended. He could not, however, change all of Hamilton's policies. The Bank of the United States had a 20-year charter. He had to live with it.

stop and think

In your notebook write two questions about Jefferson's presidency for which you know the answers. Share your questions and answers with a partner.

The Federalist Judiciary

Making the judicial system Republican was more difficult. The Republicans could not get rid of Federalist judges, because they served for life. Jefferson was able to block some new appointments. During his final hours in office, John Adams had appointed several judges and court officials. Jefferson ordered Secretary of State James Madison not to deliver the appointment papers.

William Marbury, one of the "**midnight appointees,**" filed a complaint with the Supreme Court. He demanded that the Court order Madison to deliver his papers. In the case of *Marbury* v. *Madison* (1803), Chief Justice Marshall declared that Marbury had no right to appeal Madison's action. He declared unconstitutional the law that gave Marbury that right. This was a major victory for the Supreme Court. It established the Court's right to declare acts of Congress unconstitutional.

Chief Justice John Marshall

The Louisiana Purchase

In early 1803, France offered to sell Louisiana to the United States. Buying Louisiana would nearly double the nation's size. It would give western farmers the unquestioned right to ship their produce down the Mississippi River. But President Jefferson believed in a strict, or narrow, interpretation of the Constitution. That document said nothing about the U.S. buying new territory.

Despite his doubts, Jefferson agreed to the **Louisiana Purchase**. He signed a treaty with France to buy Louisiana for $15 million. In the spring of 1804, Meriwether Lewis and William Clark led an expedition to explore Louisiana. They followed the Missouri River to its source, crossed the Rocky Mountains, and reached the Pacific. The **Lewis and Clark Expedition** returned in 1806 with a wealth of information about the Far West.

Meriwether Lewis

William Clark

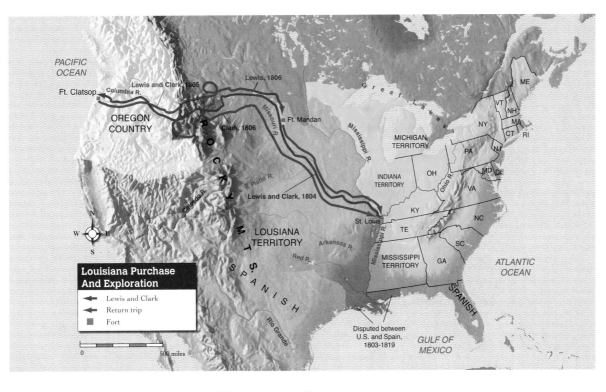

Putting It All Together

Create a web diagram in your notebook. In the middle, write the main concept, "The Republicans in Power." Go back over the section to collect facts that describe the Republicans in power. Arrange them in circles around the main concept.

Read a Primary Source

William Clark's Journal

Both Meriwether Lewis and William Clark kept journals during their expedition to the Pacific Ocean. The following entry, with Clark's inventive spelling, is from his journal on September 26, 1804. In the entry, Clark discribes his first meeting with the Sioux.

reading for understanding

Why did the men stop where they did?

How did the Sioux men and women dress?

How did Clark think women were treated in Sioux society?

"26th of Septr   Set out early and proceeded on. The river lined with Indians, [stopped] & anchored by the particular request of the Chiefs to let their Womin & Boys See the Boat. . . . Those people are Spritely . . . men particularly, they grease & Black themselves when they dress, make use of Hawks feathers about their heads, cover with a Roab. Each [has] a polecat skin to hold their Smokeables, fond of Dress, Badly armed. Ther women appear verry well, fin[e] Teeth, High Cheek [bones] Dress in Skin Peticoats, & a Roabe with the flesh Side out and harey ends turned back over their Sholders, and look well. They doe all the Laborious work, and I may say are perfect Slaves to their husbands who frequently have Several Wives."

The Journals of the Lewis & Clark Expedition
(13 vols., Lincoln, Nebraska, 1987).

Biography

Sacagawea (c.1788–1812 or 1884)

Meriwether Lewis and William Clark met Sacagawea by accident. They did not plan to take a sixteen-year-old Shoshone woman on their journey to the Pacific, especially not one with a newborn child. She was the wife of Toussaint Charbonneau, whom the explorers hired in November 1804 as an interpreter.

The explorers, led by Lewis and Clark, stopped for the winter at the Mandan Villages in present-day South Dakota. None of them could speak the languages of the Native Americans they would meet farther west. They hired Charbonneau, a French-speaking fur trapper, because he knew sign language. They soon learned that Sacagawea could speak Shoshone and Hidatsa.

Finding Sacagawea was a stroke of luck for Lewis and Clark. She showed the explorers how to find wild vegetables to add to their diet. When her husband's boat capsized on the Missouri River, he panicked, as he could not swim. Sacagawea saved the valuable compasses, books, and clothing that had washed overboard. Her very presence with her baby, Baptiste, proved helpful. It assured the Native Americans along the way that the explorers posed no threat. A war party would never bring along a woman with a baby.

Sacagawea was most valuable when the Lewis and Clark Expedition reached Shoshone country. She was the explorers' main interpreter with the Shoshone chiefs. Most important, she persuaded the chiefs to sell horses to Lewis and Clark. They could not have crossed the mountains in the winter without them.

Sacagawea traveled with the expedition to the Pacific Coast. On the return trip in 1806, she and Baptiste stopped off at the Mandan villages. She later took him to St. Louis, where William Clark placed Baptiste in school. Many historians believe she died of fever in December 1812, at age twenty-four, at a trading post on the Missouri River. However, there is an oral history that indicates she lived until 1884.

Sacagawea is honored by more monuments, markers, and mountain peaks than any other American woman. Her image also appears on the United States' one-dollar coin.

Growth and Expansion

Thinking on Your Own

Read the Focus Your Reading questions and the vocabulary words. In your notebook arrange the vocabulary words into three columns: "Words I Know," "Words I Think I Know," and "Words I Do Not Know." As you read, find the definitions of the words and write them in your notebook.

The early 1800s was a period of growth and expansion for the young American nation. More settlers moved west. In cities and towns, the number of workshops and mills increased. So did American shipping and trade with other nations. Venturing out into the world brought new opportunities and new risks.

Economic Growth

People continued to move west. They settled in the Ohio Valley and in the Lower South. Northern farmers produced corn and pork, which flatboats carried down the Mississippi River to market. By 1802, more than 500 flatboats arrived each year at the Port of New Orleans. Cotton and corn were the main crops raised in the South.

Steamboats contributed greatly to the nation's economic growth. In 1807, Robert Fulton built the *Clermont*, the first workable steamboat.

focus your reading

Why did the American economy grow during the early 1800s?

How did manufacturing change during this period?

Why was this period a golden age of American shipping?

vocabulary

spinning mill

interchangeable parts

merchant ships

tribute

neutral

embargo

On August 14, 1807, Robert Fulton's *Clermont* made the first successful steamboat trip.

Merchant shipping increased dramatically between 1793 and 1807.

Unlike flatboats, steamboats could haul goods upriver against the current. They became widely used on the Mississippi and Ohio Rivers.

Manufacturing expanded in the Northeast. In 1789, Samuel Slater built the first thread **spinning mill** in the United States. It used water power and machines to spin cotton thread. By 1815, the northeastern states had more than 200 spinning mills.

At his firearms factory in Connecticut, Eli Whitney developed a new method of machine production. His machines replaced skilled gunsmiths. They made **interchangeable parts**, which allowed unskilled workers to assemble muskets.

The early 1800s was the golden age of American shipping. The number of American **merchant ships** on the high seas doubled between 1793 and 1807. They carried farm produce being exported to foreign markets and imported goods not manufactured in the United States. This trade provided business for ship owners and work for sailors. Experienced sailors were in great demand.

stop and think

Imagine that you lived during this period. Write a newspaper advertisement for an invention that helped make the nation prosperous. Include an illustration and a caption.

Protecting American Rights

As trade expanded, American shipping faced greater risks. The Barbary States of North Africa—Algiers, Morocco, Tripoli, and Tunis—demanded **tribute**, or protection money, from ships sailing the Mediterranean Sea. In 1801, the United States went to war with Tripoli rather than meet these demands. In 1805, negotiations ended the conflict.

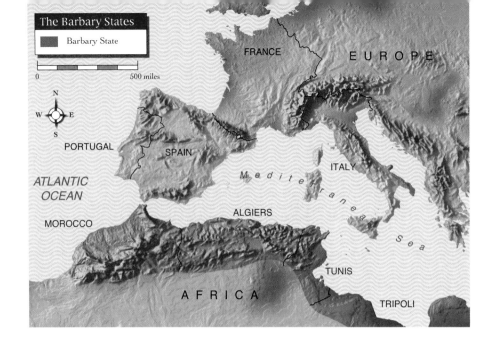

The Barbary States

■ Barbary State

0   500 miles

FRANCE   EUROPE

PORTUGAL   SPAIN   ITALY

ATLANTIC
OCEAN   *Mediterranean Sea*

MOROCCO   ALGIERS

TUNIS

AFRICA   TRIPOLI

Britain and France posed a greater threat. When these nations went to war in 1803, the United States declared itself a **neutral** country. By not taking sides, the United States could ship goods to both nations. However, neither nation respected the United States' neutral rights. In 1806, Britain began stopping all ships that traded with France. Some British officers also forced American sailors into the British navy. In reply, France declared British ports closed to neutral ships.

Stephen Decatur led a group of men who burned the *Philadelphia* in Tripoli's harbor in 1804.

To protest against these actions, President Jefferson persuaded Congress, in 1807, to pass an Embargo Act. This **embargo** stopped American ships from leaving for any foreign ports. It was a disaster for American merchants and ship owners. Congress repealed the act in 1809, replacing it with an act that reopened trade with all nations except Britain and France.

Putting It All Together

In your notebook, make a timeline of five important events included in this lesson. Below each event explain why it was significant. Then write a paragraph explaining the timeline.

The United States Goes to War

Thinking on Your Own

Read the Focus Your Reading questions and the vocabulary words. As you read, make a list of the vocabulary words and their definitions in your notebook.

In March 1809, President James Madison asked Congress to repeal the 1809 act that restricted trade with Britain and France. It had done little to protect neutral rights. Congress opened trade with both Britain and France, but promised to cut off trade with either nation if American rights were not protected. However, many Americans were losing patience with trade restrictions. They were demanding war.

focus your reading

Why did the West and South want to go to war?

Why did the United States invade Canada?

How did Andrew Jackson defeat the British?

vocabulary

Battle of Tippecanoe

War Hawks

Treaty of Ghent

The Road to War

Support for war came mainly from the South and West. Britain's seizure of American ships brought hard times to cotton and wheat farmers. Western settlers accused Britain of arming the Native Americans in the Ohio Valley. They also had their eye on good farmland in British Canada.

In the Northwest, the Shawnee posed a serious threat to the settlers. The Shawnee leader,

British ships often stopped American merchant ships and took the crews captive.

Tecumseh, tried to unite all the Ohio Valley Native American groups against the settlers. In 1811, a militia force of 1,000 men defeated the Native Americans at the **Battle of Tippecanoe**. Tecumseh and several hundred survivors escaped to Canada, where they sought British help.

stop and think

From what you have read so far, describe in your notebook the reasons America was ready for war.

In 1810, Western and Southern voters elected congressmen who shared their pro-war views. Among them were Henry Clay of Kentucky and John C. Calhoun of South Carolina. These **War Hawks**, helped persuade Congress to declare war against Britain on June 18, 1812.

The USS *Constitution*

Canada and the Great Lakes

At first, the war did not go well for the United States. To save money, Congress slashed the size of the army. The nation had to rely on poorly trained state militia troops. They made two attempts to invade Canada but were pushed back both times. That year ended with British troops in control of American forts along the Great Lakes.

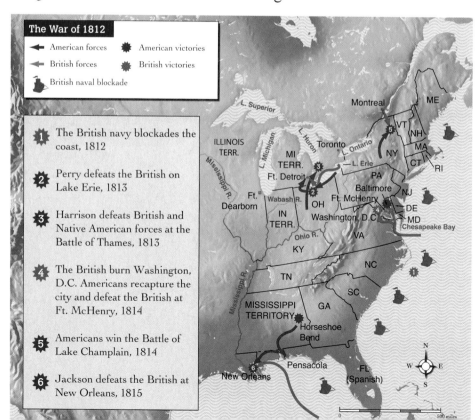

The War of 1812

→ American forces
→ British forces
British naval blockade
✸ American victories
✸ British victories

1. The British navy blockades the coast, 1812

2. Perry defeats the British on Lake Erie, 1813

3. Harrison defeats British and Native American forces at the Battle of Thames, 1813

4. The British burn Washington, D.C. Americans recapture the city and defeat the British at Ft. McHenry, 1814

5. Americans win the Battle of Lake Champlain, 1814

6. Jackson defeats the British at New Orleans, 1815

The navy had more success. The USS *President* and the USS *Constitution* each defeated British ships in individual combat. The USS *Constitution* earned its nickname "Old Ironsides" when British cannonballs bounced off its thick oak planks. In 1813, Captain Oliver Hazard Perry defeated a fleet of British gunboats on Lake Erie.

The Chesapeake and New Orleans

In 1814, Britain attacked the United States. British ships sailed up the Chesapeake Bay, landing troops near Washington, D.C. The militia defending the city fled. The British marched into the city, setting fire to the White House and the Capitol. They tried unsuccessfully to capture Baltimore.

Dolley Madison saved many documents during the British attack on the nation's capital.

Andrew Jackson led the U.S. to victory at the Battle of New Orleans in 1815.

In December, Britain launched its major attack against the United States. General Sir Edward Packenham landed an army of 7,500 troops south of New Orleans. His goal was to capture the city and use it as a base to occupy the Mississippi Valley. General Andrew Jackson blocked his advance with 4,500 militia lined up behind an earth barrier. When the British attacked on January 8, 1815, Jackson's frontier hunters stopped the Redcoats. During the half-hour battle, the British suffered 2,000 casualties, including General Packenham. The survivors withdrew. Unknown to either general, the **Treaty of Ghent** (Belgium), which ended the war, had been signed two weeks earlier.

Putting It All Together

Go back to the vocabulary words in your notebook. Use the definitions that you wrote to write a sentence using each word. Make sure that your sentences relate to why the United States went to war and include facts about each event.

Chapter Summary

President Thomas Jefferson wanted to make public life more **republican**. Jefferson refused to deliver appointment papers to one new Federalist judge. This "**midnight appointee**," William Marbury, complained to the Supreme Court. For the first time, the Supreme Court declared an act of Congress unconstitutional. In 1803, the **Louisiana Purchase** nearly doubled the size of the United States. Jefferson sent the **Lewis and Clark Expedition** to explore the Far West.

The early 1800s was a period of growth and expansion for the United States. Samuel Slater built the first thread **spinning mill**. Eli Whitney used machine-made **interchangeable parts** to make muskets. As trade expanded, American **merchant ships** faced greater risks. The Barbary States of North Africa demanded **tribute**. To protest against France and Britain stopping American ships, Congress declared an **embargo**.

By 1809, Americans were preparing for war. They had found no other way to stop Britain from interfering with their **neutral** rights. The **Battle of Tippecanoe** ended the Native American threat. In 1812, the **War Hawks** led the nation to war. In 1814, British troops set fire to the While House and the Capitol. The attack on New Orleans was halted by troops led by General Andrew Jackson. The **Treaty of Ghent** ended the war.

Chapter Review

1 Imagine that you are a Boston merchant during the Republican era. Write a letter to a friend in another country explaining the effect of the Embargo Act on your business.

2 Create a three-column chart with the labels "The Republicans in Power," "Growth and Expansion," and "The U.S. Goes to War." Fill in the columns with words or phrases that best describe each label. Use the information to write a short paragraph about the Republican era.

3 Choose five events about the Republican era that stand out for you. Create a concept web using the events.

Skill Builder

Diaries as Primary Sources

Diaries or journals can be valuable primary sources. They often present eyewitness accounts of the events they describe. The writer usually provides a day-by-day account of what was happening. However, diaries must be used critically. A critical reader should ask the following questions of a diary entry:

- Who wrote it?
- Was the writer well informed?
- What biases did the writer display?
- What problems does the vocabulary present?
- Was it written at the time of the events described?
- Why did the author write the diary entry?

Read the entry from William Clark's journal on page 190. It is a report of this explorer's first encounter with the Sioux. Read the entry critically by asking the following questions:

1 Where and when did Clark write this entry?

2 What biases did Clark show in this entry?

3 List words he used that are unfamiliar to you and explain what they mean.

4 Why do you think Clark's spelling is not accurate?

UNIT 7

THE EXPANDING NATION

After the War of 1812, the United States entered a new era of expansion. Americans headed west in larger numbers than ever. They pushed the frontier to the Mississippi River and beyond. Five new states entered the Union.

The American people seemed more united than ever before. The war had encouraged national feelings. Congress and the Supreme Court seemed to place the nation before local or regional concerns. But this Era of Good Feelings did not last long. This period of expansion also was the era of Andrew Jackson. His presidency created controversy and conflict.

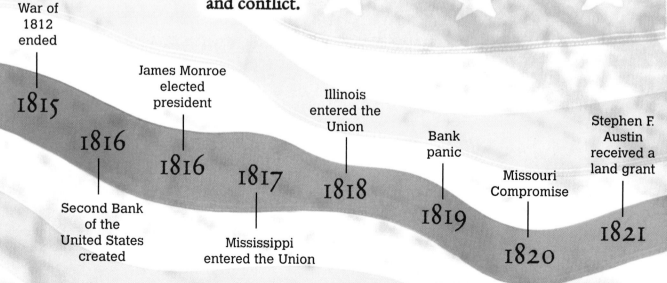

War of 1812 ended

1815

James Monroe elected president

1816

Second Bank of the United States created

1816

Mississippi entered the Union

1817

Illinois entered the Union

1818

Bank panic

1819

Missouri Compromise

1820

Stephen F. Austin received a land grant

1821

Why did more Americans head west than ever before?

What struggles did early settlers face on the frontier?

What sectional and political issues divided Americans?

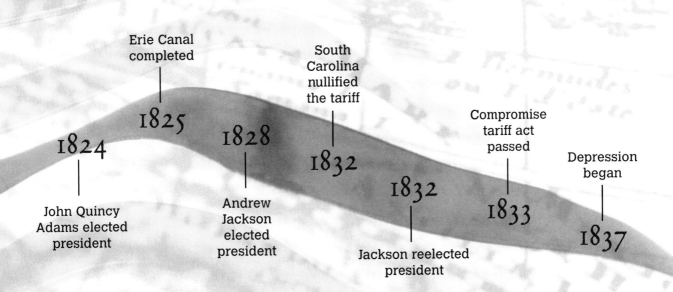

1824
John Quincy Adams elected president

1825
Erie Canal completed

1828
Andrew Jackson elected president

1832
South Carolina nullified the tariff

1832
Jackson reelected president

1833
Compromise tariff act passed

1837
Depression began

Chapter 13 WESTWARD EXPANSION

Getting Focused

Skim this chapter to predict what you will be learning.

- Read the lesson titles and subheadings.
- Look at the illustrations and read the captions.
- Examine the maps.
- Review the vocabulary words and terms.

In your notebook write a sentence or two explaining what you think the chapter is about. Compare your ideas with those of a partner.

A People on the Move

Thinking on Your Own

Think about a time when you or someone you know moved to another area. Why did the move take place? What kind of transportation was used? Then create two columns in your notebook with the headings "Today" and "In the Past." Using the vocabulary and the Focus Your Reading questions, compare and contrast a person moving today with a person moving during the period of American expansion westward.

By 1815, Americans were a people on the move. Each summer thousands of Americans headed west. They left their homes in the eastern United States and set out for the Ohio Valley, Kentucky, and Tennessee. They went to make a better living for themselves and their families.

focus your reading

Why did people move west?

What advantages did river travel have?

What were the advantages of canal boats?

vocabulary

wagon roads   canal

flatboat

Wagon Roads

Most people traveled in wagons pulled by teams of horses or oxen. It was the cheapest way for a family to travel. The wagons carried food, clothing, and farm equipment. Adults usually walked alongside. They led the teams or herded pigs and cows. Young children rode in the wagons. "The wagons swarm with children," wrote one traveler. "I heard today of three together, which contain forty-two of these young citizens."

Travelers made use of various roads. The Wilderness Road led across Virginia to Tennessee. The Cumberland Road extended from Maryland to the Ohio River. The Forbes Road crossed Pennsylvania.

Wagon trains carried supplies and provided protection.

Travel by wagon was difficult and often dangerous. Most **wagon roads** in the West were only dirt paths through the forests. The worst had tree

stumps standing in the middle of the road. Wagons often broke down because of these rough roads. The roads also became muddy when it rained or snowed. To avoid mud and stumps, some roads were covered with logs. These roads were called corduroy roads because they looked like corduroy fabric.

It was much easier to travel west by water in 1815. Most travelers who reached the Ohio River stopped to buy or build a **flatboat**. These wooden, flat-bottomed boats were easy and cheap to make. They did not run aground when the river was low. When travelers reached their destination, they took the boats apart and sold the boards for lumber.

Going down river by flatboat was the fastest way to travel. But the boats had shortcomings. People ate and slept on the open decks along with their cows and chickens. They huddled under sheets of canvas when it rained.

stop and think

Turn your book face down. In your notebook or with a partner, explain what you remember having read to this point.

Flatboats provided fast river travel.

Canals

After 1825, people could go to the Michigan Territory, northern Ohio, Indiana, and Illinois by **canal** boat. In that year, the state of New York opened the Erie Canal between the cities of Albany and Buffalo. This canal linked the Hudson River to the Great Lakes.

Canal boats provided travelers with meals and a place to sleep.

The Erie Canal was a great success. By 1840, New York and other states had built hundreds of miles of canals.

Canal boats were the most comfortable way to travel west. Passengers sat on benches in the cabin or on top of the cabin roof. At night the benches were made into beds. The boat's crew served passengers hot meals prepared in towns along the canal.

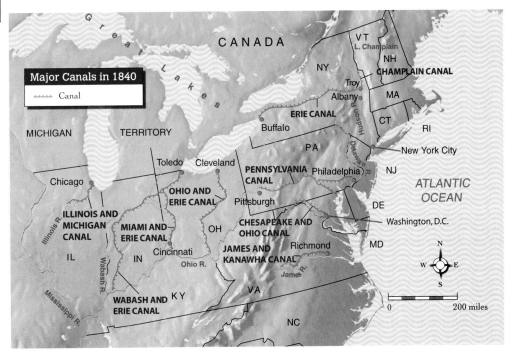

Putting It All Together

Create a newspaper advertisement for the canal boats. Persuade your audience that canal boats are the best way to travel west.

Settling the Frontier

Thinking on Your Own

Before reading this section, make a three-column chart in your notebook. Give the columns these titles: "Hunters," "Farmers," and "Townspeople." Use the vocabulary and the Focus Your Reading questions to help you describe each group. Compare your descriptions with a partner.

After 1815, thousands of white settlers moved into the Ohio Valley. They pushed the frontier (the edge of settlement) west across Indiana and Illinois. South of the Ohio River, the frontier extended into Kentucky, Tennessee, Alabama, Mississippi, and Louisiana. The area beyond the frontier was still known as Indian country.

focus your reading

Why were hunters the first white settlers?

How did farmers clear the forests?

Why did newly settled areas need villages and towns?

vocabulary

lean-tos   gristmill

blacksmith

Frontier Hunters

In most areas, the first white settlers were hunters. Wild game was plentiful on the frontier. The hunters shot deer, bear, and other wild game, bringing back meat and hides. "His manners are rough," wrote one traveler. "He wears . . . a long beard . . . He carries a knife . . . and when in the woods has a rifle on his back and a pack of dogs at his heels." Women tanned and cut up the skins to make clothing for the family.

Frontier hunters lived in **lean-tos** and in small cabins. A lean-to is a shelter with a roof

Hunting on the frontier was often dangerous.

that slopes from the front to the back. It is open to the weather on the front side. Even the cabins were hastily built, as the hunters expected to move on in a short time.

The frontier was a lonely place for women and children. The men spent most of their time hunting. Bears, panthers, and wildcats made it unsafe for women and children to go very far from home. The nearest neighbors lived miles away.

Farmers were the next to arrive. They cleared the forests, chasing away the wild game. The farmers chopped down the smaller trees with axes. They killed the larger trees by cutting off a ring of bark. Then they set these dead trees on fire. The next spring they planted crops between the blackened stumps.

Farmers often burned trees to clear space for their crops.

Corn was the main crop. It provided food for the family and feed for farm animals. Corn-fattened hogs provided ham and bacon for the dinner table. Farmers traded corn and hams at the village store for things they could not make themselves.

Frontier farmers depended mostly on themselves. They raised most of their own food. The women made most of the family's clothes. Farmers did help one another. They got together to build log cabins and to have dinners and dances. They also helped one another harvest crops.

stop and think

Sketch a symbol or logo to represent each kind of settlement in the West: hunters' cabins, farms, towns.

Villages and Towns

Every settlement had at least one village. The village served the needs of the farmers who lived nearby. Most villages included a cluster of houses, a **blacksmith** shop, a **gristmill**, and a general store. The blacksmith made and repaired iron tools. The gristmill ground grain into flour. Farmers bought salt, pots and pans, and other items at the general store. They paid with hams, eggs, corn, and potatoes more often than cash.

Some small villages grew to become towns. Most towns had a doctor's office, a newspaper, and several stores. Pittsburgh became a manufacturing center. Its skilled workers specialized in making boats, iron tools, and glassware. Cincinnati, Louisville, and other river towns became busy port cities. Other towns also grew into cities and profited as farmers began shipping their products along the river routes.

Towns and villages often provided farmers with a blacksmith.

New States

People who moved west also created new states. They wanted their own state courts, lawmakers, and governors. The new states added to the Union north of the Ohio River included Ohio (1803), Indiana (1816), and Illinois (1818). States south of the river included Louisiana (1812), Mississippi (1817), and Alabama (1819). Missouri (1820) was the first state to be added west of the Mississippi River.

Putting It All Together

Return to your three-column chart. Based on your reading, add to your descriptions of hunters, farmers, and townspeople.

Read a Primary Source

The Versatile Farmer

William Cobbett, a British writer and politician, lived in the United States from 1817 to 1819. During this time he lived with his family on a farm in Long Island, New York. He wrote the description below of the typical American farmer.

> " . . . Besides the great quantity of work performed by the American [farmer], his skill, the versatility of his talent, is a great thing. Every man can use an axe, a saw, and a hammer. Scarcely one who cannot do any job at rough carpentering, and mend a plough [plow] or a wagon. Very few indeed, who cannot kill and dress pigs and sheep, and many of them oxen and calves. Every farmer is a neat butcher; a butcher for market; and, of course, 'the boys' must learn. This is a great convenience. It makes you so independent as to a main part of the means of housekeeping. All are ploughmen [plowmen]. In short, a good labourer here can do anything that is to be done upon a farm . . . . "

William Cobbett, *A Year's Residence in the United States of America* (London, 1818).

reading for understanding

What does Cobbett mean by the "versatility" of the American farmer's talent?

Why would "versatility of talent" be useful to a frontier farmer?

What skills did American farmers have?

Why is the farm in the drawing surrounded by forest?

What animals were hunted by the farmers?

An early American farm

Biography

Kit Carson (1809–1868)

When this notice appeared in a Missouri newspaper, Kit Carson was headed west. He had joined a wagon caravan going to Santa Fe to trade. This young apprentice, valued at one cent in Missouri, proved his true worth in the West.

NOTICE TO WHOM IT MAY CONCERN

That Christopher Carson, a boy about sixteen years old, small for his age, but thick-set, light hair, ran away from the subscriber to whome he had been bound to learn the saddler's trade on or about the first day of September last. . . . One cent reward will be given to any person who will bring back said boy.

(signed) David Workman

Franklin [Missouri], October 6, 1826

After arriving in the Mexican town of Santa Fe, Kit Carson became a trapper. For nearly fifteen years he trapped beaver in the Rocky Mountains. When beaver trapping was over, he traded with the Native Americans for buffalo hides. His first wife was an Arapaho woman.

Kit Carson knew the mountains better than most men. During the 1840s, Lieutenant John Charles Frémont hired Carson as a guide to help survey the Rocky Mountains. When the Mexican War began, Carson led General Stephen Kearney's army across the mountains to California. He fought with Kearney in California. He later fought in the Civil War as a colonel in the Union army.

After the Civil War, Kit Carson served as a government agent for the Ute and Apache People. He lived among the Native Americans and tried to keep the peace. Kit Carson died peacefully in 1868 at the age of fifty-nine. A monument in Santa Fe sums up his life in these words: "He led the way."

Beyond the Mississippi

Thinking on Your Own

Read the vocabulary and Focus Your Reading questions. Discuss with a partner what you think are the main ideas of this section. Write your predictions in your notebook.

By the 1820s, some Americans had moved west of the Mississippi River. They settled in Texas, went to Santa Fe to trade, and trapped beaver in the Rocky Mountains.

focus your reading

Why did Texas declare its independence from Mexico?

Why did Missouri merchants go to Santa Fe?

Who were the Mountain Men?

vocabulary

land grant   rendezvous

Mountain Men

Texas

Americans first settled in Texas in the 1820s. Texas was then part of Mexico, which had recently won its independence from Spain. In 1821, the Mexican government offered Stephen F. Austin a large **land grant**, or gift of land, if he would bring settlers to Texas. Mexico needed American settlers to help defend its Texas frontier.

Austin helped Americans settle in Mexico. At first, the settlers were happy. Each family received thousands of acres of ranch land at little cost. In time, however, they came to dislike Mexican laws and customs. They wanted to govern themselves.

In 1836, the American settlers in Texas declared their independence. General Antonio Lopez de Santa Anna, the Mexican president, led an army to put down the revolt. The Mexicans killed 187 Texans at the Alamo, including Davy Crockett and James Bowie. "Remember the Alamo" became a famous Texas battle cry. A Texas army led by General Sam Houston finally defeated the Mexicans at the Battle of San Jacinto. Texas, nicknamed the "Lone Star Republic," was independent until 1845, when it joined the Union as a state.

Stephen F. Austin

The Alamo was the site of a battle between Mexico and Texas.

Santa Fe Trade

In 1821, William Becknell set out for Mexico. Becknell, a Missouri merchant, took with him packhorses loaded with cloth, hardware, and other goods. He sold these goods in the Mexican town of Santa Fe for a big profit.

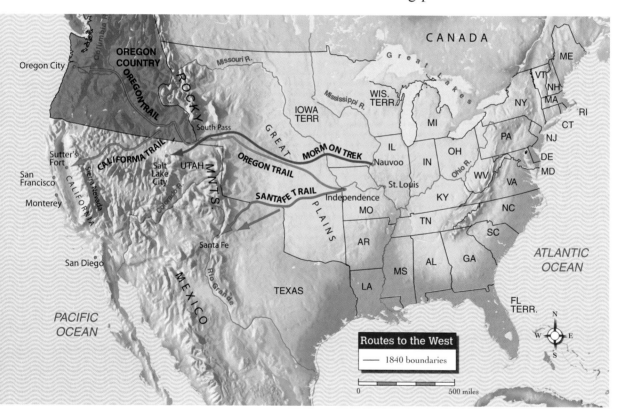

Each spring thereafter, Becknell and other merchants set out for Santa Fe in wagon caravans. They opened a new road across the plains. It was called the Santa Fe Trail. The 800-mile journey took 10 weeks. The trip was well worth the time spent. In 1824, the merchants paid $30,000 for the goods they bought in Missouri. They sold them in Santa Fe for $180,000. Many of these merchants settled in Santa Fe.

The Mountain Men

In 1822, William H. Ashley advertised in a St. Louis, Missouri, newspaper for "enterprising young men" to work for him in the Rocky Mountains. The men who answered Ashley's ad were known as the **Mountain Men**. These men trapped beaver in the Rocky Mountains for Ashley's Rocky Mountain Fur Company. Beaver pelts brought high prices in eastern cities like New York and also in Europe. The pelts were used to make men's dress hats.

Fur trapping was a dangerous life. The trappers spent all winter in the mountains. They fought off grizzly bears. Hostile Native Americans attacked them. They faced harsh winter blizzards. Those who survived met during the summer at a **rendezvous** or meeting place to deliver their furs. The company paid the trappers and sold them supplies for the coming year.

Beaver trapping came to an end in the 1840s. Beaver hats fell out of fashion. Men preferred to wear silk top hats instead. Many of the Mountain Men stayed in the West. Some settled down as farmers. Kit Carson and others worked as guides. They showed explorers and settlers the way from place to place.

Mountain Men

Putting It All Together

Pretend that the year is 1817. You have moved west with your family. Write a letter to a friend back east describing your life. Include as many details from this section as you can. You may want to do some additional research.

Chapter Summary

By 1815, Americans were a people on the move. Most travelers set out overland by **wagon road**. Wagon travel was slow and difficult. Floating down the Ohio River on a **flatboat** was quicker. The easiest way to go was by **canal** boat.

The first people to reach the frontier were backwoods hunters who lived in **lean-tos** or rough cabins. Later, farmers moved west. They cleared the forests to make room for fields. **Blacksmiths**, storekeepers, and doctors settled in nearby villages and towns to serve the farmers' needs. Some towns grew into cities. **Gristmills** were built to grind grain into flour.

By the 1820s, settlers had crossed the Mississippi River. The government of Mexico gave Stephen F. Austin a **land grant** to help settle Texas. Texas was then the northern frontier of Mexico. In 1836, Texas won its independence when Sam Houston defeated the Mexican army at the Battle of San Jacinto. In the 1820s, merchants from Missouri opened trade with Mexico over the Santa Fe Trail. Some merchants settled down in Santa Fe. By then other Americans had reached the Rocky Mountains. The **Mountain Men** trapped beaver all winter and brought the furs to a **rendezvous** in the spring.

Chapter Review

1 Draw a picture that shows one of the following in detail:

 A family going west by flatboat
 A frontier farm
 A Mountain Man at work

2 Look again at the prediction you made at the beginning of this chapter. You were asked what the chapter would be about. What would you add or change?

3 Pretend that you are a British visitor traveling in the American West in 1817. Using information from this chapter, write a letter home that describes what you have seen.

Skill Builder

Reading a Map

Most maps contain different kinds of information. This map of routes to the West in 1840 shows different methods of transportation. The map shows roads, canals, and rivers. These are identified on the Map Key.

Using the map, answer the following questions:

1 What roads would a traveler from Richmond, Virginia, take to get to Tennessee?

2 Which two waterways would a family use to get from New York City to Buffalo?

3 The National Road, commonly called the Cumberland Road, began in Cumberland, Maryland. Through which states did it run?

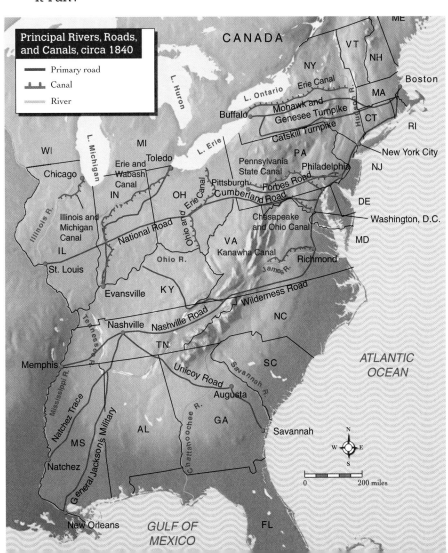

Chapter
14
THE ERA OF ANDREW JACKSON

Getting Focused

Skim this chapter to predict what you will be learning.

- Read the lesson titles and subheadings.
- Look at the illustrations and read the captions.
- Examine the maps.
- Review the vocabulary words and terms.

Recall a time when you felt content in your life. Nations, too, can have times when people feel content. With a partner, talk about what these experiences might have in common.

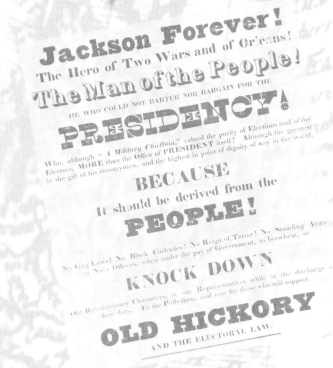

Jackson Forever!
The Hero of Two Wars and of Or'eans!
The Man of the People!
HE WHO COULD NOT BARTER NOR BARGAIN FOR THE
PRESIDENCY!

Who, although "A Military Chieftain," valued the purity of Elections and of the Electors, MORE than the Office of PRESIDENT itself! Although the greatest in the gift of his countrymen, and the highest in point of dignity of any in the world,

BECAUSE
It should be derived from the
PEOPLE!

No Gag Laws! No Black Cockades! No Reign of Terror! No Standing Army or Navy Officers, when under the pay of Government, to browbeat, or

KNOCK DOWN

Old Revolutionary Characters, or our Representatives while in the discharge of their duty. To the Polls then, and vote for those who will support

OLD HICKORY
AND THE ELECTORAL LAW.

A Nation United

Thinking on Your Own

Read the Focus Your Reading questions. Then make a concept map with "Era of Good Feelings" in the middle. While you read, add events and situations to the concept map that would produce good feelings for the nation.

In 1816, Americans were more united than ever before. They were proud of Andrew Jackson's victory over the British at New Orleans. "The people," said Albert Gallatin, "are more American; feel and act more as a nation." Party politics no longer divided the nation. In 1816, the voters elected James Monroe, a Republican, by a landslide. It was the beginning, one newspaper reported, of "an **Era of Good Feelings**."

focus your reading

Why was this period called the Era of Good Feelings?

How did the American System strengthen the United States?

How did President Monroe's foreign policy make the country stronger?

vocabulary

Era of Good Feelings

American System

Monroe Doctrine

The American System

After the war, leaders in Congress from the North and the South agreed upon a plan to strengthen the nation's economy. They called it the **American System**.

The plan included a Bank of the United States, which Congress approved in 1816. The bank issued U.S. Bank Notes, which became the nation's new currency. Its branch banks also loaned money, which benefited farmers and merchants alike.

To help factory owners, Congress passed the Tariff of 1816. American manufacturers could not produce goods as cheaply as British factory owners. Placing a tariff or tax on imports

helped them by raising the prices of those goods. In 1817, Congress agreed to provide federal funds to help states build roads and canals.

Supreme Court Decisions

During this period, the Supreme Court also helped strengthen the national government. Several court decisions, written by Chief Justice John Marshall, placed limits on the states. The Court's decision in *Dartmouth College v. Woodward* (1819) ruled that states could not overturn private business agreements. In *Gibbons v. Ogden* (1824), the Supreme Court ruled that only Congress could regulate trade between the states.

Chief Justice John Marshall

stop and think

Discuss with a partner why limiting state power would strengthen the national government. In your notebook write three ways this could happen.

Bold Foreign Policies

President James Monroe gave the United States a larger role in world affairs. He expanded the nation's boundaries by persuading Spain to sell Florida. His secretary of state, John Quincy Adams, signed a treaty with Britain that removed troops from both nations from the border with Canada. In 1823, Adams also wrote a bold policy statement for the president that closed the Western Hemisphere to future European colonization. This is known as the **Monroe Doctrine**.

President James Monroe

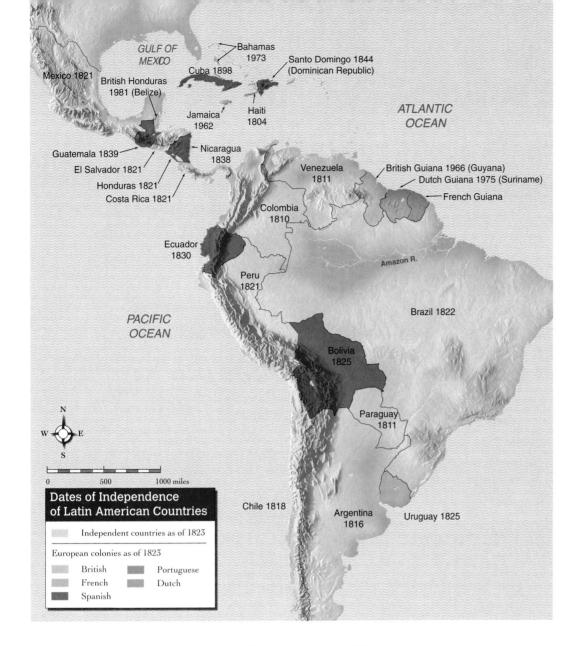

Dates of Independence of Latin American Countries

Independent countries as of 1823

European colonies as of 1823

British
French
Spanish
Portuguese
Dutch

National Prosperity

The Era of Good Feelings was a period of prosperity. A food shortage in Europe led to high prices for American wheat, pork, and cheese. Land values rose as farmers bought more land. They also bought more plows, shovels, and farm wagons from American manufacturers.

Putting It All Together

In your notebook make a two-column chart. Label the columns "Problem" and "Solution." On the problem side, write problems that President Monroe addressed in his foreign policy. On the solution side, note how he solved the problems. Use the Internet or the library to research more about President Monroe's foreign policy and add to the chart.

Sectional Conflicts and Party Battles

Thinking on Your Own

Read the Focus Your Reading questions and vocabulary. Write one sentence that predicts how the existence of slavery could threaten American unity or the union of states.

The Era of Good Feelings was short-lived. It could not survive the hard times of the 1820s. The South's efforts to admit Missouri as a slave state caused ill feelings in the North. The revival of party politics also helped divide Americans.

focus your reading

What demands did people make after the panic of 1819?

What was the Missouri Compromise?

Why did the House of Representatives decide who was elected president in 1824?

vocabulary

panic of 1819

Tallmadge Amendment

Missouri Compromise

Electoral College

Economic Hard Times

The first blow to the Era of Good Feelings was the **panic of 1819**. The Bank of the United States helped cause the panic by forcing western banks to call in their loans. Its directors were afraid the bank would lose the money it had loaned. Unable to pay back their loans, many farmers lost their farms.

As farmers placed fewer orders, factories had to close. Their owners demanded help from Congress. Congress helped them by raising tariff rates. The new Tariff of 1824 made southern planters angry. It increased the price of cloth, tools, furniture, and other items they needed. The farmers blamed northern factory owners for high prices.

The Second Bank of the United States, built in 1816, is located in Philadelphia.

The Missouri Crisis

In 1819, Missouri asked to be admitted to the Union as a slave state. This would destroy the balance that existed in Congress of eleven slave and eleven free states. Congressman James W. Tallmadge of New York demanded that Missouri be admitted as a free state. This led to an intense debate in and out of Congress. Most people in the North supported the **Tallmadge Amendment**. The South opposed it.

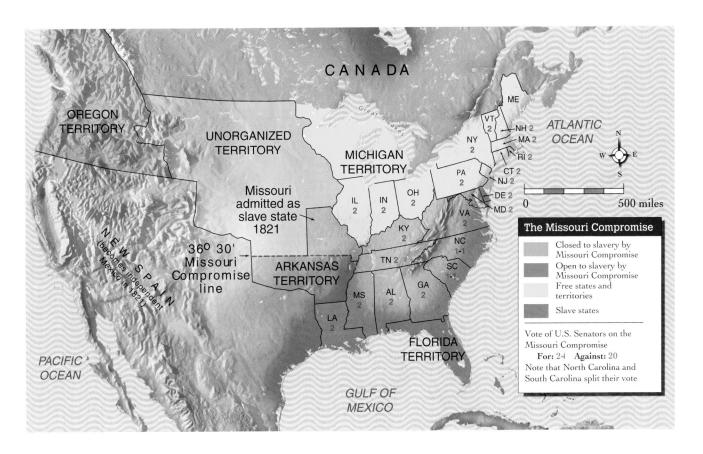

Afraid that the issue would destroy the Union, Congress agreed to a compromise. The **Missouri Compromise** (1821) admitted Missouri as a slave state. To restore the balance, it admitted Maine as a free state. To settle the question for the future, Congress drew a line on a map from Missouri to the Rocky Mountains. Any new state south of that line would be admitted as a slave state; any north of it would be a free state.

The Democratic Spirit

By the 1820s, the United States was more democratic. The very term "democracy" had a more favorable meaning. Earlier generations viewed democracy as a threat. The Constitution had placed limits on democracy. Politicians of the 1820s put much greater trust in the people.

Politics was more democratic in many ways. At the time of the American Revolution, only property owners could vote. The new western states, added to the Union between 1810 and 1820, let every white adult male vote. The older eastern states soon dropped their property requirements as well. As a result, more people voted and took part in public life.

Andrew Jackson was popular as a "self-made man" in the 1824 elections.

JACKSON TICKET

Honor and gratitude to the man who has filled the measure of his country's glory—*Jefferson*

FOR THE ASSEMBLY
GEORGE H. STEUART,
JOHN V. L. McMAHON.

Americans placed greater value on social equality. In hotels, steamboats, and marketplaces, people of all classes mixed together as equals. Inherited wealth and family name had once determined social rank. That was no longer the case. The hero of the day was the "self-made man." He was a man like Andrew Jackson, who had climbed to the top on his own.

Political Conflict

In 1824, the rising tide of democracy almost swept Andrew Jackson into the White House. Among the four candidates running for president, he won the most electoral and popular votes. But he did not win a majority in the **Electoral College**. In such a case, the House of Representatives must decide the election.

President John Quincy Adams

Henry Clay, one of the four candidates, persuaded his friends to vote for John Quincy Adams. Adams had come in second. Congress elected Adams, who then appointed Clay as his secretary of state.

Henry Clay

Andrew Jackson was furious. He accused Adams of defeating the will of the people by making a deal with Clay. For the next four years, Jackson's friends in Congress blocked nearly every bill that Adams wanted passed. President John Quincy Adams accomplished very little as president.

Putting It All Together

Create a two-column chart in your notebook entitled "Conflicts" and "Feelings." In the left column, list three conflicts of the period 1819–1824. Explain in the right column how these conflicts created bad feelings among Americans.

Biography

John Quincy Adams (1767–1848)

In December 1825, President John Quincy Adams delivered his first address to Congress. It called for Congress to build federal roads and canals, and establish a national university. The president also wanted a naval academy, a national observatory, a uniform system of weights and measures, and closer cooperation with Latin America. Few presidents have taken office with such a bold plan for the future.

Adams was born in Massachusetts in 1767. He was the eldest son of John and Abigail Adams. At age eleven, he went to Europe to watch his father negotiate a treaty of alliance with France. He graduated from Harvard College at age twenty, and chose to study and practice law.

John Quincy Adams gave up his law practice in 1794 to represent the United States in Europe. During the next twenty years he served as United States minister to the Netherlands, Prussia, and Great Britain. He returned home to win election to the United States Senate. In 1817, President James Monroe appointed him secretary of state. As secretary of state, he wrote the Monroe Doctrine, which warned Europe not to meddle in the affairs of the Western Hemisphere.

Despite such preparation, John Quincy Adams's presidency, from 1825–1829, was a failure. Andrew Jackson's friends in Congress blocked every measure he wanted passed. They fought him at every turn, and defeated him for reelection.

In 1830, the people of Adams's Massachusetts district elected him to Congress. He spent the next twelve and a half years serving in the House of Representatives. In Congress, he supported the Bank of the United States, fought for freedom of speech, and attempted to introduce amendments to the Constitution that would prevent any person born in the United States from being born a slave.

In 1839, fifty-three African captives aboard the *Amistad* mutinied off the coast of Cuba. They killed the captain and cook, and attempted to sail the ship back to Africa. The ship was stopped off the coast of Connecticut and the Africans arrested. Adams joined the team of lawyers who fought for the freedom of the Africans. In 1841, he argued their case before the Supreme Court. Adams's efforts helped gain the captives their freedom and eventual return to Africa. John Quincy Adams died in the Capitol Building on February 23, 1848, at age seventy-six.

LESSON 3 The Jacksonian Democrats

Thinking on Your Own

Read the Focus Your Reading questions and vocabulary. Make a two-column chart in your notebook with the title "Andrew Jackson's Decisions." Label one column "Made National Government Stronger" and the other column "Made State Government Stronger." As you read about the decisions Jackson made as president, list them in one column or the other.

The election campaign of 1828 was hard fought. John Quincy Adams ran for reelection as the National Republican candidate. Andrew Jackson was the candidate of the new Democratic-Republican Party. The Democrats promised that Jackson would give the government back to the people. Andrew Jackson won the election with 56 percent of the popular vote.

focus your reading

What did Andrew Jackson mean by restoring government to the people?

What limits did Jackson place on states' rights?

Why was Jackson's war against the Bank of the United States good politics?

vocabulary

doctrine of nullification

trail of tears

depression of 1837

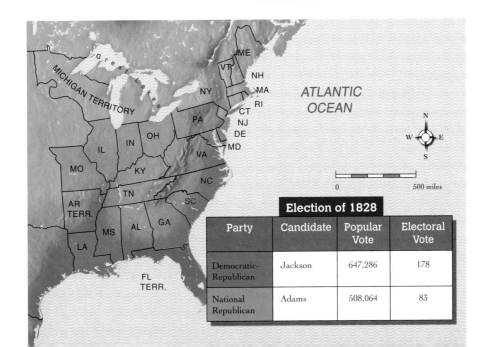

Election of 1828

Party	Candidate	Popular Vote	Electoral Vote
Democratic-Republican	Jackson	647,286	178
National Republican	Adams	508,064	83

225

Andrew Jackson

Jacksonian Democracy

Jackson wanted the people to know that he was their president. On his first day in office, he invited everyone to the White House for refreshments. Fifteen thousand people showed up. It is the largest crowd ever to attend a White House event.

President Jackson fired many of the government clerks in Washington, D.C. He replaced them with Democrats. "Rotation in office," he said, was another way to return government to the people. It also rewarded workers of the Democratic Party.

Jackson reduced the work of the federal government. He had more faith in state governments, as they were closer to the people. In 1830, Congress passed a bill to build a national road in Kentucky. Jackson vetoed it. He thought that each state should be responsible for its own roads.

Nullification Crisis

Democrats from South Carolina had their own ideas about the rights of the states. John C. Calhoun argued that states did not have to enforce acts of Congress that they thought violated the U.S. Constitution. He called this the **doctrine of nullification**. In 1832, South Carolina refused to enforce the tariff acts of 1828 and 1832. Its leaders thought the tariffs benefited northern factory owners at the expense of the South.

Jackson opposed South Carolina's action. It placed the state above the federal government. He threatened to send troops to South Carolina to enforce the tariff laws. The state's leaders agreed to repeal

John C. Calhoun

the acts of nullification if Congress would reduce the tariff. Congress passed a compromise tariff act in 1833 that reduced the rates. That ended the nullification crisis.

Indian Removal

Jackson did not include Native Americans in his promise to restore government to the people. When he took office, the State of Georgia was trying to force the Cherokee off their land. The Cherokee, who could read and write, knew how to protect their rights. The tribe filed suit against the state in the Supreme Court.

stop and think

Imagine that you are a journalist writing a report on President Jackson's treatment of the Cherokee. Write the article. Include facts about the Cherokee and American state and national governments. Research to learn more about this topic.

Andrew Jackson took Georgia's side. When the Court ruled in the Cherokee's favor in 1831, he refused to enforce its decision. Instead, he ordered the army to remove the Cherokee and other eastern people. The army relocated them to "Indian Territory" west of the Mississippi River. Thousands of Cherokee died on the forced march, or "**trail of tears**," to their new home.

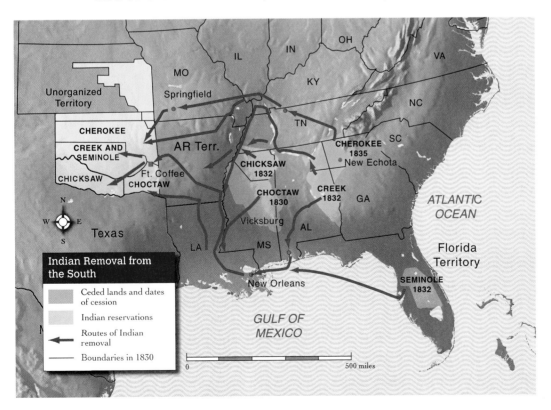

Jackson's War Against the Bank

In 1831, Jackson declared war against the Bank of the United States. He saw the bank as a powerful institution that the people did not control. When Congress passed a bill to renew the bank's charter, Jackson vetoed it. He used the bank veto in the election of 1832 to win votes in the West and the South. Many voters there blamed the bank for the panic of 1819. Jackson won reelection, defeating Henry Clay.

This cartoon shows Andrew Jackson demolishing the Bank of the United States by withdrawing federal funds.

Although Jackson's veto was good politics, it was bad for the economy. Jackson moved the U.S. Treasury's money to state banks. They loaned it out to land buyers. Many farmers lost their farms when they could not repay the loans. Destroying the bank helped bring about the **depression of 1837**, another period of hard times. By then Jackson's second term as president was over.

Putting It All Together

Review the Thinking on Your Own chart you have kept while reading this section. On the basis of Jackson's decisions during his first four years in office, would you have voted to reelect him as president in 1832?

Read a Primary Source

The Trail of Tears

Groups of Cherokee set out on the "trail of tears" to Indian Territory late in September 1838. In the following account, a traveler from Maine described the condition of the Cherokee when they passed through Kentucky.

reading for understanding

What season of the year did the Cherokee's journey take place?

How were they dressed?

What was the condition of their health?

"We met several detachments [of Cherokee] in the southern part of Kentucky on the 4th, 5th, and 6th of December. . . . The sick and feeble were carried in wagons . . . a great many ride on horseback and multitudes go on foot—even aged females, apparently nearly ready to drop into the grave, were traveling with heavy burdens attached to the back—on the sometimes frozen ground, and sometimes muddy streets, with no covering for the feet except what nature had given them. . . . We learned from the inhabitants on the road where the Indians passed, that they buried fourteen or fifteen at every stopping place."

Quoted in John Ehle, *Trail of Tears: The Rise and Fall of the Cherokee Nation* (New York: Doubleday, 1988).

Chapter Summary

The War of 1812 helped to unite Americans. The result was an **Era of Good Feelings**. During this period, Congress developed a plan called the **American System** to strengthen the economy. It included a national bank, higher tariffs, and federal funds to build roads and canals. The **Monroe Doctrine** closed the Western Hemisphere to future European colonies.

The **panic of 1819** led to economic hard times. Missouri's request to be admitted as a slave state caused ill will between the North and the South. The North supported the **Tallmadge Amendment,** which would admit Missouri as a free state. The South opposed it. The **Missouri Compromise** settled the issue. The election of 1824 created still more bad feelings. Andrew Jackson won the most votes, but he did not have a majority in the **Electoral College**. The House of Representatives decided the election in favor of John Quincy Adams.

In the presidential election of 1828, Andrew Jackson defeated John Quincy Adams. Jackson forced South Carolina to back down from its **doctrine of nullification.** Jackson supported Georgia's effort to remove the Cherokee from the state. Thousands of Cherokee died on the "**trail of tears.**"

In 1831, Jackson vetoed a bill to continue the Bank of the United States. Destroying the bank helped bring on the **depression of 1837.**

Chapter Review

1 Use information from the chapter and additional research to write a paragraph about the Era of Good Feelings.

2 Review the section on the doctrine of nullification. If a state today tried to nullify a federal law, how would you respond? Write a letter to the editor of a newspaper explaining your position.

3 Suppose you could interview any person in this chapter. Who would you choose? Why? Write a series of questions you would ask during the interview. Include questions about economics, geography, society, technology, politics, and culture.

Skill Builder

Analyzing Political Cartoons

Political cartoons have a long history in America. In 1747, Benjamin Franklin published the first political cartoon to appear in an American newspaper. In the 1830s, newspapers often used political cartoons to attack politicians. Some cartoons focused on President Andrew Jackson. The anti-Jackson cartoon below appeared during the 1832 presidential contest.

To understand political cartoons, the reader must identify the character, the topic, and the opinion of the artist. As you examine the cartoon, discuss these three items with a partner.

This cartoon shows Andrew Jackson with a "veto" message in his right hand. On the floor are scraps of paper identified as "Constitution of the United States of America" and a tattered copy of a book entitled "Judiciary of the U States."

Examine the cartoon and use information from the lesson to answer these questions:

1 How does the cartoon present Jackson as a monarch or despot?

2 What veto by President Jackson is the cartoon most likely attacking?

3 How does the cartoon show Jackson's disregard of Supreme Court decisions?

4 To which Supreme Court decision is the cartoon most likely referring?

5 Identify the character, topic, and opinion of this cartoon.

UNIT 8

DIVERGING WAYS OF LIFE

Since colonial times, Americans followed different ways of life depending on where they lived. The South had more slave owners and large plantations. People in the Northeast were more likely to live in towns. Western pioneers relied heavily on themselves.

After the 1830s, the ways of life between the Northeast and the South diverged even further. People in the North became interested in the rights of various groups. Literature and painting flourished. The South focused on growing cotton and became dependent on African American slave labor.

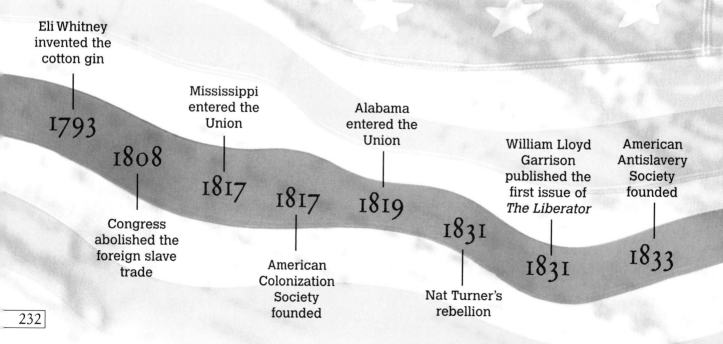

Eli Whitney invented the cotton gin
1793

Congress abolished the foreign slave trade
1808

Mississippi entered the Union
1817

American Colonization Society founded
1817

Alabama entered the Union
1819

Nat Turner's rebellion
1831

William Lloyd Garrison published the first issue of *The Liberator*
1831

American Antislavery Society founded
1833

Why did the South focus on growing cotton?

How did the abolitionist movement relate to the women's rights movement?

What contributed to the increased interest in the arts?

1836
Arkansas entered the Union

1843
Dorothea Dix reported on the mentally ill in Massachusetts

Florida entered the Union
1845

1845
Henry David Thoreau published *Walden*

First women's rights convention held at Seneca Falls
1848

1851
Sojourner Truth spoke at Ohio Women's Rights Convention

Walt Whitman published *Leaves of Grass*
1855

Chapter

15 THE SLAVE SOUTH

Getting Focused

Skim this chapter to predict what you will be learning.

- Read the lesson titles and subheadings.
- Look at the illustrations and read the captions.
- Examine the maps.
- Review the vocabulary words and terms.

What do you already know about the slave South? Discuss your ideas with a partner. Write a couple of sentences in your notebook that sum up your ideas.

The Cotton South

Thinking on Your Own

In your notebook, create a concept map with a circle in the center. Write the word "Cotton" in the circle. Read the Focus Your Reading questions and the vocabulary. Then, with a partner, brainstorm ideas related to growing cotton and arrange them on lines connected to the circle.

In 1793, Eli Whitney invented the **cotton gin**. It was a simple machine that removed the seeds from raw cotton. The amazing thing was that it did the work fifty times faster than by hand. Besides that, a gin was cheap and easy to make. This machine changed the South and its way of life.

Eli Whitney

focus your reading

What was the cotton gin?

How did the cotton gin affect the South?

What impact did cotton growing have on southern society?

vocabulary

cotton gin   lower South

The Cotton Gin's Impact on the South

The cotton gin gave the South a new cash crop. Cotton brought much higher returns than tobacco or wheat. W. S. Hyland, who owned a large plantation in Mississippi, made $6,500 to $10,000 per year growing cotton. At that time, a New England factory worker earned about $300 a year.

The promise of getting rich growing cotton helped settle the lower South. Farmers headed west to buy land to grow cotton. They helped add new states to the Union, including Mississippi (1817), Alabama (1819), Arkansas (1836), and Florida (1845). Native American tribes that stood in the way were quickly removed.

Eli Whitney received a patent for the cotton gin in 1793.

Cotton gave slavery a new lease on life. In the 1790s, slavery seemed to be dying out in the South. Farmers were planting less tobacco and more wheat, a crop that required less manual labor. Cotton made owning slaves profitable again.

Cotton also helped keep the South a rural society. While the North invested in factories and shops, the South put its money into cotton land. The only cities to rise in the South were seaports that shipped farm products to market.

Cotton Production, 1820–1860

■	Area produces up to 45 bales of cotton per square mile, 1820
☐	Area produces up to 45 bales of cotton per square mile, 1860
▨	Area produces more than 45 bales of cotton per square mile, 1860

VA
NC
TN
AR
SC
MS
AL
GA
ATLANTIC OCEAN
LA
FL
GULF OF MEXICO

N W E S

0   250 miles

stop and think

Write a bulleted list of ways that the cotton gin changed the South.

Cotton Reshaped Southern Society

Cotton growing and slavery created a new kind of society in the South. The most powerful families were the big plantation owners. They were the upper class, along with the merchants who bought and sold their cotton. Wealthy planters like W. S. Hyland owned thousands of acres. They had hundreds of slaves who worked under an overseer. The planters lived in big plantation houses filled with fine furniture.

Owners of larger plantations built large mansions on their estates.

The majority of the whites in the South were middle-class farmers. They owned small farms and perhaps a slave or two. These farmers worked alongside their slaves in the cotton field. They owned modest farm houses.

The white lower class consisted of poor farmers. They owned neither slaves nor land. Most worked as hired farm laborers. Competing with cheap slave labor kept them in poverty. These "poor whites" lived in tumbledown cabins.

Cotton plantations could be thousands of acres in size.

"Free people of color" occupied the bottom rung of free society in the South. They were African Americans who had gained their freedom. The shacks in which they lived were only a little better than slave shacks.

African American slaves were at the very bottom of southern society. The majority worked on plantations and farms in the **lower South**, the major cotton-growing region. They lived in crowded slave shacks. By 1860, they made up more than one-third of the population of the South.

Putting It All Together

Return to your concept map about cotton. Add as many new lines as you can with information you have read in this section. Use the information from your concept map and your bulleted list to write a paragraph about the cotton South.

Slave Labor

Thinking on Your Own

Read the Focus Your Reading questions and the vocabulary. In your notebook list all the words that you associate with the concept of slave labor. Then arrange the words in categories. Discuss the categories with a partner.

Cotton was an ideal crop for slave labor. It required a lot of handwork. Planters used groups of slaves to cut the weeds out of cotton fields with hoes. The slaves slowly advanced through a field using their hoes to till the soil. In the fall, picking cotton required still more hand labor.

focus your reading

Why was cotton well suited to slave labor?

What was a slave's workday like?

How did slaves resist?

vocabulary

overseer   house slaves

field slaves   slave rebellion

Work in Cotton Fields

Slaves on large cotton plantations worked under an **overseer**. This man was hired to supervise the slaves' work. He also disciplined them. Overseers whipped slaves for getting to the field late, not picking enough cotton, not obeying orders quickly enough, and for talking back. One Alabama overseer regularly whipped the last slave to get up each morning.

Field slaves had long workdays. They were in the field each morning at dawn. After a brief midday break they worked until dark. Sundays, Christmas, and the Fourth of July usually were their only days off.

Life as a field slave was difficult.

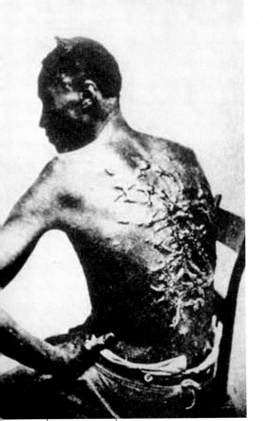

This slave is showing scars from the overseer's violence.

Other Work

Field slaves' work varied with the season. In the fall, they picked and shucked corn, dug sweet potatoes, and brought in pumpkins. They mended fences and repaired buildings during the winter. Planters also kept slaves busy clearing new cotton land. A well-managed plantation had no "slack" time, a time when no work took place.

About one out of four slaves were **house slaves**. That is, they worked in the plantation owner's house instead of in the fields. House slaves cooked, did kitchen chores, cleaned the house, and did laundry. They also helped raise the planter's children. This was easier than fieldwork. However, being a house slave had disadvantages. House servants had little privacy and little time of their own. They were always working, even on Sunday.

stop and think

Make three columns in your notebook. Label them "Overseer," "Field Slave," and "House Slave." Under each heading write descriptions of these workers.

Work as a house slave was less strenuous than work in the fields.

Nat Turner led a slave rebellion in Southampton, Virginia.

Slave Resistance

Slaves did not always follow the orders of their overseers and masters. Slaves found ways to resist the overseer's demands. They deliberately slowed down the pace of work. Slaves also avoided work by pretending to be sick. They got back at the overseer by breaking tools and damaging crops. Sometimes they ran away, although most were soon caught and severely beaten.

On rare occasions, slaves rebelled. In 1800, Gabriel Prosser tried to organize a **slave rebellion** in Virginia. The plan was discovered, and he was executed. Nat Turner did lead a slave uprising in 1831. He and forty other slaves killed more than sixty white people. The revolt was put down. Turner was tried and hanged. About fifteen other slaves were also killed.

Putting It All Together

Imagine that you are a newspaper reporter at Nat Turner's trial. Write a short article about slavery and the trial. Include the words you listed at the beginning of the Lesson and the descriptions from the Stop and Think.

Biography

Nat Turner (1800–1831)

In 1800, the slave Nat Turner was born on a plantation in Virginia. He was a bright young man. By the age of five or six, he had learned to read the Bible. His master regularly took him to prayer meetings. There the slave boy impressed everyone by reciting Bible stories. His mother said that someday he would become a prophet, a holy man. Even his master, Benjamin Turner, said he was too smart to be a field slave.

At age twelve, Turner's world turned upside down. This was the age at which all young slaves were put to work. Turner was certain he would be made a house slave. Maybe he would even be freed. However, by this time his old master had died. His new owner sent him to work in the cotton fields. Being made a field slave was a terrible experience for Turner.

As he grew older, Turner turned inward. He spent more time reading the Bible. He read about Moses, who had led his people out of slavery. Turner also had many visions. In one vision he watched a great battle

between masters and slaves. He believed that his mission in life was to lead a rebellion against the slave owners of Virginia.

Before dawn on August 22, 1831, Nat Turner began his rebellion. He set out with six loyal followers. They went from farm to farm butchering whites with axes and knives. By the end of the day, the number of slaves in the rebellion had increased to forty. They had killed about sixty whites. The next day, planters armed with muskets ended the rebellion. Nat Turner and fifteen other slaves were arrested, convicted of murder, and hanged.

Nat Turner's rebellion sent a shock wave through the South. Slave owners would never again feel safe. They looked for someone to blame for Nat Turner's anger. They did not blame themselves. Instead, they linked Turner's uprising to the abolitionist movement that had started in the North.

The Slave Community

Thinking on Your Own

Read the vocabulary and the Focus Your Reading questions. What mental pictures do you have about the slave community? In your notebook, sketch or describe one or two scenes that come to mind. Compare your sketches with those of a partner.

Most slaves had families. They tried their best to create a loving and caring home life. Planters did not object to slaves having a family. Most slave owners encouraged slaves to have more children to give their owners more slaves and more workers. They knew that slaves with spouses and children were less likely to run away. The greatest threat to the family was the possibility of a parent or child being sold and taken away to another plantation.

focus your reading

How well did slave families live?

Why was the slave trade a threat to African American families?

What kind of community life did slaves have?

vocabulary

slave quarters

slave trade

slave auction

Slave quarters were often one room.

Slave Family Life

Family life took place in the **slave quarters**. These were clusters of shacks where slaves ate, slept, and lived when not working in the fields. The shacks were small and crowded, with six to eight slaves sharing a single room.

Most planters allowed their slaves to plant gardens next to the cabin. Fresh vegetables were a welcomed addition to the salt pork and cornmeal

<table>
</table>

stop and think

As you read, write bulleted notes about slave life. Be sure to include the vocabulary words and other key terms.

the planters provided. However, some planters believed that well-fed slaves would not work, so they kept their slaves near starvation.

Slave Trade

The **slave trade**, the buying and selling of slaves, was a profitable business. Traders often bought slaves in Virginia or Maryland, states that had a surplus. The slaves were then marched in groups to the cotton states of Alabama and Mississippi. The trip was long and difficult, and many slaves died during the ordeal.

After they arrived, the traders sold the slaves at a **slave auction**. That is, the slaves were put on display and sold to the highest bidder. To make sure the slaves were healthy, buyers inspected their skin and teeth—just as they would animals. Then they bid on those they wanted.

Slave sales were heartbreaking scenes. Bidders often bought only one member of a family. One observer saw a woman sold who had two children. "She begged and implored her new master on her knees to buy her children also, but . . . he would not do it. She then begged him to buy her little girl (about 5 years old) but all to no purpose."

It was common for newspapers to advertise upcoming slave auctions.

TO BE SOLD on board the Ship Bance-Island, on tuesday the 6th of May next, at Ashley-Ferry; a choice cargo of about 250 fine healthy NEGROES, juſt arrived from the Windward & Rice Coaſt. —The utmoſt care has already been taken, and ſhall be continued, to keep them free from the leaſt danger of being infected with the SMALL-POX, no boat having been on board, and all other communication with people from Charles-Town prevented.
Auſtin, Laurens, & Appleby.
N. B. Full one Half of the above Negroes have had the SMALL-POX in their own Country.

Family members were often separated on the auction block.

The Slave South 243

Although laws prohibited slaves from legally marrying, family bonds were strong.

The Slave Community

Slaves who lived in the slave quarters formed a tightly knit community. They tried to take care of one another. Slaves without families had "aunts," "uncles," or other stand-in relatives to help them. They helped each other through injuries, sickness, childbirth, and family deaths.

If a slave wanted to see his wife or children on another plantation, he required a written pass from his owner. Anyone caught outside the plantation without such a pass was punished—often with a severe beating. However, slaves sometimes visited after dark without anyone knowing.

In the autumn, plantation owners brought their slaves together for "shucking parties." These were working parties. While they stripped the husks from corn, slaves exchanged family information and news.

Putting It All Together

Use your bulleted notes to write a paragraph about slave life. Review the notes or sketch you made at the beginning of this Lesson and your bulleted notes if you need ideas.

Read a Primary Source

Sold at Auction: Louis Hughes

As a boy, Louis Hughes was sold to a Mississippi cotton planter. Working as a house slave, he waited on the table at meals, dusted the furniture, and swept the yard. Life as a house slave was somewhat easier than working in the fields. Read Hughes's description of how he was sold.

reading for understanding

Why did Hughes's previous owner want to sell him?

Why was he worth less than other slaves?

Based on the tone of the narrative, how do you think Hughes felt about being a Christmas gift?

"I was sick a great deal—in fact, I had suffered with chills and fever ever since Mr. Reid bought me. He, therefore, concluded to sell me, and, in November, 1844, he took me back to Richmond, placing me in the Exchange building, or auction rooms, for the sale of slaves.

"When I was placed upon the block, a Mr. McGee came up and felt of me and asked what I could do. . . . The bidding commenced, and I remember well when the auctioneer said: "Three hundred eighty dollars—once, twice and sold to Mr. Edward McGee" As near as I can recollect, I was not more than twelve years of age, so did not sell for very much. Servant women sold for $500 to $700. . . . Good blacksmiths sold for $1,600 to $1,800.

"At length, after a long and wearisome journey, we reached Pontotoc, McGee's home, on Christmas eve. Boss took me into the house and into the sitting room, where all the family were assembled, and presented me as a Christmas gift to the madam, his wife."

From *Thirty Years a Slave: The Autobiography of Louis Hughes.*
(New York: Negro Universities Press, 1970).

Chapter Summary

In 1793, Eli Whitney invented the **cotton gin**. This machine allowed the South to grow more cotton, which became the South's new cash crop. Men who owned large plantations got rich growing it. Cotton also speeded up the settlement of the **lower South**. Cotton growing kept the South rural, since rich people spent their money on land and slaves, not on building factories.

Most slaves in the South worked in cotton fields. White men called **overseers** forced them to work hard. **Field slaves** often worked from before sunup until after dark. About one out of four slaves were **house slaves** who worked in the plantation owner's house. They did kitchen work, cleaned the house, and helped raise the planter's children.

Slaves found ways to resist, such as working more slowly than they could have. Some slaves ran away, but if they were caught, they were whipped severely. In 1831, Nat Turner led a **slave rebellion** in which more than sixty white people were killed.

Some slaves had a family life. They and their children lived in small, crowded cabins called **slave quarters**. The biggest danger to family life was the **slave trade**. Planters often broke up families by selling only the husband or some of the children. These slaves were sold again at a **slave auction** to whoever offered the most money.

Chapter Review

1 Slaves often sang as they worked to give themselves courage and to forget how hard the work was. Write the words to a song that you think a field slave might have composed.

2 Imagine that you are W. S. Hyland, the plantation owner. Write a letter to relatives in the North describing a day in your life.

3 Create a poster that shows one aspect of life in the South from each of the lessons in this chapter. Include plantations, slave labor, and the slave community.

Skill Builder

Reading Graphs

Graphs are useful tools that can present a large amount of information in a small space. Graphs usually present information vertically on the left side of the graph and horizontally across the bottom.

In the graphs below, the columns at the left represent numbers of cotton bales and number of slaves. The note "in thousands" means that three zeros have been left off the numbers. The dates at the bottom represent periods of time. The dots and lines on the graphs show how the two kinds of information are related.

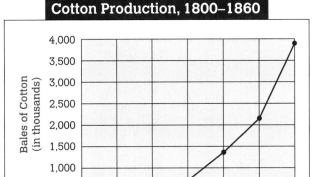

Cotton Production, 1800–1860

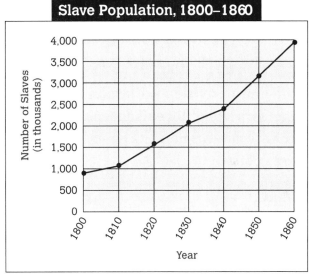

Slave Population, 1800–1860

Use the graphs above to answer these questions:

1. In what year did the South produce the smallest number of cotton bales?

2. In what year did the South produce the largest number of bales?

3. About how many bales did the South produce in 1830?

4. In what year did the South have 2,000,000 slaves?

5. How long did it take the South to double the number of slaves it had in 1830?

Chapter 16 Toward a More Perfect Society

Getting Focused

Skim this chapter to predict what you will be learning.

- Read the lesson titles and subheadings.

- Look at the illustrations and read the captions.

- Examine the maps.

- Review the vocabulary words and terms.

Read the chapter title and lesson headings. In two or three sentences, explain how the title and the headings might be related.

Religion and Reform

Thinking on Your Own

Look at the vocabulary and the Focus Your Reading questions. What do they tell you about how preachers reached people spread out over a wide country? Write two ideas in your notebook. Compare your ideas with those of a partner.

In the early 1800s, Americans had a renewed interest in religion. To save their own souls, they flocked to religious meetings called **revivals**. These revivals are called the **Second Great Awakening**. It is called the "second" because an earlier religious awakening had taken place during the 1740s. Many people decided to make life better for others as well as themselves. They set out to **reform**, or improve, society.

focus your reading

Why were revival meetings popular?

What social reforms did people propose?

What new communities were founded?

vocabulary

revivals

Second Great Awakening

reform

An early revival meeting

The Second Great Awakening

The revivals began during the 1790s in the West. Church leaders worried about people who lived in Kentucky and the Ohio River valley. Few churches existed in that newly settled area. Preachers were sent to save the souls of people on the frontier. A minister would find a clearing in the woods, stand on a stump, and begin preaching. Settlers came from miles around. They pitched their tents, visited, and listened to the preacher.

Charles G. Finney

The preachers had a powerful message: If people did not change their ways, they would be destined to burn forever and not go to heaven. Preachers like Charles G. Finney could make people tremble from fear. Determined to lead better lives, many people felt "born again" as Christians.

From the frontier, the revivals spread to the East. Ministers in eastern cities invited preachers to hold revivals at their churches. Few church members had ever heard such preaching before. They liked it and kept coming back for more.

The Second Great Awakening made revivals popular. It gave many Americans a deeper religious faith. The awakening also brought more people to church more often.

stop and think

Write two or three impressions that you have about revivals and the Second Great Awakening.

Reforming Society

For many Americans, saving their own souls was not enough. They wanted to reform, or uplift, American society as well. By the 1830s, many thought that liquor was evil. They worked to end the sale of whiskey, beer, and wine. Others wanted free public schools. Still others set out to build better prisons and to open hospitals for the mentally ill. Dorothea Dix was shocked at how mentally ill people were treated. She found them locked up in "cages, closets, cellars, stalls, pens!" She worked to create asylums for those suffering from mental illness.

Reformers also set up new communities. "We are all a little wild here with . . . projects of social reform," wrote Ralph Waldo Emerson in 1840. "Not a reading man but has a draft of a new community in his waistcoat pocket." The group known as the Shakers led strict, religious lives. The Oneida, New York, group did away with private property, choosing to share everything they owned. People at Brook Farm, Massachusetts, shared all the farm labor. Few of these new communities lasted long.

A Shaker community

Putting It All Together

Imagine that you have just returned from a revival. In your notebook, write a letter to a friend describing this event. Explain who was there, what happened, and why people went to revivals.

Read a Primary Source

The Claims of Suffering Humanity: Dorothea Dix

In 1843, Dorothea Dix made a report to the Massachusetts legislature. In it she described how mentally ill people were treated in that state. The following is an excerpt from her report.

reading for understanding

What did Dorothea Dix hope to gain by making this report?

Where were mentally ill people kept?

How were these people treated?

"I tell you what I have seen—painful and shocking as the details often are—that from them you may feel more deeply [your] obligation . . . to prevent . . . a repetition . . . of such outrages upon humanity. . . .

I come to present the strong claims of suffering humanity. I come to place before the Legislature of Massachusetts the condition of the miserable, the desolate, the outcast. I come as the advocate of helpless, forgotten, insane, and idiotic men and women; of beings sunk to a condition from which the most unconcerned would start with real horror; of being wretched in our prisons, and more wretched in our almshouses [homes for the poor]. . . .

I proceed, gentlemen, briefly to call your attention to the present state of insane persons, confined within this Commonwealth, in cages, closets, cellars, stalls, pens! Chained, naked, beaten with rods, and lashed into obedience."

From Dorothea L. Dix, "Memorial to the Legislature of Massachusetts, 1843," *Old South Leaflets* (Boston, 1904).

Dorothea Dix

252

LESSON 2 Antislavery and Women's Rights

Thinking on Your Own

"Equal rights for women is as important as freedom for slaves!" Write this statement in your notebook. Below it, make two columns and label them "I Agree" and "I Disagree." Write the thoughts that you have under each heading. Discuss your conclusions with a partner.

By the 1830s, more people opposed slavery than ever before. Revival preachers denounced slave owning as a sin. Quakers had always said it was wrong to own slaves. Many reformers opposed slavery. They saw that it violated the Declaration of Independence, which stated, "We hold these truths to be self-evident, that all men are created equal . . ." Many people thought that the Declaration applied to women as well as men. Those who opposed slavery often worked for women's rights too.

focus your reading
What method of freeing slaves did whites first propose?
How did the abolitionist movement lead to the women's rights movement?
What did William Lloyd Garrison propose?

vocabulary
gradual emancipation
abolitionists
crusade

Emancipation and Abolition

By the 1820s, most reformers called for the **gradual emancipation** of slaves. They encouraged owners to free their slaves as soon

Frederick Douglass

as they could. However, they did not expect freed slaves to remain in the United States. The American Colonization Society, established in 1816 by Robert Finley and other notable Americans, worked to send freed slaves to Liberia, a colony in Africa. Free blacks in northern cities had a different point of view.

They wanted slavery to be abolished immediately. **Abolitionists**, people who wanted to abolish slavery, opposed sending freed slaves to Africa. Among them were Frederick Douglass and Sojourner Truth, both freed slaves. They gave speeches, wrote books against slavery, and fought for all slaves to be set free.

William Lloyd Garrison

In January 1831, the abolitionists found a new voice. William Lloyd Garrison, a white newspaper editor in Boston, published the first issue of *The Liberator*. The newspaper demanded that all slaves be freed immediately. Garrison denounced slavery as sinful. He attacked slavery like a revival preacher. Black abolitionists supported him, as did many white reform leaders who saw slavery as the greatest evil of all. In 1833, Garrison and other abolitionists met in Philadelphia to found the American Antislavery Society. The goal of the group was the complete abolition of slavery.

The Liberator was a popular abolitionist newspaper.

Many women also supported abolition. They attended meetings, helped raise money, and signed antislavery petitions. A few brave women stood up to speak at public meetings. Angelina and Sarah Grimke became well-known public speakers. Their father was a South Carolina slave owner. The Grimke sisters shocked listeners with their

stop and think

Imagine that you are a young woman living during this period. What reforms would interest you? Which would you feel threatened by?

The Seneca Falls Convention of 1848

firsthand accounts of the evils of slavery. New England ministers scolded Angelina Grimke for lecturing in public.

The women abolitionists shocked many men. Women in the 1830s lacked many of the rights that men enjoyed. It was believed that a woman's place was in the home. Women could not vote or hold public office. Even a married woman's property belonged to her husband. Women factory workers earned only one-third to one-half as much as men.

Elizabeth Cady Stanton and Susan B. Anthony fought for women's right to vote.

The abolitionist **crusade** paved the way for equal rights for women. "The investigation of the rights of the slave has led me to a better understanding of my own," Angelina Grimke wrote. Two female abolitionists organized the first national women's rights convention in the United States. They were Lucretia Mott and Elizabeth Cady Stanton. The meeting took place in 1848 in Seneca Falls, New York. It called for equal rights for women, including the right to vote.

The Seneca Falls Convention attracted nearly 300 women and forty men. This was the start of the women's rights movement. The organizers of the meeting wrote a "Declaration of Sentiments" that they modeled after the Declaration of Independence. This declaration stated, "We hold these truths to be self-evident: that all men and women are created equal." Just as the Declaration of Independence listed the colonists' grievances with Great Britain, the Declaration of Sentiments listed grievances against men. They included denying women the right to vote and limiting education for women.

Putting It All Together

Make a T-chart in your notebook. On one side write the names of people or groups involved in reform. On the other side briefly describe their work. Compare your list with that of a partner.

Biography

Sojourner Truth (1797? – 1883)

Sojourner Truth was a forceful public speaker. Her speeches urged Congress to free the slaves and give women equal rights. The crowds that came to hear this African American woman were not always friendly. Men often hissed at her. "I am sorry to see them so short  minded," she said at a speech in New York City. "But we'll have our rights; see if we don't; and you can't stop us from them; see if you can. You may hiss as much as you like, but it is comin'." No one could stop her from speaking her mind.

Sojourner Truth drew on her own experience. She was born in the 1790s as a slave in rural New York State. Her slave name was Isabella Baumfree. She grew up being whipped and abused by her white owners. Baumfree married another slave named Thomas, and they had five children. She lost two children to slave traders. Baumfree was a slave until 1826, when New York freed its slaves.

Once free, she made herself into a new person. She went to Methodist revival meetings, where she was "born again" as a Christian. She found she could preach and became a traveling preacher. Then she changed her name to Sojourner Truth. *To sojourn* means to not stay in one place very long. The name fit her, as she was always on the move. She also told the truth exactly as she saw it.

In the 1840s, Truth lived in a commune near Boston. There she met William Lloyd Garrison and Frederick Douglass. They asked her to travel with them, giving speeches opposing slavery. Women she met at these speeches invited her to women's rights meetings. In 1851, she spoke at the Ohio Woman's Rights Convention. After that, she traveled throughout the North speaking against slavery and for women's rights.

In 1864, Sojourner Truth visited President Abraham Lincoln at the White House in Washington, D.C. She asked President Lincoln to free the slaves. The president asked her to remain in Washington, D.C., to work as a counselor to freed slaves.

Sojourner Truth died in 1883 at about eighty-six years of age. She had lived to see half of her goal accomplished. The Thirteenth Amendment (1865) abolished slavery. Securing equal rights for women remained in the future.

Literature and the Arts

Thinking on Your Own

Read the vocabulary and the Focus Your Reading questions for clues. What themes do you think American artists and writers explored during this period? Discuss the themes with a partner. Write two or three ideas in your notebook.

In the 1830s, American writers and artists also wanted reform. Until then, they had mainly used European ideas in their literature and art. It was time, said Ralph Waldo Emerson, for them to declare their "**intellectual independence.**" This feeling was widely shared. The result was a flood of truly American essays, books, and paintings.

Ralph Waldo Emerson

focus your reading

How did the spirit of reform influence writers and artists?

What American themes did writers explore?

What American scenes did painters include in their work?

vocabulary

intellectual independence

American Renaissance

Hudson River School

A New American Literature

Ralph Waldo Emerson of Concord, Massachusetts, took the lead. He wrote essays and gave lectures on the importance of the individual. People, he thought, should stand on their own feet. They should think for themselves and decide what is right. They should solve their own problems. Emerson saw these as American values.

Henry David Thoreau, Emerson's friend, did not just reject Europe. He declared

WALDEN;

OR,

LIFE IN THE WOODS.

BY HENRY D. THOREAU,
AUTHOR OF "A WEEK ON THE CONCORD AND MERRIMACK RIVERS."

I do not propose to write an ode to dejection, but to brag as lustily as chanticleer in the morning, standing on his roost, if only to wake my neighbors up. — Page 92.

BOSTON:
TICKNOR AND FIELDS.
M DCCC LIV.

Walden was published by Henry David Thoreau in 1854.

Henry David Thoreau

independence from modern society. "Nature is sufficient," he said. He lived alone in a cabin for two years. His book about those years, *Walden* (1854), is widely read today. Thoreau had his own ideas about politics, as well. He criticized the government for protecting slavery. Once, he went to jail for refusing to pay a poll tax.

The writer Walt Whitman best reflected the spirit of American democracy. His book, *Leaves of Grass* (1855), praised the diversity of American life. "Here is not merely a nation but a teeming nation of nations," he wrote.

Nathaniel Hawthorne (*The Scarlet Letter*, 1850) and Herman Melville (*Moby Dick*, 1851) also used American themes and settings in their writings. Edgar Allen Poe was an exception. Many of his tales were set in Europe. This period produced so many good writers that it is sometimes called the **American Renaissance**.

stop and think

In your notebook identify two American authors and explain what they wrote about.

Walt Whitman

The Notch of the White Mountains, by Thomas Cole (1839)

American Art

Painters had already started to paint American scenes. A group called the **Hudson River School** specialized in painting scenes along that river. They tried to show the beauty of the American landscape. The best-known painters were Thomas Cole, Thomas Doughty, and Asher Durand.

George Caleb Bingham painted pictures of the American West. He knew the West firsthand. He grew up in Missouri when it was being settled. Among his paintings are *Fur Traders Descending the Missouri, Jolly Flatboat Men,* and *Daniel Boone Coming through Cumberland Gap.*

George Catlin also painted about the West from personal experience. His subjects were Native Americans. He traveled through the Great Plains in the 1830s, painting portraits of Native Americans. His paintings now are important historical documents. They show what Native Americans wore and how they decorated themselves.

Putting It All Together

Create a concept web. In the center circle write "Writers and Artists." On lines coming from the circle, write the names of writers and artists of this period. On lines below their names, write the titles of their works.

Chapter Summary

In the early 1800s, thousands of Americans went to **revival** meetings where preachers told them to lead better lives. These meetings were part of the **Second Great Awakening** of religion in the United States. This new interest in religion began on the western frontier, but soon reached cities of the East. Many religious men and women also wanted to **reform** American society by stopping the sale of liquor, building better prisons, and improving conditions for the mentally ill.

By the 1830s, many Americans also opposed slavery. Most called for the **gradual emancipation** of slaves. However, **abolitionists** wanted all slaves to be freed immediately, without delay. Freed slaves like Sojourner Truth and Frederick Douglass were abolitionists. The abolitionist **crusade** paved the way for women's rights.

In the 1830s, American writers and artists also called for reform. They declared their **intellectual independence** from Europe. They began to write books and to paint pictures with American themes. The period 1830 to 1860 is sometimes called the **American Renaissance** because it produced so many good writers and painters. Among them were the **Hudson River School** artists, who painted scenes along that river.

Chapter Review

1 Garrison and other abolitionists created the American Antislavery Society. Create a poster for the American Antislavery Society.

2 Imagine that you are listening to a conversation between Ralph Waldo Emerson and Henry David Thoreau. Write the dialogue that you would expect to hear.

3 Now that you have finished the chapter, reread the chapter title and lesson headings. Now how do you think the title and headings are related?

Skill Builder

Critically Reading Primary Sources

Primary sources are powerful documents. They include letters, diaries, and newspaper articles written by people from that time period. Many were written by eyewitnesses. However, this does not mean they are always accurate.

The accuracy of Sojourner Truth's 1851 "Ar'n't I a Woman?" speech is one primary source that has been questioned. Did she actually say the famous phrase "Ar'n't I a woman?" Historian Nell Irvin Painter has her doubts. The account of the speech was published in the *New York Independent* in April 1863. The author, Frances Dana Gage, attended the convention and listened to the speech.

To understand why Professor Painter has doubts, compare the date of the speech and the published account.

- What was the date of the speech?
- What was the date of the published account?

You will see that Gage published her account of the speech twelve years after the event. Would she have remembered the speech word for word after that much time had passed?

Painter's doubts led her to look for accounts closer to the time of the convention. *The Salem Anti-Slavery Bugle* reported the speech in June 1851. *The Bugle*'s editor took notes as he listened. The main points in his account are the same as Gage's. But the wording is different. Gage mentions the "Ar'n't I a woman?" phrase four times. *The Bugle* account does not mention it once. Surely the editor would have reported such a memorable phrase.

When you read a primary source, be sure to ask:

- How close to the time of the event was it written?
- Was the author biased in any way?
- Can I check it against other accounts?
- Could one account be more reliable than another?

9 UNIT

A SOCIETY IN CHANGE

The 1830s and 1840s was a period of rapid change. Change affected nearly every aspect of American life. New machines helped farmers raise more crops and helped factories produce more goods. Towns and cities grew as more people sought work. The makeup of American society changed as immigrants flooded into the United States to work in factories.

Political change also was under way. During the 1840s, the United States extended its boundary to the Pacific Ocean. Expansion brought the slavery issue back into American politics. The country needed to decide if new territories and states would allow slavery or not.

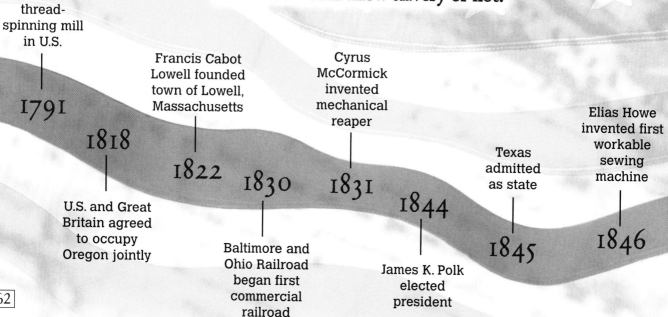

Samuel Slater built first thread-spinning mill in U.S.

1791

1818

U.S. and Great Britain agreed to occupy Oregon jointly

Francis Cabot Lowell founded town of Lowell, Massachusetts

1822

1830

Baltimore and Ohio Railroad began first commercial railroad

Cyrus McCormick invented mechanical reaper

1831

1844

James K. Polk elected president

Texas admitted as state

1845

Elias Howe invented first workable sewing machine

1846

Why did the United States go to war with Mexico?

How did the policy of manifest destiny impact the United States?

How did machines change everyday life in the United States?

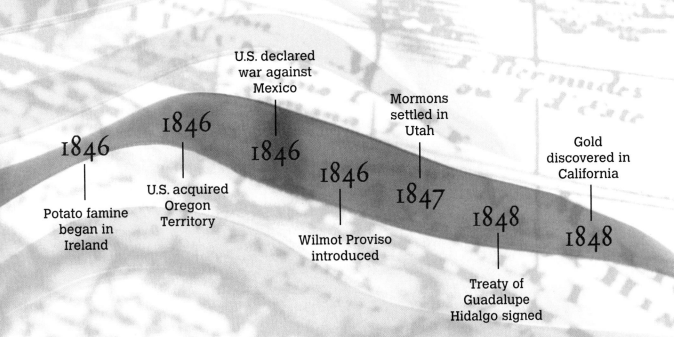

1846
Potato famine began in Ireland

1846
U.S. acquired Oregon Territory

U.S. declared war against Mexico
1846

1846
Wilmot Proviso introduced

Mormons settled in Utah
1847

Treaty of Guadalupe Hidalgo signed
1848

Gold discovered in California
1848

Chapter 17 CHANGING TIMES

Getting Focused

Skim this chapter to predict what you will be learning.

- Read the lesson titles and subheadings.
- Look at the illustrations and read the captions.
- Examine the maps.
- Review the vocabulary words and terms.

Think about a time when you or someone you know underwent a change. How did the change affect you? What led to the change? What were some of the outcomes? Write two or three sentences about this experience in your notebook.

Changes in Everyday Life

Thinking on Your Own

Examine the illustrations in this lesson. Read the section headings. What clues do they give you about the changes that occurred during the 1840s? Discuss your ideas with a classmate. Take notes in your notebook.

B y the 1840s, everyday life in the United States was changing. Americans focused more on making money. The pace of life was quicker. New inventions changed the way people worked.

focus your reading

How did farming change between 1800 and 1840?

How did farm work change?

How did housework change?

vocabulary

cash crops

scythe

mechanical reaper

Rural Life

Life on American farms was changing. In 1800, most farmers raised or made most of what they used. They traded corn or pork for the salt, nails, and other things they could not make. The only farmers who depended on **cash crops** were Southern planters. By the 1840s, farmers in the North also farmed to make money. They sold most of the corn, wheat, and hemp that they raised. With the cash they bought things they had once made at home.

A scythe was a slow method of reaping grain.

Farm work, too, was changing. In earlier days, farmers cut wheat by hand. Each farmer walked through the field swinging a long curved blade called a **scythe**. In 1831, Cyrus McCormick invented a **mechanical reaper**. It cut as much wheat in one day as a man with a scythe could harvest in two weeks.

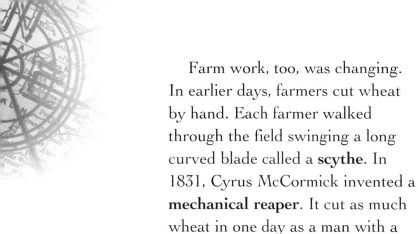

MC CORMICK.

REAPING MACHINE.

The mechanical reaper made farming profitable.

stop and think

In your notebook describe two machines that created significant changes on American farms or in the home.

By the 1840s, it was in wide use. Farmers bought reapers so they could plant more wheat and make more money. They also bought mowing machines to cut hay.

Housework in the Early 1800s

Women spent much of their time making clothes for their family. They spun wool or flax into yarn and wove it into cloth. Using needle and thread, they made dresses, shirts,

Farmers earned money by selling their crops at market.

Elias Howe's sewing machine greatly improved women's lives.

and coats by hand. "I somehow or somewhere got the idea, when I was a small child," wrote Lucy Larcom, "that the chief end of woman was to make clothing for mankind." Cooking also was a difficult chore. To cook, women had to stoop over heavy iron pots hanging in a hot fireplace.

Women's work was changing by the 1840s. Inexpensive, factory-made cloth replaced home-woven fabric. In 1846, Elias Howe invented a sewing machine. As this machine was improved, women would spend less time sewing clothes. An invention that made cooking easier was the cast-iron cookstove. This stove had a flat, iron top that was heated from beneath by a wood fire. Because the stove top was waist high, women no longer had to bend over kettles when they cooked. They also used new, lighter-weight pots and pans that were specially made for the cookstove.

Putting It All Together

Imagine that you are a newspaper reporter in the 1840s. Write a brief article about how a typical housewife's work changed with the invention of the sewing machine and cookstove.

The cookstove changed the way people cooked at home.

Read a Primary Source

An Irish Immigrant: Told by Herself

The following is an account by an Irish-American cook. She tells the story of leaving Ireland during the famine years and coming to America to find a better life.

reading for understanding

Why did this family decide to leave Ireland?

Why did Tilly leave first?

How did the family pay for the two tickets?

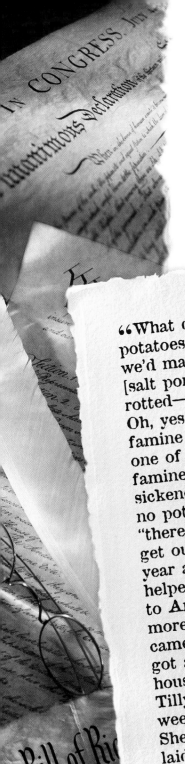

"What did we eat? Well, just potatoes. On Sundays, once a month, we'd maybe have a bit of flitch [salt pork]. When the potatoes rotted—that was the hard times. Oh, yes, I . . . [remember] the famine years. . . . Maria—she was one of the twins—she died the famine year of the typhus and—well, she sickened of the herbs and roots we ate—we had no potatoes. Mother said when Maria died, "there's a curse on old green Ireland and we'll get out of it." So we worked an' saved for four year an' then Squire Varney helped a bit an' we sent Tilly to America. She had always more head than me. She came to Philadelphia and got a place for general housework at Mrs. Bent's. Tilly got but two dollars a week, bein' a greenhorn. . . . She had no expenses and laid by money enough to bring me out before the year was gone. I sailed from Londonderry. . . . The passage was $12. . . . The steerage was a dirty place and we were eight weeks on the voyage— over time three weeks."

"The Life Story of an Irish Cook," Hamilton Holt, ed., *The Life Stories of Undistinguished Americans as Told by Themselves* (New York, 1906).

"Coffin ships" brought immigrants to the United States.

Towns, Factories, and Railroads

Thinking on Your Own

Look over the vocabulary and the Focus Your Reading questions. With a partner share what you already know about early American towns and factories. Create two questions that you think this lesson may answer. Make notes in your notebook.

By the 1840s, life was changing for Americans who lived in towns and cities. New machines and factories changed where and how people worked. The growth of factories attracted more people to the towns and cities of the Northeast.

focus your reading

Why did more Americans go to work in factories?

Why did towns and cities grow larger?

How did factories create a need for railroads?

vocabulary

spinning machines

textile mill

company town

wharves

Mills and Factories

In 1800, most skilled craftsmen worked at home or in small shops. They wove cloth or made shoes or hats with hand tools. Customers dropped by to place their orders. By the 1840s, machines were taking the place of hand tools. Machines powered by water wheels produced items faster and cheaper. The men who owned these machines put them in big shops and

Slater's Mill was the beginning of the cloth industry in New England.

factories. Skilled workers could not compete with them. They had to go to work in the factories, instead of working in small shops.

Cloth making was the first trade to move into factories. In 1791, Samuel Slater built the nation's first cotton thread-spinning mill in Rhode Island. But Slater's **spinning machines** did not weave the thread into cloth. He sent the thread to skilled weavers, who wove the cloth in their homes. In 1813, Francis Cabot Lowell built the first integrated **textile mill**. There, workers spun, wove, and dyed cloth in the same factory. His mill was a great success. It helped make New England the center of textile making in the United States.

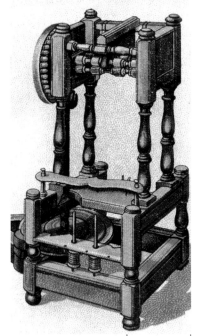

Spinning machines made cotton yarn or thread.

stop and think

In your notebook list the changes in daily life that you think are especially important. Share your ideas with a partner.

Growth of Towns and Cities

The building of mills and factories spurred the growth of towns and cities. In 1822, Francis Cabot Lowell built a new factory town almost overnight. The town of Lowell, Massachusetts, was a **company town**. That is, the investors in the textile company built and owned the town. Most new factories were built in existing towns and cities. These places grew rapidly as people moved there to get jobs.

During the 1840s, the population of large American seaports also increased. In ten years, New York, Boston, and Baltimore more than doubled their populations. The tall masts of ships towered over their skylines. Their **wharves** were piled high with goods. They also became centers of manufacturing. New factories, textile mills, and locomotive works sprang up on the edges of these cities.

Lowell, Massachusetts, was a result of the textile industry.

Cities such as New York grew as people began working in factories.

Peter Cooper

Expansion of Railroads

Railroads expanded rapidly during this period. The nation's first railroad, the Baltimore and Ohio, opened for business in 1830. Its cars were pulled by the *Tom Thumb*, the first steam locomotive built in the United States. Railroad companies built tracks between most cities in the Northeast during the 1840s. By 1855, railroad tracks connected New York to Chicago. The railroads provided the United States with a cheap and rapid way to transport goods and raw materials.

Peter Cooper's *Tom Thumb* was the first steam-powered locomotive.

Putting It All Together

Create two columns in your notebook. Label the first "Cause" and the second "Effect." First, list the changes (effects) in the early American workplace and living areas. Then write the cause of each change.

Factory Workers and Immigrants

Thinking on Your Own

Look at the vocabulary and the Focus Your Reading questions. What concerns would you have about children working in mills and young women living in boardinghouses? Discuss your thoughts with a classmate.

The mill and factory owners needed workers to run their machines. Most Americans lived on farms. They were busy raising crops. The owners had to look elsewhere for workers.

focus your reading

Where did the spinning mills find workers?

Who worked in the large textile mills?

Why did factory owners hire immigrants?

vocabulary

boardinghouses

immigrants

peasant farmers

potato famine

Child Labor

The early spinning mill companies advertised in newspapers for workers. They urged poor families to come to the mills. The entire family, they promised, would get jobs. As a result, poor families provided most of the workers in the small mills of New England. Often these were families with many children.

Children were important in mills because their small fingers could thread the machines quickly.

Children filled many of the jobs in spinning mills. Some became highly skilled workers. In one mill in Rhode Island, a thirteen-year-old boy was in charge of repairing the machines. The foreman of the Pawtucket Thread Company in Pawtucket, Rhode Island, was only nineteen. He had worked in textile mills for eleven years. Most children worked at machines for only a few pennies a day. Children who worked in the factories had a difficult life. Injuries, and even death, were common. Very few factory children received an education.

Weaving machines increased the speed of making cloth.

Mill Girls

The mills in Lowell, Massachusetts, and other company towns were able to find workers other than children. They brought in farm women in their late teens and twenties. The owners built **boardinghouses** for the "mill girls," as they were called. Older women looked after the young boarders. Most mill girls worked to save the money they would need to set up housekeeping once they got married. However, because of poor wages and because they had to pay for their room and board, mill girls had to work a long time to be able to save any money.

The women at Lowell worked long hours. The workday began at 5:00 A.M. At 7:00, the workers took off half an hour for breakfast. Then they worked until 12:30 P.M., when they stopped for lunch. Returning at 1:30, they labored until 7:00 P.M., which was quitting time.

stop and think

Imagine you are a mill girl. In your notebook, describe one day in your life.

Immigrants made up a large part of the workforce.

Immigrant Workers

In the 1840s, factory owners found a new source of cheap labor. More **immigrants** were arriving from Europe than ever before. From 1820 to 1840, 700,000 immigrants came to the United States. Between 1840 and 1860, the number jumped to 4,200,000. They came from Ireland and Germany, with large numbers also from England, the Netherlands, Norway, and Sweden. The majority of the newcomers were **peasant farmers**.

The Irish came because they were starving due to the **potato famine**. Potatoes were their principal food. In the mid-1840s, a plant disease ruined the potato crop for several years. A million Irish people died of starvation and disease. Another million and a half left the country, most coming to the United States. In Germany and elsewhere, land owners combined the peasants' small plots of land into large farms. This forced the peasants off the land. For many, their only choice was to immigrate or to starve.

American factory owners welcomed the new arrivals. Unskilled and starving, the immigrants gladly worked long hours for low wages. By 1860, immigrants had replaced most of the young farm women in the textile mills.

Putting It All Together

Where people lived and worked changed during this time in history. Create a three-column chart in your notebook. In the first column write each of these topics on a line: "Farm Machines," "Cookstoves," "Spinning Machines," "Company Towns," and "Railroads." In the next column, briefly note what you have learned about each. In the last column, write questions you still have about these topics.

Biography

Lucy Larcom (1824–1893)

Lucy Larcom was a "mill girl." At the age of twelve, she worked in a textile mill in Lowell, Massachusetts. Her job was to remove spools of thread from a spinning machine. "We were not occupied more than half the time," she remembered. "The intervals were spent frolicking around among the

spinning-frames, teasing and talking to the older girls, or entertaining ourselves with games and stories in a corner." The work was not hard, but she hated the noisy machinery. Most of all, she missed going to school.

Larcom was a quick learner. Her older sisters had taken her to school with them since she was two years old. She could read the Bible at age two and a half, and when she was five she read her first novel. She liked her teachers. She loved poetry and wrote verses. Larcom wanted to be a teacher and a poet when she grew up.

In 1835, when Larcom was eleven, her father died. With eight children to support, her mother had to go to work. She moved the children to the mill town of Lowell, Massachusetts. There she opened a boardinghouse. She did not earn enough to feed her large family. To help pay the bills, twelve-year-old Larcom went to work in the mill.

Larcom never lost her love for poetry. After work, she spent her free time reading and writing poems. She met John Greenleaf Whittier, who came to Lowell to read his poems. He encouraged her to publish her verses. Larcom published several poems in the *Lowell Offering*, a magazine produced by the mill workers. After leaving Lowell at age twenty-two, she went to school to become a teacher. She taught for several years but continued writing poetry. She published five books of poetry and her autobiography, *A New England Girlhood* (1889). Lucy Larcom died in 1893 at the age of sixty-nine.

Chapter Summary

By the 1840s, everyday life in the United States was changing. Farm families who once raised most of their own food and made their own clothing were now raising **cash crops** and buying what they needed. Farmers who once cut wheat with a **scythe** now used **mechanical reapers** that could harvest more grain and make more money. Housework also was changing. Women no longer had to weave their own cloth, and the new cookstove made cooking easier.

The 1840s also saw more people living in towns and cities, especially in the Northeast. Many people moved there to work in **textile mills** and factories. In 1791, Samuel Slater built a factory to make thread with **spinning machines**. Some of the mills and factories were located in **company towns**, such as Lowell, Massachusetts. American seaports grew as shipping increased, and **wharves** were piled high with goods.

The factory and mill owners encouraged poor New England families to move to the mill towns. As a result, many of the new workers were children and teenage girls. They lived in supervised **boardinghouses**. These children and "mill girls" worked long hours under poor conditions for very little money.

Many **immigrant** workers were **peasant farmers** who fled Ireland due to the **potato famine**. Unskilled and starving, they gladly worked long hours for low wages. In time, they replaced the young farm women in the textile mills.

Chapter Review

1 Create an ad for the mechanical reaper to distribute to farmers in the 1840s.

2 Imagine that you are a young person who moved to the city in the 1840s. Write a letter to your family back on the farm about city life and work.

3 Organize a concept web with "Factory Workers" as the main topic in the center circle. In lines going out from the circle, add information related to the topic.

Skill Builder

Mapping Change over Time

Maps serve different purposes. All maps show where cities, rivers, mountains, or other places are located. Maps also can show change over time.

This map shows the growth of railroads in the Northeast, Midwest, and South. Railroads that existed in 1850 are shown in purple. Those built between 1850 and 1860 are shown in orange. The locations of major cities are also shown.

Use the map to answer the following questions:

1 Which section (Northeast, Midwest, or South) had the most railroads by 1850?

2 Which section (Northeast, Midwest, or South) added the most railroads between 1850 and 1860?

3 Which section (Northeast, Midwest, or South) had the fewest railroads by 1860?

4 Which cities were major rail centers by 1860?

5 What advantage did the Northeast have by 1860?

6 Why was New Orleans at a disadvantage?

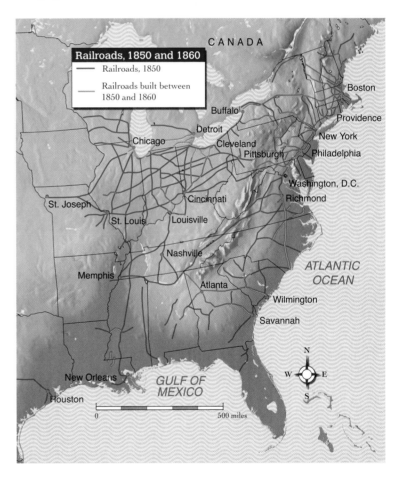

Chapter
18 Manifest Destiny

Getting Focused

Skim this chapter to predict what you will be learning.

- Read the lesson titles and subheadings.
- Look at the illustrations and read the captions.
- Examine the maps.
- Review the vocabulary words and terms.

Use the headings to create questions about what you expect to learn from this chapter. Compare your questions with those of a partner. Write your questions in your notebook.

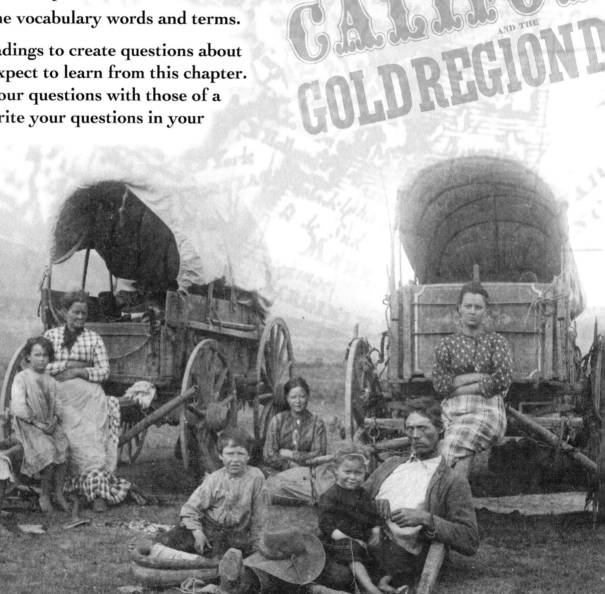

Westward Expansion

Thinking on Your Own

Look over the vocabulary and the Focus Your Reading questions. Write three predictions about the topic "Westward Expansion" in your notebook. Compare your predictions with a partner's.

By 1840, the line of settlement had reached the edge of the woodland and prairies. People settled as far west as Missouri and Arkansas. Beyond were the Great Plains and the Rocky Mountains. The next wave of settlement would be different from any that had gone before. This time farmers did not gradually push the frontier line west. Rather, they leapfrogged over the plains and mountains. They used Native American trails and mountain passes as highways to the Pacific Coast.

focus your reading

Why were settlers attracted to Oregon?

What religious group settled in Utah?

What did the expansionists want?

vocabulary

missionaries

Oregon fever

expansionists

manifest destiny

Oregon Fever

An important area of settlement was the Oregon Country. This area extended from the Columbia River in Oregon north into Canada. In 1840, both Great Britain and the United States claimed this territory.

A variety of covered wagons were used for the trip west.

The first Americans to settle in Oregon were **missionaries**. In the 1830s, preachers went there to convert Native Americans to the Christian faith. They were not very successful. Their letters home, however, contained glowing accounts of Oregon's rich farmland.

Oregon's fertile land drew settlers like a magnet. "Whoo ha! Go it, boys! We're in a perfect **Oregon fever**," exclaimed a Missouri newspaper editor. The fever spread. The Oregon Trail became the key route to the Oregon Country. By the end of 1843, more than 1,500 settlers had arrived. The number climbed to 9,000 by 1849.

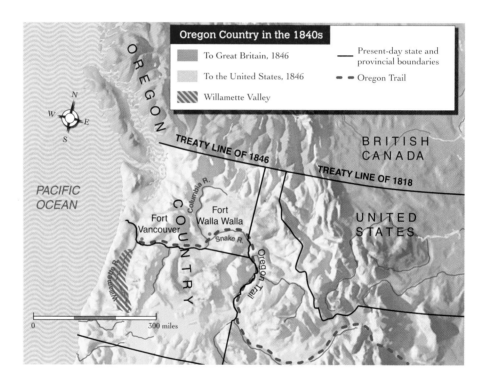

Oregon Country in the 1840s

- To Great Britain, 1846
- To the United States, 1846
- Willamette Valley
- Present-day state and provincial boundaries
- Oregon Trail

OREGON

PACIFIC OCEAN

TREATY LINE OF 1846

BRITISH CANADA

TREATY LINE OF 1818

Columbia R.

Fort Vancouver

Fort Walla Walla

Snake R.

Oregon Trail

C O U N T R Y

UNITED STATES

0   300 miles

Utah

The people known as Mormons did not go all the way to Oregon. They stopped at the Great Salt Lake in Utah. The Mormons belonged to the Church of Jesus Christ of Latter-day Saints. Joseph Smith had founded this religion in New York in 1830. Harassed by their neighbors, the Mormons left New York and settled in Nauvoo, Illinois. There an anti-Mormon mob murdered Smith. In 1847, Brigham Young led the Mormons to Utah. It was then Mexican territory. They settled on farmland and built a town called Salt Lake City.

Brigham Young

The Mormon trek to Utah

Acquiring New Territory

In the 1840s, many Americans wanted to acquire new territory. The **expansionists** wanted to add Texas and Oregon to the United States. They also had their eyes on California, which was still Mexican territory. Extending the nation's boundaries to the Pacific Ocean was, they said, our "**manifest destiny**," or God-given right.

President James K. Polk

stop and think

"Whoo ha! Go it, boys!" was the slogan used by people moving to Oregon. Design another slogan that reflects the mood of the times about westward expansion.

In 1844, James K. Polk, an expansionist Democrat, was elected president. The Democrats called the election a vote for expansion. In February 1845, Congress admitted Texas as a state. The next year Polk threatened a war with Great Britain over Oregon. The British agreed to sign a treaty that gave the United States most of what it wanted. It included the area that is now the states of Oregon and Washington.

Putting It All Together

Write the statement "America has a God-given right to extend her boundaries" in your notebook. Under it make two columns labeled "Agree" and "Disagree." In one column or the other, explain why you either agree or disagree. Compare your reasons with those of a partner.

Read a Primary Source

The Fall of Mexico City: Two Accounts

Below are two accounts of the capture of Mexico City at the end of the Mexican War. The first is by an American reporter, and the second is by a Mexican merchant. The American army, led by General Winfield Scott, occupied the city in September 1847.

"At 7 o'clock this morning Gen. Scott, with his staff, rode in and took quarters in the national palace, on the top of which the regimental flag of the gallant rifles and the stars and stripes were already flying, and an immense crowd [of Mexicans] . . . were congregated in the plaza as the commander-in-chief entered it. They pressed our soldiers, and eyed them as though they were beings of another world. . . . They [the soldiers] were told, however, not to injure or harm a man in the mob—as they were all our friends."

George W. Kendall, newspaper reporter for the *New Orleans Picayune*, September 14, 1847.

reading for understanding

How did the American reporter describe the relations between the soldiers and the Mexican people?

How does the Mexican merchant's account differ?

Why do you think these accounts are different?

"Seeing further resistance useless, our [Mexican] soldiers ceased firing, and on the 16th of September (sad day!) the enemy was in possession of the Mexican capital. Though we inflicted havoc and death upon the Yankees, we suffered greatly ourselves. Many were killed by the blowing up of the houses, many by the bombardment, but more by the confusion which prevailed in the city, and altogether we cannot count our killed, wounded and missing since the actions commenced yesterday at less than 4,000 among whom are many women and children. . . . What a calamity!"

Anonymous Mexican merchant, September 16, 1847, quoted in George W. Smith and Charles Judah, eds., *Chronicles of the Gringos: The U.S. Army in the Mexican War, 1846-1848* (Albuquerque: University of New Mexico).

War with Mexico

Thinking on Your Own

Look over the vocabulary and the Focus Your Reading questions. Think of a time when you or someone you know disagreed about who owned something. What created the problem? How did you resolve the issue?

In 1845, Mexico and the United States were headed for war. Mexico refused to accept the U.S. **annexation** of Texas. The two nations also could not agree on the boundary between Texas and Mexico. Thousands of square miles of land were in dispute. President James K. Polk wanted to buy New Mexico and California. Mexico refused to sell.

focus your reading

On what issues did the United States and Mexico not agree?

Why did the United States and Mexico go to war?

What did the United States get from the war?

vocabulary

annexation

disputed zone

negotiate

Treaty of Guadalupe Hidalgo

Going to War

In January 1846, President Polk was ready for war. He ordered General Zachary Taylor's army into the **disputed zone**. Mexico, in turn, sent in its troops. A clash was only a matter of time. In April, the Mexicans attacked Taylor's army, killing eleven American soldiers. When the news reached Washington, Polk sent a message to Congress. "Mexico . . . has invaded our territory and shed American blood on the American soil," he wrote. "War exists . . . by the act of Mexico herself." He did not mention that the attack took place in a zone claimed by both nations. On May 13, 1846, Congress declared war.

General Zachary Taylor

Captain Frémont fighting at Monterey

The Mexican War

The United States quickly got the territory it wanted. General Taylor's army drove the Mexicans out of Texas. A second army occupied New Mexico. When news of the war reached California, Americans there revolted against Mexico. Sailors stationed in California on American ships joined the revolt. Captain John C. Frémont, who was surveying in California, also sent troops. After a month of fighting, California was in American hands.

Having got what he wanted, Polk tried to end the war. But the Mexicans would not **negotiate**. The United States had to

General Winfield Scott entered Mexico City on September 14, 1847.

stop and think

Words can shape emotions. What emotion do you think President Polk tried to stir up with his statement, "Mexico . . . shed American blood on the American soil?" Write your thoughts in your notebook. Compare them with a partner's and share with the class.

force Mexico to the peace table. In March 1847, an American army invaded Mexico. Led by General Winfield Scott, the troops fought their way into Mexico City. The fighting finally ended in September 1847.

The Peace Treaty

President Polk finally got the peace treaty he wanted. The treaty was signed on February 2, 1848. In the **Treaty of Guadalupe Hidalgo**, Mexico agreed to sell to the United States approximately 529,000 square miles of territory. This area now consists of California, Nevada, Arizona, and the western parts of New Mexico and Colorado. In return, the United States agreed to pay Mexico $15 million. That was about five cents per acre.

The United States won the Battle of Buena Vista.

Putting It All Together

In your notebook design a timeline of events that led to the annexation of Texas, New Mexico, and California. Add information you find from your own research.

The Slavery Issue

Thinking on Your Own

Read the vocabulary and the Focus Your Reading questions. Draw three columns in your notebook. In the first column, on separate lines, write "The Slavery Issue," "The Wilmot Proviso," and "Miners' Law in California." In the second column, write what you already know about these topics. In the third column, write questions you have about each topic.

The slavery issue divided Americans along sectional lines. Many realized that it could destroy the Union. Leaders in the House of Representatives and the Senate had tried to keep the issue out of Congress. The Missouri Compromise had put the issue of slavery to rest in the Louisiana Territory. In 1820, Congress agreed to the Missouri Compromise, which banned slavery from the area north of the 36° 30' line of latitude. It allowed slavery in any territories created below that line, but not in any areas north of the line. In 1836, the House of Representatives passed a **gag rule** that banned the discussion of slavery in its debates.

focus your reading

Why did Congress try to avoid the slavery issue?

How did the Wilmot Proviso bring the issue back into Congress?

Why did the miners in California make up their own rules?

vocabulary

gag rule

Wilmot Proviso

Free-Soil Party

Revival of the Slavery Issue

The Mexican War renewed interest in the slavery issue. Many antislavery people in the North had opposed the war. President Polk, they argued, went to war only to add new slave territory to the Union.

In August 1846, Congressman David Wilmot of Pennsylvania brought the issue back into Congress.

David Wilmot

He introduced a resolution that banned slavery from any territory acquired from Mexico. The **Wilmot Proviso**, as it was called, passed in the House in 1846 and 1847, but the Senate never voted on it.

The Wilmot Proviso showed once again the power of the slavery issue to divide the nation along sectional lines. Northern Democrats and Whigs voted in favor of it. All but three of the sixty-four congressmen from the South voted against it.

Deadlock over Slavery

In the presidential election of 1848, the candidates avoided the issue. Whig candidate Zachary Taylor and Democrat Lewis Cass knew they would lose votes in the North or the South if they took a stand on slavery. Taylor, a slave owner, ignored the issue. Cass said he would let the people of a territory decide for themselves.

Some of the antislavery people formed a third party, the **Free-Soil Party**. Their candidate was former president Martin Van Buren. Van Buren was president from 1837 to 1841. While the new party did not carry a single state, it did send a warning: Avoiding the slavery issue could destroy the existing two-party political system.

Slavery was avoided during the election of 1848.

Gold in California

The discovery of gold in California brought the slavery issue to a crisis. In early 1848, James W. Marshall found gold deposits at Sutter's Mill along the American River. By May, word of the gold strike had reached San Francisco. Within a month, the city was virtually a ghost town. Everyone rushed to the gold diggings. In December, President Polk reported the discovery in his annual message to Congress. That helped trigger the great California gold rush.

California "gold fever" infected thousands of Americans. The rumor was that anyone could make $1,000 a day in the California foothills.

In the spring of 1849, some 80,000 people set out to find gold. These people became known as "forty-niners" because they moved to California in 1849. Most people went by wagon across the plains or by ship around Cape Horn. Upon arriving in California, they staked out mining claims.

Thousands of miners searched for gold in 1849.

Very few of the newcomers knew anything about gold mining. They dug gravel and sand from streambeds and swirled it in shallow pans filled with water. The sand and pebbles washed out, leaving the heavier gold in the bottom of the pan. They also used boxes mounted on rockers and long wooden troughs called sluices for this purpose. California miners took out more than $81 million in gold by using these simple techniques.

By the winter of 1849, the residents of California faced a crisis. They realized that they needed a government that could make real laws, but Congress could not act. It could not agree on the status of slavery in the territory of California.

Putting It All Together

Take turns with a partner naming the issues that a miner living in California during 1848 to 1849 had to face. Write the issues in your notebook.

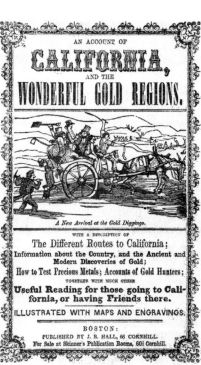

Biography

James W. Marshall (1812–1885)

On the morning of January 24, 1848, James W. Marshall walked along the millrace of the sawmill he was building. The race, or canal, brought water from the American River to power the mill. In the sand at the bottom, Marshall saw the glint of a gold nugget. To make sure it was gold, he weighed it. It was heavier than silver. He bit it and made a dent in the metal. It flattened out when he pounded it with a rock. Then he rushed off to tell John Sutter, his partner, that he had discovered gold.

James W. Marshall was born in 1812 in New Jersey. When he was twenty-one, Marshall moved to Missouri to farm. Looking for better land, he left for Oregon in 1844. He settled in California in 1845 near a trading post called Sutter's Fort.

John Sutter's trading post was the center of American settlement in California. Sutter sold farmland to the new settlers. He also hired men to make shoes, saddles, and farm tools, which he sold to the newcomers. In 1847, John Marshall agreed to help Sutter build a sawmill. They could make money selling lumber to the settlers.

When Marshall found gold, Sutter made him promise not to tell anyone about the nugget. Sutter was afraid his shoe and saddle makers would quit work to look for gold. The word of the gold discovery got out anyway. Sutter's workers took off for the hills. During the next year, more than 80,000 gold seekers rushed to California.

Neither Sutter nor Marshall benefited from the gold discovery. Without workers, Sutter's businesses failed. Hundreds of gold seekers settled on his land but refused to pay him for it. Claim jumpers took over Marshall's mining claims. They tore down the sawmill to build cabins with the lumber. Marshall spent the rest of his life cleaning out wells, making gardens, and doing odd jobs. He died a poor man in 1885 at age seventy-three.

Chapter Summary

The first Americans to settle in the Oregon Territory were **missionaries**. People in the eastern United States read the glowing accounts of the region and became so excited that newspapers said they had caught **Oregon fever**. After the United States annexed Texas in 1845, **expansionists** wanted to buy California from Mexico or take it by force, if necessary. They said it was our "**manifest destiny**" to extend our country to the Pacific Ocean.

In 1845, the United States and Mexico were headed for war because Mexico opposed the **annexation** of Texas. Fighting broke out when President James K. Polk sent troops into the **disputed zone**, and Congress declared war on May 13, 1846. In 1848, the United States **negotiated** the **Treaty of Guadalupe Hidalgo** in which Mexico agreed to sell to the United States all the land it owned north of the Rio Grande.

The issue of slavery almost destroyed the Union in 1820 when Missouri was admitted as a slave state. Congress passed a **gag rule** in 1836 to keep the issue from being debated. In August 1846, Congressman David Wilmot proposed the **Wilmot Proviso**, which stated that slavery would be banned from any territory acquired from Mexico. During the presidential election of 1848 the **Free-Soil Party** ran an antislavery candidate. The discovery of gold in California in 1848 brought the slavery issue to a new crisis as gold miners wanted to make California a free territory.

Chapter Review

1 Imagine that you are a farmer traveling west to Oregon. Write a journal entry explaining your experiences along the trail.

2 Make a cartoon sketch of two characters debating. One argues the Mexican position about the Mexican War. The other takes the American position. Include facts from the text.

3 Write a newspaper editorial arguing for California either to be a free state or a slave state. Include information from your own research.

Skill Builder

Mapping Movement

As you have learned, maps can serve many purposes.
The railroad map in Chapter 17 presented change over time.
Maps can also show locations of places and movement.

The map below shows the movement of armies during the
Mexican War. The lines in red represent the Mexican army. The
blue lines are the movements of United States troops. This map
also shows which side won each major battle. Study the Map
Key carefully. What other information does this map include?

Use the map to answer the following questions.

1 How many battles did General Taylor fight after leaving
Corpus Christi?

2 Approximately how many miles did General Kearny travel to
reach San Gabriel in California?

3 Which general led
United States troops
to Mexico City?

4 How many Mexican
victories were
there? How many
American victories?

5 How did this war
affect the size of the
United States?

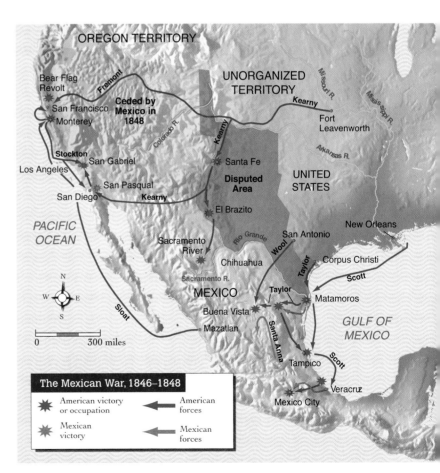

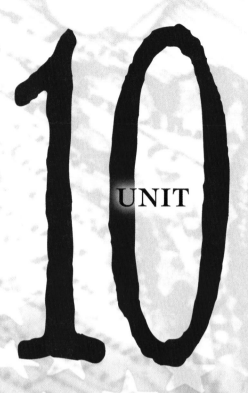

10 UNIT

A NATION IN CRISIS

The 1850s was a critical decade. The nation faced the difficult question of whether slavery should be allowed to expand into new territories. The South demanded protection for its slave property in territories that belonged to all the states. The North wanted to confine slavery to the states where it already existed. A minority wanted to abolish it altogether.

Americans had never faced a political issue as divisive as slavery. It split the political parties along sectional lines. It resisted every attempt at compromise. Time and again, it threatened to destroy the Union. The final crisis over slavery led to the bloodiest war in American history.

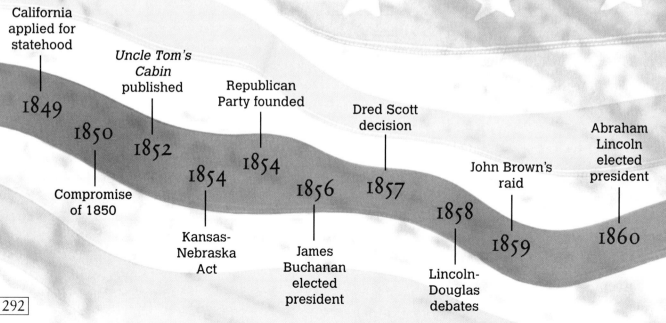

California applied for statehood

Uncle Tom's Cabin published

Republican Party founded

Dred Scott decision

Abraham Lincoln elected president

John Brown's raid

1849

1850

1852

1854

1854

1856

1857

1858

1859

1860

Compromise of 1850

Kansas-Nebraska Act

James Buchanan elected president

Lincoln-Douglas debates

How did the Civil War resolve the slavery issue?

Why did Abraham Lincoln's election cause slave states to secede?

How did westward expansion create a crisis over slavery?

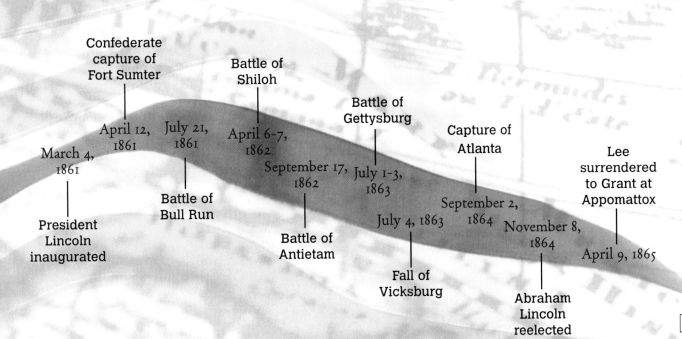

Confederate capture of Fort Sumter

April 12, 1861

Battle of Shiloh

July 21, 1861

April 6–7, 1862

Battle of Gettysburg

March 4, 1861

September 17, 1862

July 1–3, 1863

Capture of Atlanta

Lee surrendered to Grant at Appomattox

President Lincoln inaugurated

Battle of Bull Run

September 2, 1864

July 4, 1863

November 8, 1864

Battle of Antietam

April 9, 1865

Fall of Vicksburg

Abraham Lincoln reelected

Chapter

19 The Sectional Crisis

Getting Focused

Skim this chapter to predict what you will be learning.

- Read the lesson titles and subheadings.
- Look at the illustrations and read the captions.
- Examine the maps.
- Review the vocabulary words and terms.

The North and South disagreed about slavery. The U.S. Senate tried to reach a compromise. Can you remember a time in your life when an argument led to a compromise? Did it end the argument? Write your thoughts in your notebook.

Compromise of 1850

Thinking on Your Own

As you read, pay attention to the vocabulary words in the lesson. In your notebook, use each word in a sentence to show how it relates to the North-South conflict and to the compromise over slavery.

In 1849, Congress was deadlocked over the slavery issue. The people of California had asked to be admitted as a free territory. Congress responded along sectional lines. Northern congressmen favored the request. The South was solidly opposed. The result was a **sectional crisis** that threatened to destroy the Union.

The Crisis over California

To break the deadlock, President Zachary Taylor urged Californians to skip the **territorial stage**—one step in the process of a region being added to the United States. He asked them to organize a state government. No one questioned the right of a state to decide the issue of slavery for itself. They took Taylor's advice and drew up a state constitution. Taylor urged Congress to admit California as a free state.

Southern leaders in Congress were furious. They called Taylor a traitor to the South. They were afraid that all the new land acquired from Mexico would be carved up into free states. Upsetting the balance of power in Congress might mean that the North could abolish slavery. The most extreme proslavery men called for the South to **secede** from the Union.

> **focus your reading**
>
> Why were Southern congressmen angry at President Taylor?
>
> What was the Compromise of 1850?
>
> Why was the Fugitive Slave Law unpopular in the North?
>
> **vocabulary**
>
> sectional crisis
>
> territorial stage
>
> secede
>
> compromise
>
> Fugitive Slave Law
>
> personal liberty laws

The Compromise of 1850

Both sides looked for a way out. In January 1850, Senator Henry Clay of Kentucky proposed a **compromise**. His set of proposals gave the North and the South part of what each wanted. It included:

1 admitting California as a free state

2 organizing the remainder of the land acquired from Mexico as territories with no restrictions on slavery

Henry Clay

3 outlawing the buying and selling of slaves in the District of Columbia

4 passing a new federal law to help slave owners recover runaway or fugitive slaves

The compromise also included two less important measures that settled Texas's boundary dispute with New Mexico and paid Texas's $10 million debt. Together, these proposals were known as the Compromise of 1850.

stop and think

Imagine that you and your friends are creating a documentary film about California in 1849. From what you have read so far, write the film's main idea in your notebook and suggest a title for the film. As you read, note facts to include in the film.

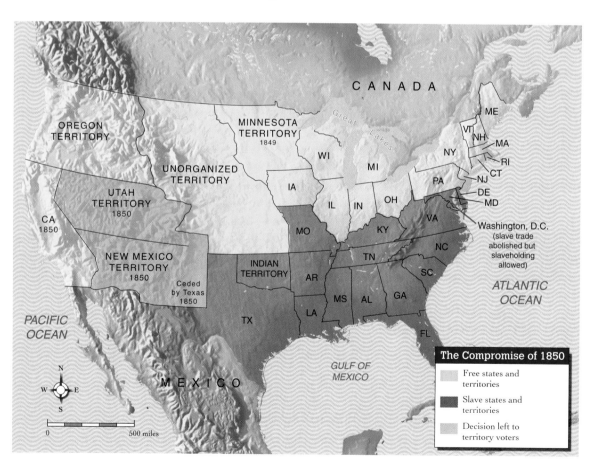

The Compromise of 1850
- Free states and territories
- Slave states and territories
- Decision left to territory voters

Reaction to the Compromise of 1850

The Compromise of 1850 led to a heated debate in Congress. Henry Clay defended his proposals. John C. Calhoun of South Carolina opposed the compromise. He wanted the compromise to state that there would

John C. Calhoun

be no restrictions on slavery in any of the territories. Daniel Webster of Massachusetts urged both sections to compromise. Otherwise, he warned, the slavery issue would destroy the Union. The compromise finally passed in September 1850.

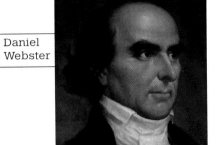

Daniel Webster

The **Fugitive Slave Law** caused an uproar in the North. The law required U.S. marshals in the North to help catch runaway slaves. It filled free blacks throughout the North with terror. When an ex-slave named Shadrack was arrested in Boston, a mob broke into the jail. They freed Shadrack and sent him to Canada. Nine northern states passed **personal liberty laws** that prevented local officials from capturing ex-slaves.

The Compromise of 1850 settled the slavery issue in Congress. It did not remove it from the minds of the people.

CAUTION!!

COLORED PEOPLE

OF BOSTON, ONE & ALL,

You are hereby respectfully CAUTIONED and advised, to avoid conversing with the

Watchmen and Police Officers of Boston,

For since the recent ORDER OF THE MAYOR & ALDERMEN, they are empowered to act as

KIDNAPPERS

AND

Slave Catchers,

And they have already been actually employed in KIDNAPPING, CATCHING, AND KEEPING SLAVES. Therefore, if you value your LIBERTY, and the *Welfare of the Fugitives* among you, *Shun* them in every possible manner, as so many *HOUNDS* on the track of the most unfortunate of your race.

Keep a Sharp Look Out for KIDNAPPERS, and have TOP EYE open.

APRIL 24, 1851.

Northern abolitionists posted signs to warn freed slaves of the Fugitive Slave Law.

In 1852, Harriet Beecher Stowe published *Uncle Tom's Cabin*, a novel that described the evils of slavery. The novel told the story of a fictitious slave family. For the first time slave life was explained in human terms. It sold one million copies in its first two years and was turned into a play. The issue of slavery was on the minds of many and could not be avoided by Congress for long.

Eliza and her child being chased when she tried to escape

Harriet Beecher Stowe

In 1854, Boston abolitionists tried to rescue Anthony Burns, a runaway slave from Virginia. They were turned away by marshals after breaking down the courthouse door. The next day Burns was put on a ship and returned to Virginia.

Anthony Burns and Thomas Sims

Putting It All Together

Create a concept map in your notebook with "Compromise of 1850" in the middle circle. Add circles on the right and left, one for "North" and one for "South." Discuss the effects of the compromise for each section and list them in smaller circles under "North" and "South."

Kansas and Nebraska

Thinking on Your Own

Look over the Focus Your Reading questions. As you read the lesson, take notes on how free-soilers may have reacted to Douglas's bill. How might the bill have affected their attitudes toward political parties? Discuss your notes with a partner. Write your thoughts in your notebook.

In 1854, a new crisis erupted over slavery. As before, the issue involved slavery in the territories. Senator Stephen A. Douglas of Illinois introduced a bill to create the Kansas and Nebraska Territories. Organizing that area for settlement would benefit Chicago, Douglas's hometown. This time, Northern antislavery people were angry. Once again, the issue threatened to tear the Union apart.

focus your reading

Why did Senator Douglas's bill open Kansas and Nebraska to slavery?

Who opposed the Kansas-Nebraska bill?

What impact did the Kansas-Nebraska Act have on the political parties?

vocabulary

popular sovereignty

free-soilers

Kansas-Nebraska Act

The Kansas-Nebraska Bill

Senator Douglas proposed to carve the Kansas and Nebraska Territories out of the northern part of the Louisiana Purchase. The Missouri Compromise already had outlawed slavery there. Douglas needed Southern votes in Congress for his bill. He also knew that no Southern congressman would vote to admit free territories. So he agreed to open these territories to slavery if the people there voted for it. He called this the principle of **popular sovereignty**.

Douglas knew that most of the settlers in Kansas and Nebraska would be farmers from free states. They would vote against slavery when the issue came to a vote.

Stephen A. Douglas introduced the Kansas-Nebraska Bill in 1854.

Reaction to the Kansas-Nebraska Bill

The Kansas-Nebraska bill created a furor. Its opponents held protest meetings throughout the North. They denounced the bill as "a gross violation of a sacred pledge [the Missouri Compromise], a criminal betrayal of precious rights." Douglas was surprised that so many people in the North opposed the bill.

Most of the bill's opponents were known as **free-soilers**. They did not intend to abolish slavery, but they strongly opposed its expansion westward. They did not think that free farmers could compete with slave labor.

stop and think

Senator Douglas's principle of popular sovereignty appeared to be fair to the North and the South. Was it really? In your notebook, argue either in favor of popular sovereignty or against it. Support your argument with three reasons.

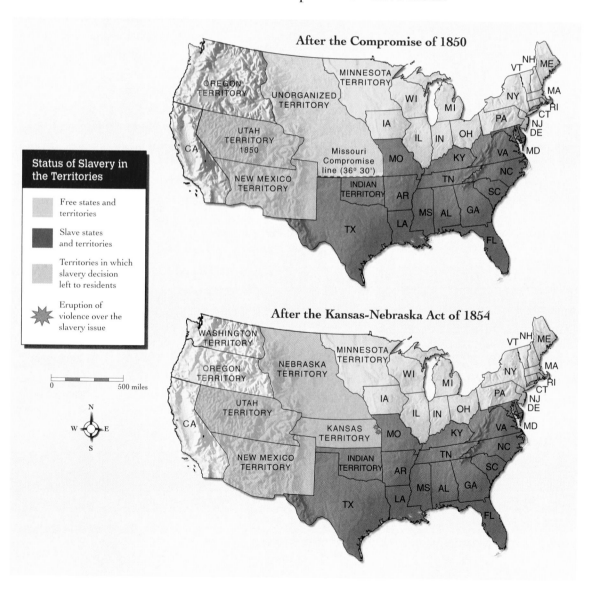

After the Compromise of 1850

After the Kansas-Nebraska Act of 1854

Status of Slavery in the Territories

- Free states and territories
- Slave states and territories
- Territories in which slavery decision left to residents
- Eruption of violence over the slavery issue

0   500 miles

Proslavery people from Missouri, known as border ruffians, attacked free-soilers in Kansas.

After three months of angry debate, the Kansas-Nebraska bill was passed by Congress. It became the **Kansas-Nebraska Act**. It was signed into law in May 1854.

A Time of Political Upheaval

The Kansas-Nebraska Act tore the Whig Party apart. Northern or "Conscience" Whigs denounced it. Southern or "Cotton" Whigs supported it. The party soon collapsed. Many northern Democrats also left their party in protest.

In the summer of 1854, a new anti-Nebraska party had emerged. It was called the Republican Party. That fall, it ran candidates for the House of Representatives. In 1856, the Republicans nominated John C. Frémont as their candidate for president. Although defeated by Democrat James Buchanan, Frémont carried eleven northern states. Most of Buchanan's votes came from the South. The slavery question again had divided the nation along sectional lines.

Putting It All Together

Imagine that you have joined the new Republican Party in the summer of 1854. After researching the founding of the party, design a campaign slogan for the party.

Read a Primary Source

The Kansas-Nebraska Debate

In January 1854, Senator Stephen A. Douglas introduced the Kansas-Nebraska bill. To attract southern support, Douglas agreed to let the people in these new territories vote on whether to allow slavery. That, in effect, repealed the Missouri Compromise.

reading for understanding

What principle does the Kansas-Nebraska bill rest upon, according to Douglas?

Why does Douglas think slavery will not expand to these territories?

On what grounds does Theodore Parker oppose the bill?

Senator Stephen A. Douglas Supports the Bill

In the following letter to a newspaper in February 1854, Senator Stephen A. Douglas defended his bill.

❝The [Kansas-Nebraska] bill rests upon . . . the great fundamental principle of self-government. . . . It does not propose to legislate slavery into the Territories, nor out of the Territories. . . . The bill, therefore, does not introduce slavery; does not revive it; does not establish it; does not contain any clause designed to produce that result. . . . All candid men who understand the subject admit that the laws of climate, and production, and of physical geography . . . have excluded slavery from that country. . . . Mr. Badger of North Carolina [declared] . . . that he and his southern friends did not expect that slavery would go there; that the climate and productions were not adapted to slave labor . . . but they insisted upon [the right of the settlers to vote for or against it] as a matter of principle, and of principle alone.❞

—From Robert W. Johannsen, ed., *The Letters of Stephen A. Douglas.*

Theodore Parker Opposes the Bill

Theodore Parker, a Congregational minister in Boston, spoke out against the bill on February 12, 1854. The following is an excerpt from his sermon.

❝So the question is, shall we let Slavery into the two great territories Kansas and Nebraska? . . . Shall men work with poor industrial tools, or with good ones? Shall they have the varied industry of New England and the North, or the Slave labor of Virginia and Carolina? Shall their land be worth five dollars and eight cents an acre, as in South Carolina, or thirty dollars and a half as in Connecticut? Shall the people all be comfortable, engaged in honest work . . . or shall a part be the poorest of the world that a few may be idle and rich?

"It is a question of political morality. Shall the Government be a commonwealth where all are citizens, or an aristocracy where man owns his brother man?❞

—From *The Nebraska Question. Some Thoughts upon Freedom in America,* by Theodore Parker.

National Crisis

Thinking on Your Own

Read the Focus Your Reading questions. Make three columns in your notebook with the headings "Dred Scott," "John Brown," and "Abraham Lincoln." As you read the lesson, take notes about how each person was involved in a national crisis.

In 1856, civil war broke out in Kansas. Settlers from free and slave states chose sides on the slavery issue. Proslavery men set fire to Lawrence, Kansas, a free-soil town. In response, a free-soil fanatic named John Brown killed five proslavery settlers.

In May 1856, the violence spread to Washington, D.C. There, Senator Charles Sumner of Massachusetts gave a speech entitled "The Crime Against Kansas." He was attacked and beaten on the floor of the Senate by Congressman Preston Brooks of South Carolina.

> ### focus your reading
>
> Why did the slave Dred Scott claim to be a free person?
>
> Why did John Brown raid the federal arsenal?
>
> Why was the South shocked by Abraham Lincoln's election?
>
> ### vocabulary
>
> chief justice
>
> annals
>
> federal arsenal
>
> uprising

Rep. Brooks attacks Senator Sumner in 1856.

The Dred Scott Decision

In March 1857, the Supreme Court ruled on the slavery issue in the Dred Scott case. Dred Scott, a slave, sued for his freedom because his owner had once taken him to live in Illinois and then to Wisconsin Territory. He claimed that residence in a free state and a free territory made him a free person.

The Supreme Court ruled against Scott. The decision, written by **Chief Justice** Roger B. Taney, said that Scott was still a slave. It also ruled that Scott should not have gone to court, as slaves had no legal rights. Finally, the Supreme Court struck down the Missouri Compromise. It ruled that Congress had no right to exclude slavery from any territory.

The Dred Scott decision drove another wedge between the North and the South. The South applauded it. Republican leaders in the North called the decision "the greatest crime in the **annals** of the republic."

In 1858, the decision was the focus of a senatorial debate in Illinois between Senator Stephen A. Douglas and Abraham Lincoln. Douglas, who defended the decision, defeated Lincoln and won reelection to the Senate. Although he lost the election, Lincoln's opposition to the court decision made him a leader of the Republican Party.

The Dred Scott case highlighted the issue of slavery.

stop and think

Add new information to the three columns you made for Thinking on Your Own. Update the columns as you continue reading.

John Brown's capture after his raid on Harper's Ferry

John Brown's Raid

In October 1859, the South got shocking news. John Brown, a militant abolitionist, and eighteen men had attacked the **federal arsenal** at Harper's Ferry, Virginia. They tried to get weapons from the arsenal to arm the slaves for a massive **uprising**. A slave uprising was the slave owners' worst nightmare. They also were shocked when northern abolitionists made a hero of John Brown. Although Brown was captured, tried, and hanged, the raid drove the wedge between the sections ever deeper.

John Brown being led to his execution

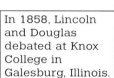

In 1858, Lincoln and Douglas debated at Knox College in Galesburg, Illinois.

The Election of 1860

In 1860, the future looked bleak for the South. Three new western states (California, 1850; Minnesota, 1858; and Oregon, 1859) gave the North a majority in the Senate.

Free-soil states also had a majority in the House of Representatives. The South's only hope was to elect a proslavery president. In November 1860, that hope also vanished.

The election of 1860 was a four-way contest. Stephen A. Douglas ran as the Democratic Party candidate. The Southern Democrats chose John C. Breckinridge from Kentucky as their proslavery candidate. The Republicans nominated Abraham Lincoln. The Constitutional Union Party, made up of former Whigs, made John C. Bell their candidate.

Abraham Lincoln

The Republicans won the election. Lincoln got more electoral votes than all of his opponents combined. He also received more popular votes than any other candidate. With Lincoln's victory, the South had become a powerless, minority section. That winter, seven slave states seceded from the Union.

Putting It All Together

Design a triangle with "Loss of Southern Power" in the middle. On each point of the triangle include one fact that indicates how the South lost power.

Biography

Dred Scott (1795?–1858)

Dred Scott was born a slave in Virginia about 1795. His owner, Peter Blow, was a cotton planter. Scott probably worked as a field slave. In 1830, the Blow family quit farming and moved to St. Louis, Missouri, taking Dred Scott with them.

As a "city slave," he was hired to work for wages. Scott worked on steamboats traveling up and down the Mississippi River. In 1832, Peter Blow sold Scott to John Emerson, a U.S. Army doctor.

In 1833, the army sent Dr. Emerson to Fort Armstrong in northern Illinois. He took Scott along. Three years later, Emerson was assigned to Fort Snelling in Wisconsin Territory. During the seven years Scott spent there, he married Harriet Robinson, a slave woman. In 1840, Emerson

was transferred to a fort in Florida. On his way south, he left Dred and Harriet Scott with his wife Irene in St. Louis. When Dr. Emerson died in 1843, Scott became Irene Emerson's slave.

In 1846, Dred Scott sued in a Missouri court for his freedom. He claimed that living on free soil in Illinois and Wisconsin Territory made him a free man. He also asked for the freedom of his wife and their children, Eliza and Lizzie. When the state court ruled in their favor, Irene Emerson appealed to the Missouri Supreme Court. It reversed the lower court's decision. In the meantime, she had sold the Scotts to her brother, John Sanford of New York.

Dred Scott sued again. As residents of two states were now involved, he could sue in a federal court. He lost again. With the help of a St. Louis lawyer, Roswell M. Field, Scott appealed to the United States Supreme Court.

On March 6, 1857, the Supreme Court ruled that the Scotts were still slaves. It also said that as a slave, Dred Scott had no right to sue in the courts. It held, finally, that Congress had no right to ban slavery from a territory.

Although they lost in the courts, the Scotts did gain their freedom. Irene Emerson married Calvin Chaffee, an antislavery congressman who objected to his wife owning slaves. In May 1858, Emerson gave the Scott family to Taylor Blow, the son of Peter Blow, Dred Scott's first owner. He freed the Scotts and helped them pay their legal bills.

Dred Scott died a free man on September 17, 1858.

Chapter Summary

In 1849, to avoid the slavery issue, California skipped the territorial stage and asked to be admitted as a free state. Congress was facing a **sectional crisis** over the issue. Some Southern leaders even threatened to **secede** from the Union. The matter was settled when the **Compromise** of 1850 admitted California as a free state. The rest of the land acquired from Mexico would become slave territories. **Fugitive Slave Laws** made it easier for slave owners to recover runaway slaves, while **personal liberty laws** prevented officials from capturing ex-slaves.

The **Kansas-Nebraska Act** let territories decide the slavery issue for themselves. This was called the principle of **popular sovereignty**. Northern **free-soilers** were angry, as the Missouri Compromise had already excluded slavery from that area.

During the next four years, the issue of slavery split the nation apart. In 1857, **Chief Justice** Tanney wrote that Congress could not exclude slavery from any territory. Antislavery people in the North believed it was "the greatest crime in the **annals** of the republic." The South was alarmed in 1859 by John Brown's raid on a **federal arsenal**. He tried to steal weapons for a slave **uprising**. Realizing they were now a minority, seven Southern states seceded from the Union before Lincoln took office.

Chapter Review

1 Imagine that you are a Kansas farmer. Your neighbor wants you to join a raid against settlers in another county who favor slavery. Make a list of reasons for and against the raid.

2 In her novel *Uncle Tom's Cabin*, Harriet Beecher Stowe described how slaves suffered. If you could design a cover for the book, what pictures would you include?

3 Choose six vocabulary words from the chapter. Draw a box for each word and divide it into three parts. In the parts, write 1) the word, 2) its definition, and 3) a sentence that includes the word.

Skill Builder

Reading a Presidential Election Map

In a presidential election in the United States, electoral votes are awarded by state. The party that has the most votes in each state wins all of its electoral votes. The results usually are presented on a map by showing the states, in different colors, that each party won.

The map below shows the results of the presidential election of 1860. The key in the center identifies the color used for each party and its candidate. It also indicates the total number of electoral and popular votes that each candidate received. The circle graphs at the bottom show the percentage of the total votes that each candidate won.

Use the map to answer the following questions:

1 Which party carried the largest number of free states?

2 Which candidate won the most slave states?

3 Which parties carried at least one slave state?

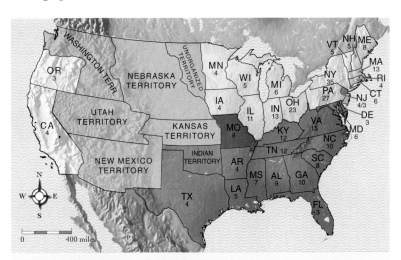

Election of 1860	Electoral Votes	Popular Votes
Lincoln (Republican)	180	1,865,593
Breckinridge (S. Democratic)	72	848,356
Bell (Constitutional Union)	39	592,906
Douglas (Democratic)	12	1,382,713

Voter Turnout — 81.2%

Electoral Votes — 12.9% | 4% | 23.7% | 59.4%

Popular Votes — 29.5% | 39.8% | 12.6% | 18.1%

Chapter

20 THE CIVIL WAR

Getting Focused

Skim this chapter to predict what you will be learning.

- Read the lesson titles and subheadings.
- Look at the illustrations and read the captions.
- Examine the maps.
- Review the vocabulary words and terms.

During the Civil War, the Union lost more than 360,000 soldiers. The Confederacy lost approximately 260,000 soldiers. Why do you think the mortality rate was so high? Write your prediction in your notebook.

The War Begins

Thinking on Your Own

Use the Glossary at the end of the book to find the definitions of the vocabulary words. Then work with a partner to use the words in sentences. Each sentence should show the meaning of the word.

In the spring of 1861, seven states in the Lower South (Alabama, Florida, Georgia, Louisiana, Mississippi, South Carolina, and Texas) seceded from the Union. They formed the new Confederate States of America, with Jefferson Davis as their president. Eight slave states in the Upper South remained in the Union. They waited to see what Abraham Lincoln would do about the slavery issue.

Abraham Lincoln

focus your reading

Why did Union troops try to capture Richmond?

Why did the North lose the Battle of Bull Run?

What did Ulysses S. Grant do in 1862?

vocabulary

inaugural address

militia

gunboats

blockade

In his **inaugural address** on March 4, 1861, President Lincoln said that he would not abolish slavery, but he would defend the Union. He stated that he would not strike the first blow: "In your hands, my dissatisfied fellow-countrymen, and not in mine, is the momentous issue of civil war." Lincoln was afraid the states of the Upper South would secede if the North attacked first.

Jefferson Davis

The War Begins

On the morning of April 12, 1861, Jefferson Davis's government took action. Confederate guns fired on Fort Sumter, a federal fort in the harbor of Charleston, South Carolina. The fort surrendered the next afternoon. With the outbreak of war, Virginia, North Carolina, Tennessee, and Arkansas decided to join the Confederacy. Four border states—Missouri, Kentucky,

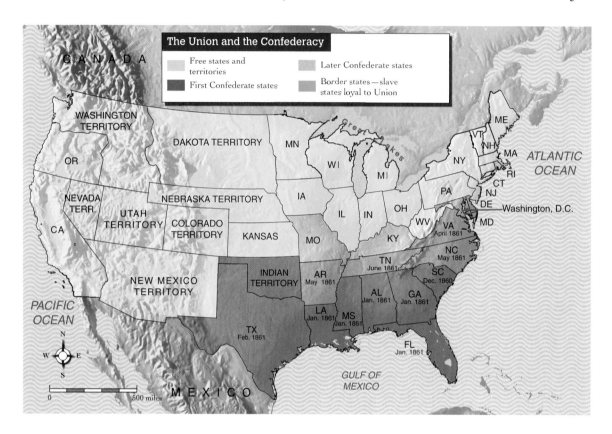

The Union and the Confederacy

- Free states and territories
- First Confederate states
- Later Confederate states
- Border states—slave states loyal to Union

Maryland, and Delaware—remained in the Union. The western counties of Virginia also remained loyal. In 1863, they joined the Union as the state of West Virginia.

The Battle of Bull Run

President Lincoln prepared the North for war. He asked the loyal states for 75,000 state **militia** troops. That spring trainloads of volunteers arrived in Washington, D.C. They were young men with little or no military experience. Lincoln hoped they could end the war quickly by capturing the Confederate capital of Richmond, Virginia.

Union soldier

The Battle of Bull Run

"Forward to Richmond!" Northern newspapers cried out. Marching toward Richmond, the Union troops were defeated by a Confederate army at the Battle of Bull Run on July 21, 1861. This battle was a shock to the North and taught them a serious lesson. They would need a large and well-trained army to defeat the Confederates.

stop and think

With a partner, role-play a conversation between two people in Virginia. One supports the Confederates; the other is loyal to the Union. They know they soon may face each other as enemy soldiers. Write the most important facts for each side in your notebook.

The War in 1862

In 1862, Union troops again tried to take Richmond. This time, Lincoln sent General George B. McClellan with a well-trained army. A Confederate army led by General Robert E. Lee stopped McClellan's advance. After a seven-day battle, the Union army withdrew. The North had again failed to defeat the Confederates.

Confederate soldier

In September, General Lee tried to invade the North. He attacked Union troops in Maryland. This battle was the bloodiest one-day battle of the Civil War. At the Battle of Antietam, 4,800 men were killed and 18,550 were wounded.

Union forces did, however, make headway in the West. A Union army captured the state capital at Nashville. General Ulysses S. Grant captured two Confederate forts in Tennessee. The Confederates finally stopped Grant at the bloody Battle of

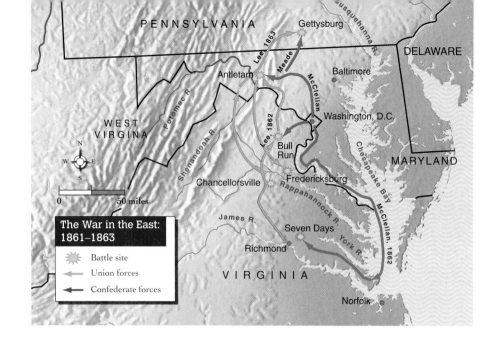

Shiloh on April 6 and 7, 1862. By the end of that summer, Union **gunboats** also controlled most of the Mississippi River.

Along the Atlantic and Gulf coasts, the Union navy blockaded Confederate ports. It wanted to keep the Confederates from getting supplies from Europe. The Confederate navy sent out an ironclad ship, the CSS *Virginia*, to break the **blockade**. The USS *Monitor*, a Union ironclad, attacked the *Virginia*. This first battle ever of ironclad ships ended in a draw.

The CSS *Virginia* and the USS *Monitor* battle along the coast of Virginia.

Putting It All Together

Several battles took place in 1862. Create a timeline that places them in the sequence in which they occurred. Use the map if you need help.

Biography

Kate Cumming (1835–1909)

Kate Cumming was born in Scotland in 1835. Her family moved to Canada and then to Mobile, Alabama, when she was a child. When the Civil War began, she was twenty-six and a true daughter of the Confederacy. At first she kept busy helping to put on concerts and plays to raise money for the troops. The advancing Union army soon brought that happy and patriotic time to an end.

In April 1862, Union and Confederate troops clashed near the village of Shiloh, Tennessee. The Confederate army needed volunteers to care for the wounded. On April 7, 1862, Cumming and other women from Mobile left for Corinth, Mississippi, where the Confederates had set up a hospital. The town was twenty miles south of the battlefield at Shiloh.

Cumming was totally unprepared for what she found at Corinth. "Nothing that I had ever heard or read had given me the faintest idea of the horrors witnessed here," she wrote in her diary. "Gray-haired men—men in the pride of manhood— beardless boys—Federals and all, mutilated in every imaginable way, lying on the floor . . . so close together it was almost impossible to walk without stepping on them."

Cumming was surprised at how quickly she got used to the horror. "The foul air from this mass of human beings at first made me giddy and sick, but I soon got over it. We have to walk, and when we give the men anything, kneel in blood and water; but we think nothing of it at all." Nearly all of the seriously wounded men died within a day or two. The nurses bathed the men's wounds, gave them bread and crackers, and helped them write their last letters home.

For the next three years, Cumming journeyed from one Confederate hospital to another. After leaving the hospital at Corinth, she wrote in her diary, "I shall ever look back on these two months with sincere gratification, and feel that I have lived for something."

At the end of the war, Cumming returned to Mobile, Alabama. There she published her diary, *A Journal of Hospital Life in the Confederate Army* (1866). Afterward she moved to Birmingham, Alabama, where she taught school and music. Cumming never married. She died in June 1909 at the age of seventy-four.

Read a Primary Source

Front-Line Realities

Young men marched off to the Civil War glad to do their patriotic duty. Many soldiers changed their view of the war after fighting on the battlefield. The following excerpts are examples of Confederate and Union soldiers whose perspectives had changed.

The South

❝Yesterday evening we was in one of the hardest fought battles ever known. . . . I don't think the [4th Texas Regiment] could muster this morning over 150 or 200 men & there were 530 yesterday. . . . I never had a clear conception of the horrors of war until that night and the [next] morning. On going round on that battlefield with a candle searching for my friends I could hear on all sides the dreadful groans of the wounded and their heart piercing cries for water and assistance. . . . I assure you I am heartily sick of soldiering.❞

A. N. Erskin to his wife,
June 28, 1862

The North

❝As far as I can judge from what I have heard, there is very little zeal or patriotism in the army now, the men have seen so much more of defeat than of victory & so much bloody slaughter that all patriotism is played out. Even in this regiment only out five months . . . I don't believe there are twenty men but are heartily sick of war & want to go home.❞

Edward L. Edes to Charlotte, December 28, 1862,
Massachusetts Historical Society

reading for understanding

What changed these men's views of war?

Why were they both "heartily sick" of war?

How had their feelings of patriotism changed?

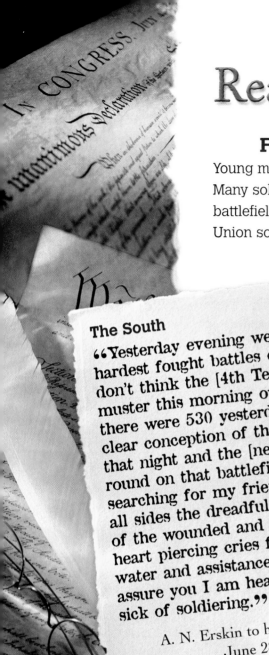

Behind the Lines

Thinking on Your Own

Read the paragraph below. What is a thimble? How much blood can one hold? In your notebook, explain the meaning of the quotation about a thimble.

I n 1861 most Americans thought the Civil War would be over quickly. "A lady's **thimble** will hold all the blood that will be shed," one Confederate said. The fighting in 1862 shattered that hope. Leaders on both sides realized that the war would be long and costly. The question was which side would best be able to fight such a war.

focus your reading

What advantages did the North have in the Civil War?

What were the South's main advantages?

How did women contribute to the war effort?

vocabulary

thimble	enlisted
stalemate	military hospitals

Iron foundries added to the strength of the North.

Railroads allowed goods to be shipped to Northern troops.

The Two Sides Compared

In a drawn-out war, the North had several advantages. It had more factories and workshops to produce weapons and clothing for its soldiers. The Union army was very well supplied. The North also had more railroads, banks, and men of military age—those between eighteen and forty-five years old. The Confederate army never had enough tents, blankets, and uniforms. Its soldiers often fought barefoot.

The South also had advantages. It could free more white men to fight because it had slaves to do part of the work at home or on the farm. As most of the battles took place in the South, the Confederates fought on familiar ground. They knew back roads that did not appear on the Union army's maps. They also knew that they did not have to defeat the North to win. The Confederate states could gain their independence by wearing down the North. A **stalemate**, or draw, was as good as a victory.

stop and think

With a partner, play the roles of a Northern and a Southern soldier. What arguments could each of you make that your side probably would win the war? Add to your list from the Stop and Think in Lesson 1.

The War on the Home Front

The war reached into every home in America. More than 1.5 million husbands, fathers, and sons joined the Union army. Over 1 million **enlisted** on the Confederate side. This created a labor shortage that made life difficult for those at home. In 1863, the South also faced a shortage of food. Women in Richmond rioted in the streets to get bread for their families.

Women supported the war by working in factories.

The war gave women new roles. They had to plant and harvest crops as well as take care of the home. "I met more women driving teams [of horses] on the road and saw more at work in the fields than men," wrote a traveler in Iowa in 1862. More women in the North worked in factories than before. In the South, planters' wives had to learn how to raise cotton.

Southern women also took over men's jobs in government and as schoolteachers.

Women also contributed directly to the war effort. Many volunteered their time to collect food and medical supplies. Women served as nurses in **military hospitals**. Dozens of women also served as Union and Confederate spies and scouts. Several hundred fought on battlefields disguised as men.

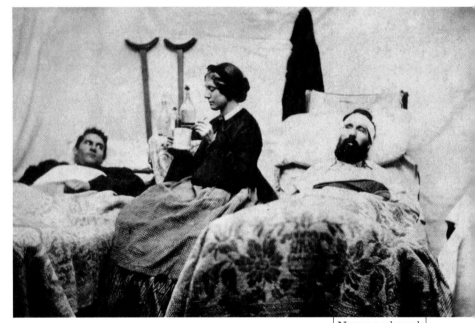

Nurses played an important role at military hospitals.

Putting It All Together

Create a T-chart. Label it "Women during the Civil War." Under the label write "Advantages" on one side and "Disadvantages" on the other side. List what you think belongs under each heading. Compare your ideas with a partner's.

Turning of the Tide

Thinking on Your Own

Read over the Focus Your Reading questions. Make predictions about what this lesson will include. Write three predictions in your notebook.

For the North, the year 1863 was a turning point in the Civil War. Until then the North had fought to save the Union, not to **abolish** slavery. On January 1, 1863, President Abraham Lincoln added a new purpose—freeing the slaves. Union generals also had more success on the battlefield that year. The war was far from over, but the North could finally see a ray of hope.

focus your reading

Why did President Lincoln emancipate the slaves?

Why are the battles at Gettysburg and Vicksburg called turning points?

How did Sherman's victory affect the 1864 presidential election?

vocabulary

abolish

Emancipation Proclamation

ratified

surrendered

Ulysses S. Grant

Emancipating the Slaves

In 1862, President Lincoln concluded that the North could not win the war without freeing the slaves. Promising them freedom would encourage slaves to leave their plantations. That would drain the Confederates' labor supply. It also would provide the Union army with additional troops.

On January 1, 1863, Lincoln issued the **Emancipation Proclamation**. It freed all the slaves behind the Confederate lines. Many slaves living in the border states would not be freed until the Thirteenth Amendment was **ratified** in 1865. The proclamation helped the Union cause. Slaves who were freed as the troops advanced into the South did join the Union army. More than 130,000 black soldiers and sailors fought on the Union side.

Robert E. Lee

Gettysburg and Vicksburg

In the summer of 1863, General Robert E. Lee led a Confederate army north from Richmond. Union armies tried to stop him at Fredericksburg and Chancellorsville, Virginia. They lost both battles. Then Lee invaded Pennsylvania hoping to break the North's will to fight. General George G. Meade met him at the town of Gettysburg with a Union army. After three days of hard fighting, from July 1 to 3, Meade stopped the Confederates, who suffered heavy losses. But Meade let Lee's army get away.

The next day, General Ulysses S. Grant won a victory at Vicksburg. The Confederates had approximately 30,000 troops dug in on the bluffs overlooking the Mississippi River at Vicksburg, Mississippi. Every Union attack had failed. Grant finally surrounded the city, cutting it off from its supply lines. On July 4, 1863, the Confederates surrendered. Vicksburg fell, giving the North control of the Mississippi River.

President Lincoln liked Grant. He won battles. In the fall of 1863, Lincoln placed Grant in command of the Union army in Virginia. General Grant, he believed, could defeat General Lee.

The Final Year

Despite the victories of 1863, the war dragged on. The North grew weary. In 1864, Abraham Lincoln doubted that he would be reelected. The Democrats ran General George B. McClellan as their candidate.

The War in the West: 1862–1863

* Battle site
← Union forces
← Confederate forces

They promised to negotiate a peace if McClellan won. The Union cause was in trouble.

In early September 1864, General William T. Sherman captured Atlanta. The loss of this railroad hub was a serious blow to the Confederacy. The North was jubilant. That November, Lincoln won a stunning election victory by winning 55 percent of the popular vote.

Roughly 46,000 Americans died at the Battle of Gettysburg, a turning point in the war.

After taking Atlanta, Sherman's army marched through Georgia to the sea. It destroyed everything in its path including railroads, farms, and cities. Then Sherman turned north to take the war into the Carolinas.

General Grant spent the year 1864 hammering away at Robert E. Lee's army. He fought Lee at the Battles of The Wilderness and at Cold Harbor. He lost more men than Lee, but that did not matter. Grant was determined to wear Lee down. In early April 1865, Grant's army finally surrounded Lee's troops in western Virginia. On April 9, 1865, General Lee **surrendered** to General Grant at Appomattox Court House, Virginia. The Civil War had finally ended, and the United States of America had been preserved.

Atlanta was destroyed during Sherman's march through Georgia.

stop and think

Imagine that you are an advisor to President Lincoln. You want to persuade him to free the slaves. What arguments would you make? Discuss your arguments with a partner and include them in your notebook.

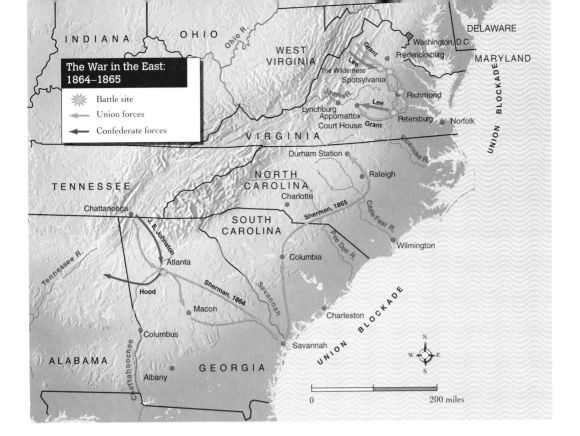

The War in the East:
1864–1865

☀ Battle site
← Union forces
◄ Confederate forces

The Civil War was the bloodiest and most costly war in American history. It took the lives of 360,000 Union and 260,000 Confederate soldiers at a cost of $20 billion. The South lost two-thirds of its wealth in property, half of its farm equipment, and two-fifths of its livestock. It paid dearly for its attempt to secede from the Union.

Robert E. Lee surrendered to Ulysses S. Grant at Appomattox Court House, Virginia.

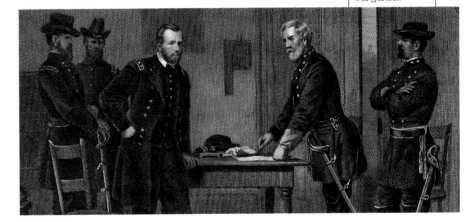

Putting It All Together

Work with a partner. Imagine that the date is late April 1865, and you have just attended a funeral of a Union soldier. Explain to a partner what might have been said in the funeral sermon. Have your partner explain what might have been said at a Confederate soldier's funeral. Include information about the battles where they fought and other information you learned about the Civil War.

Chapter Summary

In 1861, eleven slave states seceded from the Union. President Abraham Lincoln said in his **inaugural address** that he would fight to preserve the Union. When the Confederates attacked Fort Sumter in South Carolina, Lincoln asked the loyal states for 75,000 **militia** troops. The Union army failed to capture the Confederate capital at Richmond, Virginia, in 1861 and again in 1862. More than a **thimble** of blood was shed.

Union **gunboats** gained control of most of the Mississippi River in 1862. The Union navy **blockaded** Southern ports. The Confederates tried to break the blockade. The attempt failed when the USS *Monitor* stopped the CSS *Virginia*.

Both the North and the South had their own advantages. However, the South believed that a **stalemate** was as good as a victory. The war created new roles for women, and many served as nurses in **military hospitals**. So many men **enlisted** in the two armies that a labor shortage existed at home.

The year 1863 was a turning point in the Civil War. President Lincoln's **Emancipation Proclamation** made it a war to free the slaves. Slavery, however, would not be **abolished** in all states until the Thirteenth Amendment was **ratified**.

Confederate General Robert E. Lee finally **surrendered** to General Ulysses S. Grant on April 9, 1865.

Chapter Review

1 Civil War armies brought supplies to their soldiers in horse-drawn wagons. Research the conditions of delivering these supplies and write a newspaper article about the Confederate supply wagons at Vicksburg.

2 Write an editorial for either a Union or Confederate newspaper that explains why your side won or lost the war. Include as many of the vocabulary words as you can.

3 Look over the Focus Your Reading questions. Choose one that you would like to answer in more detail. Find additional information about the question in a library or on a Web site.

Skill Builder

Interpreting Multiple Graphs

Most graphs focus on one topic. However, sometimes multiple graphs are shown together.

The graphs below present advantages the Union had over the Confederacy. The topic of each is listed along the top of each graph. The values of each are presented in each graph.

Use the graphs to answer the following questions:

1 In what area did the North have the greatest advantage?

2 In what area was the South most nearly equal to the North?

3 How does the information in these graphs help explain which side won the Civil War?

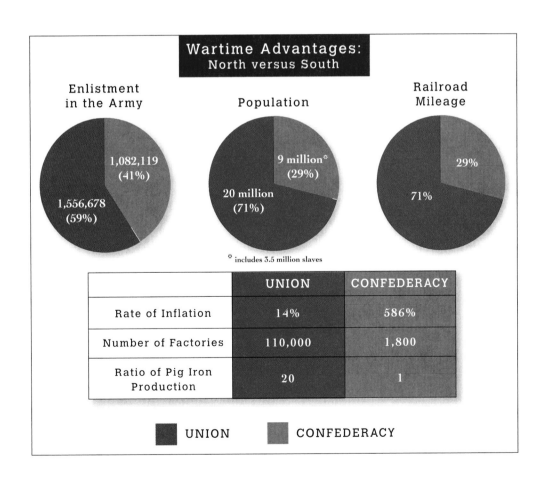

Wartime Advantages:
North versus South

Enlistment in the Army
- 1,082,119 (41%)
- 1,556,678 (59%)

Population
- 9 million* (29%)
- 20 million (71%)

Railroad Mileage
- 29%
- 71%

*includes 3.5 million slaves

	UNION	CONFEDERACY
Rate of Inflation	14%	586%
Number of Factories	110,000	1,800
Ratio of Pig Iron Production	20	1

■ UNION   ■ CONFEDERACY

Appendix
HISTORICAL DOCUMENTS AND MAPS

The Declaration of Independence

Action of Second Continental Congress, July 4, 1776

The unanimous Declaration of the thirteen United States of America

WHEN in the Course of human Events, it becomes necessary for one People to dissolve the Political Bands which have connected them with another, and to assume among the Powers of the Earth, the separate and equal Station to which the Laws of Nature and of Nature's God entitle them, a decent Respect to the Opinions of Mankind requires that they should declare the causes which impel them to the Separation.

WE hold these Truths to be self-evident, that all Men are created equal, that they are endowed by their Creator with certain unalienable Rights, that among these are Life, Liberty and the Pursuit of Happiness — That to secure these Rights, Governments are instituted among Men, deriving their just Powers from the Consent of the Governed, that whenever any Form of Government becomes destructive of these Ends, it is the Right of the People to alter or to abolish it, and to institute new Government, laying its Foundation on such Principles, and organizing its Powers in such Form, as to them shall seem most likely to effect their Safety and Happiness. Prudence, indeed, will dictate that Governments long established should not be changed for light and transient Causes; and accordingly all Experience hath shewn, that Mankind are more disposed to suffer, while Evils are sufferable, than to right themselves by abolishing the Forms to which they are accustomed. But when a long Train of Abuses and Usurpations, pursuing invariably the same Object, evinces a Design to reduce them under absolute Despotism, it is their Right, it is their Duty, to throw off such Government, and to provide new Guards for their future Security. Such has been the patient Sufferance of these Colonies; and such is now the Necessity which constrains them to alter their former Systems of Government. The History of the present King of Great- Britain is a History of repeated Injuries and Usurpations, all having in direct Object the Establishment of an absolute Tyranny over these States. To prove this, let Facts be submitted to a candid World.

HE has refused his Assent to Laws, the most wholesome and necessary for the public Good.

HE has forbidden his Governors to pass Laws of immediate and pressing Importance, unless suspended in their Operation till his Assent should be obtained; and when so suspended, he has utterly neglected to attend to them.

HE has refused to pass other Laws for the Accommodation of large Districts of People, unless those People would relinquish the Right of Representation in the Legislature, a Right inestimable to them, and formidable to Tyrants only.

HE has called together Legislative Bodies at Places unusual, uncomfortable, and distant from the Depository of their public Records, for the sole Purpose of fatiguing them into Compliance with his Measures.

HE has dissolved Representative Houses repeatedly, for opposing with manly Firmness his Invasions on the Rights of the People.

HE has refused for a long Time, after such Dissolutions, to cause others to be elected; whereby the Legislative Powers, incapable of the Annihilation, have returned to the People at large for their exercise; the State remaining in the mean time exposed to all the Dangers of Invasion from without, and the Convulsions within.

HE has endeavoured to prevent the Population of these States; for that Purpose obstructing the Laws for Naturalization of Foreigners; refusing to pass others to encourage their Migrations hither, and raising the Conditions of new Appropriations of Lands.

HE has obstructed the Administration of Justice, by refusing his Assent to Laws for establishing Judiciary Powers.

HE has made Judges dependent on his Will alone, for the Tenure of their Offices, and the Amount and Payment of their Salaries.

HE has erected a Multitude of new Offices, and sent hither Swarms of Officers to harrass our People, and eat out their Substance.

HE has kept among us, in Times of Peace, Standing Armies, without the consent of our Legislatures.

HE has affected to render the Military independent of and superior to the Civil Power.

HE has combined with others to subject us to a Jurisdiction foreign to our Constitution, and unacknowledged by our Laws; giving his Assent to their Acts of pretended Legislation:

FOR quartering large Bodies of Armed Troops among us;

FOR protecting them, by a mock Trial, from Punishment for any Murders which they should commit on the Inhabitants of these States:

FOR cutting off our Trade with all Parts of the World:

FOR imposing Taxes on us without our Consent:

FOR depriving us, in many Cases, of the Benefits of Trial by Jury:

FOR transporting us beyond Seas to be tried for pretended Offences:

FOR abolishing the free System of English Laws in a neighbouring Province, establishing therein an arbitrary Government, and enlarging its Boundaries, so as to render it at once an Example and fit Instrument for introducing the same absolute Rules into these Colonies:

FOR taking away our Charters, abolishing our most valuable Laws, and altering fundamentally the Forms of our Governments:

FOR suspending our own Legislatures, and declaring themselves invested with Power to legislate for us in all Cases whatsoever.

HE has abdicated Government here, by declaring us out of his Protection and waging War against us.

HE has plundered our Seas, ravaged our Coasts, burnt our Towns, and destroyed the Lives of our People.

HE is, at this Time, transporting large Armies of foreign Mercenaries to compleat the Works of Death, Desolation, and Tyranny, already begun with circumstances of Cruelty and Perfidy, scarcely paralleled in the most barbarous Ages, and totally unworthy the Head of a civilized Nation.

HE has constrained our fellow Citizens taken Captive on the high Seas to bear Arms against their Country, to become the Executioners of their Friends and Brethren, or to fall themselves by their Hands.

HE has excited domestic Insurrections amongst us, and has endeavoured to bring on the Inhabitants of our Frontiers, the merciless Indian Savages, whose known Rule of Warfare, is an undistinguished Destruction, of all Ages, Sexes and Conditions.

IN every stage of these Oppressions we have Petitioned for Redress in the most humble Terms: Our repeated Petitions have been answered only by repeated Injury. A Prince, whose Character is thus marked by every act which may define a Tyrant, is unfit to be the Ruler of a free People.

NOR have we been wanting in Attentions to our British Brethren. We have warned them from Time to Time of Attempts by their Legislature to extend an unwarrantable Jurisdiction over us. We have reminded them of the Circumstances of our Emigration and Settlement here. We have appealed to their native Justice and Magnanimity, and we have conjured them by the Ties of our common Kindred to disavow these Usurpations, which, would inevitably interrupt our Connections and Correspondence. They too have been deaf to the Voice of Justice and of Consanguinity. We must, therefore, acquiesce in the Necessity, which denounces our Separation, and hold them, as we hold the rest of Mankind, Enemies in War, in Peace, Friends.

WE, therefore, the Representatives of the UNITED STATES OF AMERICA, in GENERAL CONGRESS, Assembled, appealing to the Supreme Judge of the World for the Rectitude of our Intentions, do, in the Name, and by Authority of the good People of these Colonies, solemnly Publish and Declare, That these United Colonies are, and of Right ought to be, FREE AND INDEPENDENT STATES; that they are absolved from all Allegiance to the British Crown, and that all political Connection between them and the State of Great-Britain, is and ought to be totally dissolved; and that as FREE AND INDEPENDENT STATES, they have full Power to levy War, conclude Peace, contract Alliances, establish Commerce, and to do all other Acts and Things which INDEPENDENT STATES may of right do. And for the support of this Declaration, with a firm Reliance on the Protection of divine Providence, we mutually pledge to each other our Lives, our Fortunes, and our sacred Honor.

John Hancock	Charles Carroll	Geo. Taylor	Josiah Bartlett
Button Gwinnett	Of Carrollton	James Wilson	Wm. Whipple
Lyman Hall	George Wythe	Geo. Ross	Saml Adams
Geo Walton	Richard Henry Lee	Caesar Rodney	John Adams
Wm Hooper	Th Jefferson	Geo Read	Robt Treat Paine
Joseph Hewes	Benja Harrison	Tho M. Kean	Elbridge Gerry
John Penn	Thos Nelson Jr.	Wm Floyd	Step Hopkins
Edward Rutledge	Francis Lightfoot Lee	Phil. Livingston	William Ellery
Thos Heyward Junr.	Carter Braxton	Frans. Lewis	Roger Sherman
Thomas Lynch Junr.	Robt Morris	Lewis Morris	Samel Huntington
Arthur Middleton	Benjamin Rush	Richd. Stockton	Wm. Williams
Samuel Chase	Benja. Franklin	Jno Witherspoon	Oliver Wolcott
Wm. Paca	John Morton	Fras. Hopkinson	Matthew Thornton
Thos. Stone	Geo Clymer	John Hart	
	Jas. Smith	Abra Clark	

The United States Constitution

The pages that follow contain the original text of the United States Constitution. Sections that are no longer enforced have been crossed out. The spelling and punctuation of the document remain in their original format. The headings are not part of the original Constitution.

We the People of the United States, in Order to form a more perfect Union, establish Justice, insure domestic Tranquility, provide for the common defence, promote the general Welfare, and secure the Blessings of Liberty to ourselves and our Posterity, do ordain and establish this Constitution for the United States of America.

Article I
Legislative Branch

Section 1
Congress

All legislative Powers herein granted shall be vested in a Congress of the United States, which shall consist of a Senate and House of Representatives.

Section 2
House of Representatives

Clause 1: The House of Representatives shall be composed of Members chosen every second Year by the People of the several States, and the Electors in each State shall have the Qualifications requisite for Electors of the most numerous Branch of the State Legislature.

Clause 2: No Person shall be a Representative who shall not have attained to the Age of twenty five Years, and been seven Years a Citizen of the United States, and who shall not, when elected, be an Inhabitant of that State in which he shall be chosen.

Clause 3: Representatives and direct Taxes shall be apportioned among the several States which may be included within this Union, according to their respective Numbers, ~~which shall be determined by adding to the whole Number of free Persons, including those bound to Service for a Term of Years, and excluding Indians not taxed, three fifths of all other Persons.~~

The actual Enumeration shall be made within three Years after the first Meeting of the Congress of the United States, and within every subsequent Term of ten Years, in such Manner as they shall by Law direct.

The Number of Representatives shall not exceed one for every thirty Thousand, but each State shall have at Least one Representative; ~~and until such enumeration shall be made, the State of New Hampshire shall be entitled to chuse three, Massachusetts eight, Rhode-Island and Providence Plantations one, Connecticut five, New-York six, New Jersey four, Pennsylvania eight, Delaware one, Maryland six, Virginia ten, North Carolina five, South Carolina five, and Georgia three.~~

Clause 4: When vacancies happen in the Representation from any State, the Executive Authority thereof shall issue Writs of Election to fill such Vacancies.

Clause 5: The House of Representatives shall chuse their Speaker and other Officers; and shall have the sole Power of Impeachment.

Section 3
Senate

Clause 1: The Senate of the United States shall be composed of two Senators from each State, chosen ~~by the Legislature thereof,~~ for six Years; and each Senator shall have one Vote.

Clause 2: Immediately after they shall be assembled in Consequence of the first Election, they shall be divided as equally as may be into three Classes. The Seats of the Senators of the first Class shall be vacated at the Expiration of the second Year, of the second Class at the Expiration of the fourth Year, and of the third Class at the Expiration of the sixth Year, so that one third may be chosen every second Year; ~~and if Vacancies happen by Resignation, or otherwise, during the Recess of the Legislature of any State, the Executive thereof may make temporary Appointments until the next Meeting of the Legislature, which shall then fill such Vacancies.~~

Clause 3: No Person shall be a Senator who shall not have attained to the Age of thirty Years, and been nine Years a Citizen of the United States, and who shall not, when elected, be an Inhabitant of that State for which he shall be chosen.

Clause 4: The Vice President of the United States shall be President of the Senate, but shall have no Vote, unless they be equally divided.

Clause 5: The Senate shall chuse their other Officers, and also a President pro tempore, in the Absence of the Vice President, or when he shall exercise the Office of President of the United States.

Clause 6: The Senate shall have the sole Power to try all Impeachments. When sitting for that Purpose, they shall be on Oath or Affirmation. When the President of the United States is tried, the Chief Justice shall preside: And no Person shall be convicted without the Concurrence of two thirds of the Members present.

Clause 7: Judgment in Cases of Impeachment shall not extend further than to removal from Office, and disqualification to hold and enjoy any Office of honor, Trust or Profit under the United States: but the Party convicted shall nevertheless be liable and subject to Indictment, Trial, Judgment and Punishment, according to Law.

Section 4
Elections and Meetings

Clause 1: The Times, Places and Manner of holding Elections for Senators and Representatives, shall be prescribed in each State by the Legislature thereof; but the Congress may at any time by Law make or alter such Regulations, ~~except as to the Places of chusing Senators.~~

Clause 2: The Congress shall assemble at least once in every Year, ~~and such Meeting shall be on the first Monday in December, unless they shall by Law appoint a different Day.~~

Section 5
Rules of Procedure

Clause 1: Each House shall be the Judge of the Elections, Returns and Qualifications of its own Members, and a Majority of each shall constitute a Quorum to do Business; but a smaller Number may adjourn from day to day, and may be authorized to compel the Attendance of absent Members, in such Manner, and under such Penalties as each House may provide.

Clause 2: Each House may determine the Rules of its Proceedings, punish its Members for disorderly Behaviour, and, with the Concurrence of two thirds, expel a Member.

Clause 3: Each House shall keep a Journal of its Proceedings, and from time to time publish the same, excepting such Parts as may in their Judgment require Secrecy; and the Yeas and

Nays of the Members of either House on any question shall, at the Desire of one fifth of those Present, be entered on the Journal.

Clause 4: Neither House, during the Session of Congress, shall, without the Consent of the other, adjourn for more than three days, nor to any other Place than that in which the two Houses shall be sitting.

Section 6
Privileges and Restrictions

Clause 1: The Senators and Representatives shall receive a Compensation for their Services, to be ascertained by Law, and paid out of the Treasury of the United States. They shall in all Cases, except Treason, Felony and Breach of the Peace, be privileged from Arrest during their Attendance at the Session of their respective Houses, and in going to and returning from the same; and for any Speech or Debate in either House, they shall not be questioned in any other Place.

Clause 2: No Senator or Representative shall, during the Time for which he was elected, be appointed to any civil Office under the Authority of the United States, which shall have been created, or the Emoluments whereof shall have been encreased during such time; and no Person holding any Office under the United States, shall be a Member of either House during his Continuance in Office.

Section 7
How Bills Become Laws

Clause 1: All Bills for raising Revenue shall originate in the House of Representatives; but the Senate may propose or concur with Amendments as on other Bills.

Clause 2: Every Bill which shall have passed the House of Representatives and the Senate, shall, before it become a Law, be presented to the President of the United States; If he approve he shall sign it, but if not he shall return it, with his Objections to that House

in which it shall have originated, who shall enter the Objections at large on their Journal, and proceed to reconsider it. If after such Reconsideration two thirds of that House shall agree to pass the Bill, it shall be sent, together with the Objections, to the other House, by which it shall likewise be reconsidered, and if approved by two thirds of that House, it shall become a Law. But in all such Cases the Votes of both Houses shall be determined by yeas and Nays, and the Names of the Persons voting for and against the Bill shall be entered on the Journal of each House respectively.

If any Bill shall not be returned by the President within ten Days (Sundays excepted) after it shall have been presented to him, the Same shall be a Law, in like Manner as if he had signed it, unless the Congress by their Adjournment prevent its Return, in which Case it shall not be a Law.

Clause 3: Every Order, Resolution, or Vote to which the Concurrence of the Senate and House of Representatives may be necessary (except on a question of Adjournment) shall be presented to the President of the United States; and before the Same shall take Effect, shall be approved by him, or being disapproved by him, shall be repassed by two thirds of the Senate and House of Representatives, according to the Rules and Limitations prescribed in the Case of a Bill.

Section 8
Powers of Congress

Clause 1: The Congress shall have Power To lay and collect Taxes, Duties, Imposts and Excises, to pay the Debts and provide for the common Defence and general Welfare of the United States; but all Duties, Imposts and Excises shall be uniform throughout the United States;

Clause 2: To borrow Money on the credit of the United States;

Clause 3: To regulate Commerce with foreign Nations, and among the several States, and with the Indian Tribes;

Clause 4: To establish an uniform Rule of Naturalization, and uniform Laws on the subject of Bankruptcies throughout the United States;

Clause 5: To coin Money, regulate the Value thereof, and of foreign Coin, and fix the Standard of Weights and Measures;

Clause 6: To provide for the Punishment of counterfeiting the Securities and current Coin of the United States;

Clause 7: To establish Post Offices and post Roads;

Clause 8: To promote the Progress of Science and useful Arts, by securing for limited Times to Authors and Inventors the exclusive Right to their respective Writings and Discoveries;

Clause 9: To constitute Tribunals inferior to the supreme Court;

Clause 10: To define and punish Piracies and Felonies committed on the high Seas, and Offences against the Law of Nations;

Clause 11: To declare War, grant Letters of Marque and Reprisal, and make Rules concerning Captures on Land and Water;

Clause 12: To raise and support Armies, but no Appropriation of Money to that Use shall be for a longer Term than two Years;

Clause 13: To provide and maintain a Navy;

Clause 14: To make Rules for the Government and Regulation of the land and naval Forces;

Clause 15: To provide for calling forth the Militia to execute the Laws of the Union, suppress Insurrections and repel Invasions;

Clause 16: To provide for organizing, arming, and disciplining, the Militia, and for governing such Part of them as may be employed in the Service of the United States, reserving to the States respectively, the Appointment of the Officers, and the Authority of training the Militia according to the discipline prescribed by Congress;

Clause 17: To exercise exclusive Legislation in all Cases whatsoever, over such District (not exceeding ten Miles square) as may, by Cession of particular States, and the Acceptance of Congress, become the Seat of the Government of the United States, and to exercise like Authority over all Places purchased by the Consent of the Legislature of the State in which the Same shall be, for the Erection of Forts, Magazines, Arsenals, dock-Yards, and other needful Buildings;—And

Clause 18: To make all Laws which shall be necessary and proper for carrying into Execution the foregoing Powers, and all other Powers vested by this Constitution in the Government of the United States, or in any Department or Officer thereof.

Section 9
Powers Denied to the Federal Government

Clause 1: ~~The Migration or Importation of such Persons as any of the States now existing shall think proper to admit, shall not be prohibited by the Congress prior to the Year one thousand eight hundred and eight, but a Tax or duty may be imposed on such Importation, not exceeding ten dollars for each Person.~~

Clause 2: The Privilege of the Writ of Habeas Corpus shall not be suspended, unless when in Cases of Rebellion or Invasion the public Safety may require it.

Clause 3: No Bill of Attainder or ex post facto Law shall be passed.

Clause 4: No Capitation, or other direct, Tax shall be laid, unless in Proportion to the Census or Enumeration herein before directed to be taken.

Clause 5: No Tax or Duty shall be laid on Articles exported from any State.

Clause 6: No Preference shall be given by any Regulation of Commerce or Revenue to the Ports of one State over those of another: nor shall Vessels bound to, or from, one State, be obliged to enter, clear, or pay Duties in another.

Clause 7: No Money shall be drawn from the Treasury, but in Consequence of Appropriations made by Law; and a regular Statement and Account of the Receipts and Expenditures of all public Money shall be published from time to time.

Clause 8: No Title of Nobility shall be granted by the United States: And no Person holding any Office of Profit or Trust under them, shall, without the Consent of the Congress, accept of any present, Emolument, Office, or Title, of any kind whatever, from any King, Prince, or foreign State.

Section 10
Powers Denied to the States

Clause 1: No State shall enter into any Treaty, Alliance, or Confederation; grant Letters of Marque and Reprisal; coin Money; emit Bills of Credit; make any Thing but gold and silver Coin a Tender in Payment of Debts; pass any Bill of Attainder, ex post facto Law, or Law impairing the Obligation of Contracts, or grant any Title of Nobility.

Clause 2: No State shall, without the Consent of the Congress, lay any Imposts or Duties on Imports or Exports, except what may be absolutely necessary for executing it's inspection Laws: and the net Produce of all Duties and Imposts, laid by any State on Imports or Exports, shall be for the Use of the Treasury of the United States; and all such Laws shall be subject to the Revision and Controul of the Congress.

Clause 3: No State shall, without the Consent of Congress, lay any Duty of Tonnage, keep Troops, or Ships of War in time of Peace, enter into any Agreement or Compact with another State, or with a

foreign Power, or engage in War, unless actually invaded, or in such imminent Danger as will not admit of delay.

Article II Executive Branch

Section 1
President and Vice-President

Clause 1: The executive Power shall be vested in a President of the United States of America. He shall hold his Office during the Term of four Years, and, together with the Vice President, chosen for the same Term, be elected, as follows

Clause 2: Each State shall appoint, in such Manner as the Legislature thereof may direct, a Number of Electors, equal to the whole Number of Senators and Representatives to which the State may be entitled in the Congress: but no Senator or Representative, or Person holding an Office of Trust or Profit under the United States, shall be appointed an Elector.

Clause 3: ~~The Electors shall meet in their respective States, and vote by Ballot for two Persons, of whom one at least shall not be an Inhabitant of the same State with themselves. And they shall make a List of all the Persons voted for, and of the Number of Votes for each; which List they shall sign and certify, and transmit sealed to the Seat of the Government of the United States, directed to the President of the Senate. The President of the Senate shall, in the Presence of the Senate and House of Representatives, open all the Certificates, and the Votes shall then be counted. The Person having the greatest Number of Votes shall be the President, if such Number be a Majority of the whole Number of Electors appointed; and if there be more than one who have such Majority, and have an equal Number of Votes, then the House of Representatives shall immediately chuse by Ballot one of them for President; and if no Person have a Majority, then from the five highest on the~~

~~List the said House shall in like Manner chuse the President. But in chusing the President, the Votes shall be taken by States, the Representation from each State having one Vote; A quorum for this Purpose shall consist of a Member or Members from two thirds of the States, and a Majority of all the States shall be necessary to a Choice. In every Case, after the Choice of the President, the Person having the greatest Number of Votes of the Electors shall be the Vice President. But if there should remain two or more who have equal Votes, the Senate shall chuse from them by Ballot the Vice President.~~

Clause 4: The Congress may determine the Time of chusing the Electors, and the Day on which they shall give their Votes; which Day shall be the same throughout the United States.

Clause 5: No Person except a natural born Citizen, or a Citizen of the United States, at the time of the Adoption of this Constitution, shall be eligible to the Office of President; neither shall any Person be eligible to that Office who shall not have attained to the Age of thirty five Years, and been fourteen Years a Resident within the United States.

Clause 6: ~~In Case of the Removal of the President from Office, or of his Death, Resignation, or Inability to discharge the Powers and Duties of the said Office, the Same shall devolve on the Vice President, and~~ the Congress may by Law provide for the Case of Removal, Death, Resignation or Inability, both of the President and Vice President, declaring what Officer shall then act as President, and such Officer shall act accordingly, until the Disability be removed, or a President shall be elected.

Clause 7: The President shall, at stated Times, receive for his Services, a Compensation, which shall neither be encreased nor diminished during the Period for which he shall have been elected, and he shall not receive within that Period any other Emolument from the United States, or any of them.

Clause 8: Before he enter on the Execution of his Office, he shall take the following Oath or Affirmation:—"I do solemnly swear (or affirm) that I will faithfully execute the Office of President of the United States, and will to the best of my Ability, preserve, protect and defend the Constitution of the United States."

Section 2
Powers of the President

Clause 1: The President shall be Commander in Chief of the Army and Navy of the United States, and of the Militia of the several States, when called into the actual Service of the United States; he may require the Opinion, in writing, of the principal Officer in each of the executive Departments, upon any Subject relating to the Duties of their respective Offices, and he shall have Power to grant Reprieves and Pardons for Offences against the United States, except in Cases of Impeachment.

Clause 2: He shall have Power, by and with the Advice and Consent of the Senate, to make Treaties, provided two thirds of the Senators present concur; and he shall nominate, and by and with the Advice and Consent of the Senate, shall appoint Ambassadors, other public Ministers and Consuls, Judges of the supreme Court, and all other Officers of the United States, whose Appointments are not herein otherwise provided for, and which shall be established by Law: but the Congress may by Law vest the Appointment of such inferior Officers, as they think proper, in the President alone, in the Courts of Law, or in the Heads of Departments.

Clause 3: The President shall have Power to fill up all Vacancies that may happen during the Recess of the Senate, by granting Commissions which shall expire at the End of their next Session.

Section 3
Duties of the President

He shall from time to time give to the Congress Information of the State of the Union, and recommend to their Consideration such Measures as he shall judge necessary and expedient; he may, on extraordinary Occasions, convene both Houses, or either of them, and in Case of Disagreement between them, with Respect to the Time of Adjournment, he may adjourn them to such Time as he shall think proper; he shall receive Ambassadors and other public Ministers; he shall take Care that the Laws be faithfully executed, and shall Commission all the Officers of the United States.

Section 4
Impeachment

The President, Vice President and all civil Officers of the United States, shall be removed from Office on Impeachment for, and Conviction of, Treason, Bribery, or other high Crimes and Misdemeanors.

Article III
Judicial Branch

Section 1
Federal Courts

The judicial Power of the United States, shall be vested in one supreme Court, and in such inferior Courts as the Congress may from time to time ordain and establish. The Judges, both of the supreme and inferior Courts, shall hold their Offices during good Behaviour, and shall, at stated Times, receive for their Services, a Compensation, which shall not be diminished during their Continuance in Office.

Section 2
Extent of Judicial Powers

Clause 1: The judicial Power shall extend to all Cases, in Law and Equity, arising under this Constitution, the Laws of the United States, and Treaties made, or which shall be made, under their Authority;—to all Cases affecting Ambassadors, other public Ministers and Consuls;—to all Cases of admiralty and maritime Jurisdiction;—to Controversies to which the United States shall be a Party;—to Controversies between two or more States;—between a State and Citizens of another State; —between Citizens of different States, —between Citizens of the same State claiming Lands under Grants of different States, and between a State, or the Citizens thereof, and foreign States, Citizens or Subjects.

Clause 2: In all Cases affecting Ambassadors, other public Ministers and Consuls, and those in which a State shall be Party, the supreme Court shall have original Jurisdiction. In all the other Cases before mentioned, the supreme Court shall have appellate Jurisdiction, both as to Law and Fact, with such Exceptions, and under such Regulations as the Congress shall make.

Clause 3: The Trial of all Crimes, except in Cases of Impeachment, shall be by Jury; and such Trial shall be held in the State where the said Crimes shall have been committed; but when not committed within any State, the Trial shall be at such Place or Places as the Congress may by Law have directed.

Section 3
Treason

Clause 1: Treason against the United States, shall consist only in levying War against them, or in adhering to their Enemies, giving them Aid and Comfort. No Person shall be convicted of Treason unless on the Testimony of two Witnesses to the same overt Act, or on Confession in open Court.

Clause 2: The Congress shall have Power to declare the Punishment of Treason, but no Attainder of Treason shall work Corruption of Blood, or Forfeiture except during the Life of the Person attainted.

Article IV
The States

Section 1
Recognition of Each Other's Acts

Full Faith and Credit shall be given in each State to the public Acts, Records, and judicial Proceedings of every other State. And the Congress may by general Laws prescribe the Manner in which such Acts, Records and Proceedings shall be proved, and the Effect thereof.

Section 2
Citizens' Rights in Other States

Clause 1: The Citizens of each State shall be entitled to all Privileges and Immunities of Citizens in the several States.

Clause 2: A Person charged in any State with Treason, Felony, or other Crime, who shall flee from Justice, and be found in another State, shall on Demand of the executive Authority of the State from which he fled, be delivered up, to be removed to the State having Jurisdiction of the Crime.

Clause 3: ~~No Person held to Service or Labour in one State, under the Laws thereof, escaping into another, shall, in Consequence of any Law or Regulation therein, be discharged from such Service or Labour, but shall be delivered up on Claim of the Party to whom such Service or Labour may be due.~~

Section 3
New States and Territories

Clause 1: New States may be admitted by the Congress into this Union; but no new State shall be formed or erected within the Jurisdiction of any other State; nor any State be formed by the Junction of two or more States, or Parts of States, without the Consent of the Legislatures of the States concerned as well as of the Congress.

Clause 2: The Congress shall have Power to dispose of and make all needful Rules and Regulations respecting the Territory or other Property belonging to the United States; and nothing in this Constitution shall be so construed as to Prejudice any Claims of the United States, or of any particular State.

Section 4
Guarantees to the States

The United States shall guarantee to every State in this Union a Republican Form of Government, and shall protect each of them against Invasion; and on Application of the Legislature, or of the Executive (when the Legislature cannot be convened) against domestic Violence.

Article V
Amending the Constitution

The Congress, whenever two thirds of both Houses shall deem it necessary, shall propose Amendments to this Constitution, or, on the Application of the Legislatures of two thirds of the several States, shall call a Convention for proposing Amendments, which, in either Case, shall be valid to all Intents and Purposes, as Part of this Constitution, when ratified by the Legislatures of three fourths of the several States, or by Conventions in three fourths thereof, as the one or the other Mode of Ratification may be proposed by the Congress; Provided ~~that no Amendment which may be made prior to the Year One thousand eight hundred and eight shall in any Manner affect the first and fourth Clauses in the Ninth Section of the first Article; and~~ that no State, without its Consent, shall be deprived of its equal Suffrage in the Senate.

Article VI
National Supremacy

Clause 1: All Debts contracted and Engagements entered into, before the Adoption of this Constitution, shall be as

valid against the United States under this Constitution, as under the Confederation.

Clause 2: This Constitution, and the Laws of the United States which shall be made in Pursuance thereof; and all Treaties made, or which shall be made, under the Authority of the United States, shall be the supreme Law of the Land; and the Judges in every State shall be bound thereby, any Thing in the Constitution or Laws of any State to the Contrary notwithstanding.

Clause 3: The Senators and Representatives before mentioned, and the Members of the several State Legislatures, and all executive and judicial Officers, both of the United States and of the several States, shall be bound by Oath or Affirmation, to support this Constitution; but no religious Test shall ever be required as a Qualification to any Office or public Trust under the United States.

Article VII
Ratification

The Ratification of the Conventions of nine States, shall be sufficient for the Establishment of this Constitution between the States so ratifying the Same. Done in Convention by the Unanimous Consent of the States present the Seventeenth Day of September in the Year of our Lord one thousand seven hundred and Eighty seven and of the Independence of the United States of America the Twelfth In witness whereof We have hereunto subscribed our Names,

———————————————

George Washington, President and Deputy from Virginia

Delaware
George Read
Gunning Bedford, Junior
John Dickinson
Richard Bassett
Jacob Broom

Maryland
James McHenry
Daniel of St. Thomas Jenifer
Daniel Carroll

Virginia
John Blair
James Madison, Junior

North Carolina
William Blount
Richard Dobbs Spaight
Hugh Williamson

South Carolina
John Rutledge
Charles Cotesworth Pinckney
Charles Pinckney
Pierce Butler.

Georgia
William Few
Abraham Baldwin

New Hampshire
John Langdon
Nicholas Gilman

Massachusetts
Nathaniel Gorham
Rufus King

Connecticut
William Samuel Johnson
Roger Sherman

New York
Alexander Hamilton

New Jersey
William Livingston
David Brearley
William Paterson.
Jonathan Dayton

Pennsylvania
Benjamin Franklin
Thomas Mifflin
Robert Morris
George Clymer
Thomas FitzSimons
Jared Ingersoll
James Wilson
Gouverneur Morris
Attest: William Jackson, Secretary

Amendments to the Constitution

The pages that follow contain the original text of the Amendments to the United States Constitution. Sections that are no longer enforced have been crossed out. The spelling and punctuation of the document remain in their original format. The headings are not part of the original Amendments.

Amendment 1 (1791)
Religious and Political Freedom

Congress shall make no law respecting an establishment of religion, or prohibiting the free exercise thereof; or abridging the freedom of speech, or of the press; or the right of the people peaceably to assemble, and to petition the Government for a redress of grievances.

Amendment 2 (1791)
Right to Bear Arms

A well regulated Militia, being necessary to the security of a free State, the right of the people to keep and bear Arms, shall not be infringed.

Amendment 3 (1791)
Quartering of Soldiers

No Soldier shall, in time of peace be quartered in any house, without the consent of the Owner, nor in time of war, but in a manner to be prescribed by law.

Amendment 4 (1791)
Search and Seizure

The right of the people to be secure in their persons, houses, papers, and effects, against unreasonable searches and seizures, shall not be violated, and no Warrants shall issue, but upon probable cause, supported by Oath or affirmation, and particularly describing the place to be searched, and the persons or things to be seized.

Amendment 5 (1791)
Life, Liberty, and Property

No person shall be held to answer for a capital, or otherwise infamous crime, unless on a presentment or indictment of a Grand Jury, except in cases arising in the land or naval forces, or in the Militia, when in actual service in time of War or public danger; nor shall any person be subject for the same offence to be twice put in jeopardy of life or limb; nor shall be compelled in any criminal case to be a witness against himself, nor be deprived of life, liberty, or property, without due process of law; nor shall private property be taken for public use, without just compensation.

Amendment 6 (1791)
Rights of the Accused

In all criminal prosecutions, the accused shall enjoy the right to a speedy and public trial, by an impartial jury of the State and district wherein the crime shall have been committed, which district shall have been previously ascertained by law, and to be informed of the nature and cause of the accusation; to be confronted with the witnesses against him; to have compulsory process for obtaining witnesses in his favor, and to have the Assistance of Counsel for his defence.

Amendment 7 (1791)
Right to Trial by Jury

In Suits at common law, where the value in controversy shall exceed twenty dollars, the right of trial by jury shall be preserved, and no fact tried by a jury, shall be otherwise re-examined in any Court of the United States, than according to the rules of the common law.

Amendment 8 (1791)
Bail and Punishment

Excessive bail shall not be required, nor excessive fines imposed, nor cruel and unusual punishments inflicted.

Amendment 9 (1791)
All Other Rights

The enumeration in the Constitution, of certain rights, shall not be construed to deny or disparage others retained by the people.

Amendment 10 (1791)
Rights of States and the People

The powers not delegated to the United States by the Constitution, nor prohibited by it to the States, are reserved to the States respectively, or to the people.

Amendment 11 (1795)
Suits Against a State

The Judicial power of the United States shall not be construed to extend to any suit in law or equity, commenced or prosecuted against one of the United States by Citizens of another State, or by Citizens or Subjects of any Foreign State.

Amendment 12 (1804)
Election of President

The Electors shall meet in their respective states, and vote by ballot for President and Vice-President, one of whom, at least, shall not be an inhabitant of the same state with themselves; they shall name in their ballots the person voted for as President, and in distinct ballots the person voted for as Vice-President, and they shall make distinct lists of all persons voted for as President, and of all persons voted for as Vice-President, and of the number of votes for each, which lists they shall sign and certify, and transmit sealed to the seat of the government of the United States, directed to the President of the Senate;

The President of the Senate shall, in the presence of the Senate and House of Representatives, open all the certificates and the votes shall then be counted;

The person having the greatest number of votes for President, shall be the President, if such number be a majority of the whole number of Electors appointed; and if no person have such majority, then from the persons having the highest numbers not exceeding three on the list of those voted for as President, the House of Representatives shall choose immediately, by ballot, the President. But in choosing the President, the votes shall be taken by states, the representation from each state having one vote; a quorum for this purpose shall consist of a member or members from two-thirds of the states, and a majority of all the states shall be necessary to a choice.

~~And if the House of Representatives shall not choose a President whenever the right of choice shall devolve upon them, before the fourth day of March next following, then the Vice-President shall act as President, as in the case of the death or other constitutional disability of the President.~~

The person having the greatest number of votes as Vice-President, shall be the Vice-President, if such number be a majority of the whole number of Electors appointed, and if no person have a majority, then from the two highest numbers on the list, the Senate shall choose the Vice-President; a quorum for the purpose shall consist of two-thirds of the whole number of Senators, and a majority of the whole number shall be necessary to a choice. But no person constitutionally ineligible to the office of

President shall be eligible to that of Vice-President of the United States.

Amendment 13   (1865)
Abolition of Slavery

Section 1 Neither slavery nor involuntary servitude, except as a punishment for crime whereof the party shall have been duly convicted, shall exist within the United States, or any place subject to their jurisdiction.

Section 2 Congress shall have power to enforce this article by appropriate legislation.

Amendment 14   (1868)
Civil Rights in the States

Section 1 All persons born or naturalized in the United States, and subject to the jurisdiction thereof, are citizens of the United States and of the State wherein they reside. No State shall make or enforce any law which shall abridge the privileges or immunities of citizens of the United States; nor shall any State deprive any person of life, liberty, or property, without due process of law; nor deny to any person within its jurisdiction the equal protection of the laws.

Section 2 Representatives shall be apportioned among the several States according to their respective numbers, counting the whole number of persons in each State, excluding Indians not taxed. But when the right to vote at any election for the choice of electors for President and Vice President of the United States, Representatives in Congress, the Executive and Judicial officers of a State, or the members of the Legislature thereof, is denied to any of the male inhabitants of such State, being twenty-one years of age, (See Note 15) and citizens of the United States, or in any way abridged, except for participation in rebellion, or other crime, the basis of representation therein shall be reduced in the proportion which the number of such male citizens shall bear to the whole number of male citizens twenty-one years of age in such State.

Section 3 No person shall be a Senator or Representative in Congress, or elector of President and Vice President, or hold any office, civil or military, under the United States, or under any State, who, having previously taken an oath, as a member of Congress, or as an officer of the United States, or as a member of any State legislature, or as an executive or judicial officer of any State, to support the Constitution of the United States, shall have engaged in insurrection or rebellion against the same, or given aid or comfort to the enemies thereof. But Congress may by a vote of two-thirds of each House, remove such disability.

Section 4 The validity of the public debt of the United States, authorized by law, including debts incurred for payment of pensions and bounties for services in suppressing insurrection or rebellion, shall not be questioned. But neither the United States nor any State shall assume or pay any debt or obligation incurred in aid of insurrection or rebellion against the United States, or any claim for the loss or emancipation of any slave; but all such debts, obligations and claims shall be held illegal and void.

Section 5 The Congress shall have power to enforce, by appropriate legislation, the provisions of this article.

Amendment 15   (1870)
Black Suffrage

Section 1 The right of citizens of the United States to vote shall not be denied or abridged by the United States or by any State on account of race, color, or previous condition of servitude.

Section 2 The Congress shall have power to enforce this article by appropriate legislation.

Amendment 16   (1913)
Income Tax

The Congress shall have power to lay and collect taxes on incomes, from whatever source derived, without apportionment among the several States, and without regard to any census or enumeration.

Amendment 17   (1919)
Direct Election of Senators

Section 1 The Senate of the United States shall be composed of two Senators from each State, elected by the people thereof, for six years; and each Senator shall have one vote. The electors in each State shall have the qualifications requisite for electors of the most numerous branch of the State legislatures.

Section 2 When vacancies happen in the representation of any State in the Senate, the executive authority of such State shall issue writs of election to fill such vacancies: Provided, That the legislature of any State may empower the executive thereof to make temporary appointments until the people fill the vacancies by election as the legislature may direct.

Section 3 This amendment shall not be so construed as to affect the election or term of any Senator chosen before it becomes valid as part of the Constitution.

Amendment 18   (1919)
National Prohibition

Section 1 ~~After one year from the ratification of this article the manufacture, sale, or transportation of intoxicating liquors within, the importation thereof into, or the exportation thereof from the United States and all territory subject to the jurisdiction thereof for beverage purposes is hereby prohibited.~~

Section 2 ~~The Congress and the several States shall have concurrent power to enforce this article by appropriate legislation.~~

Section 3 ~~This article shall be inoperative unless it shall have been ratified as an~~ ~~amendment to the Constitution by the legislatures of the several States, as provided in the Constitution, within seven years from the date of the submission hereof to the States by the Congress.~~

Amendment 19   (1920)
Women's Suffrage

The right of citizens of the United States to vote shall not be denied or abridged by the United States or by any State on account of sex.

Congress shall have power to enforce this article by appropriate legislation.

Amendment 20   (1933)
"Lame-Duck" Amendment

Section 1 The terms of the President and Vice President shall end at noon on the 20th day of January, and the terms of Senators and Representatives at noon on the 3d day of January, of the years in which such terms would have ended if this article had not been ratified; and the terms of their successors shall then begin.

Section 2 The Congress shall assemble at least once in every year, and such meeting shall begin at noon on the 3d day of January, unless they shall by law appoint a different day.

Section 3 If, at the time fixed for the beginning of the term of the President, the President elect shall have died, the Vice President elect shall become President. If a President shall not have been chosen before the time fixed for the beginning of his term, or if the President elect shall have failed to qualify, then the Vice President elect shall act as President until a President shall have qualified; and the Congress may by law provide for the case wherein neither a President elect nor a Vice President elect shall have qualified, declaring who shall then act as President, or the manner in which one who is to act shall be selected, and such person shall act accordingly until a President or Vice President shall have qualified.

Section 4 The Congress may by law provide for the case of the death of any of the persons from whom the House of Representatives may choose a President whenever the right of choice shall have devolved upon them, and for the case of the death of any of the persons from whom the Senate may choose a Vice President whenever the right of choice shall have devolved upon them.

Section 5 Sections 1 and 2 shall take effect on the 15th day of October following the ratification of this article.

Section 6 This article shall be inoperative unless it shall have been ratified as an amendment to the Constitution by the legislatures of three-fourths of the several States within seven years from the date of its submission.

Amendment 21   (1933)
Repeal of Prohibition

Section 1 The eighteenth article of amendment to the Constitution of the United States is hereby repealed.

Section 2 The transportation or importation into any State, Territory, or possession of the United States for delivery or use therein of intoxicating liquors, in violation of the laws thereof, is hereby prohibited.

Section 3 This article shall be inoperative unless it shall have been ratified as an amendment to the Constitution by conventions in the several States, as provided in the Constitution, within seven years from the date of the submission hereof to the States by the Congress.

Amendment 22   (1951)
Presidential Term of Office

Section 1 No person shall be elected to the office of the President more than twice, and no person who has held the office of

President, or acted as President, for more than two years of a term to which some other person was elected President shall be elected to the office of the President more than once. ~~But this article shall not apply to any person holding the office of President when this article was proposed by the Congress, and shall not prevent any person who may be holding the office of President, or acting as President, during the term within which this article becomes operative from holding the office of President or acting as President during the remainder of such term.~~

Section 2 This article shall be inoperative unless it shall have been ratified as an amendment to the Constitution by the legislatures of three-fourths of the several states within seven years from the date of its submission to the states by the Congress.

Amendment 23   (1961)
Voting in the District of Columbia

Section 1 The District constituting the seat of government of the United States shall appoint in such manner as the Congress may direct:

A number of electors of President and Vice President equal to the whole number of Senators and Representatives in Congress to which the District would be entitled if it were a state, but in no event more than the least populous state; they shall be in addition to those appointed by the states, but they shall be considered, for the purposes of the election of President and Vice President, to be electors appointed by a state; and they shall meet in the District and perform such duties as provided by the twelfth article of amendment.

Section 2 The Congress shall have power to enforce this article by appropriate legislation.

Amendment 24   (1964)
Abolition of Poll Taxes

Section 1 The right of citizens of the United States to vote in any primary or other election for President or Vice President, for

electors for President or Vice President, or for Senator or Representative in Congress, shall not be denied or abridged by the United States or any state by reason of failure to pay any poll tax or other tax.

Section 2 The Congress shall have power to enforce this article by appropriate legislation.

Amendment 25 (1967)
Presidential Disability and Succession

Section 1 In case of the removal of the President from office or of his death or resignation, the Vice President shall become President.

Section 2 Whenever there is a vacancy in the office of the Vice President, the President shall nominate a Vice President who shall take office upon confirmation by a majority vote of both Houses of Congress.

Section 3 Whenever the President transmits to the President pro tempore of the Senate and the Speaker of the House of Representatives his written declaration that he is unable to discharge the powers and duties of his office, and until he transmits to them a written declaration to the contrary, such powers and duties shall be discharged by the Vice President as Acting President.

Section 4 Whenever the Vice President and a majority of either the principal officers of the executive departments or of such other body as Congress may by law provide, transmit to the President pro tempore of the Senate and the Speaker of the House of Representatives their written declaration that the President is unable to discharge the powers and duties of his office, the Vice President shall immediately assume the powers and duties of the office as Acting President.

Thereafter, when the President transmits to the President pro tempore of the Senate and

the Speaker of the House of Representatives his written declaration that no inability exists, he shall resume the powers and duties of his office unless the Vice President and a majority of either the principal officers of the executive department or of such other body as Congress may by law provide, transmit within four days to the President pro tempore of the Senate and the Speaker of the House of Representatives their written declaration that the President is unable to discharge the powers and duties of his office. Thereupon Congress shall decide the issue, assembling within forty-eight hours for that purpose if not in session. If the Congress, within twenty-one days after receipt of the latter written declaration, or, if Congress is not in session, within twenty-one days after Congress is required to assemble, determines by two-thirds vote of both Houses that the President is unable to discharge the powers and duties of his office, the Vice President shall continue to discharge the same as Acting President; otherwise, the President shall resume the powers and duties of his office.

Amendment 26 (1971)
Eighteen-Year-Old Vote

Section 1 The right of citizens of the United States, who are 18 years of age or older, to vote, shall not be denied or abridged by the United States or any state on account of age.

Section 2 The Congress shall have the power to enforce this article by appropriate legislation.

Amendment 27 (1992)
Congressional Salaries

No law varying the compensation for the services of the Senators and Representatives shall take effect until an election of Representatives shall have intervened.

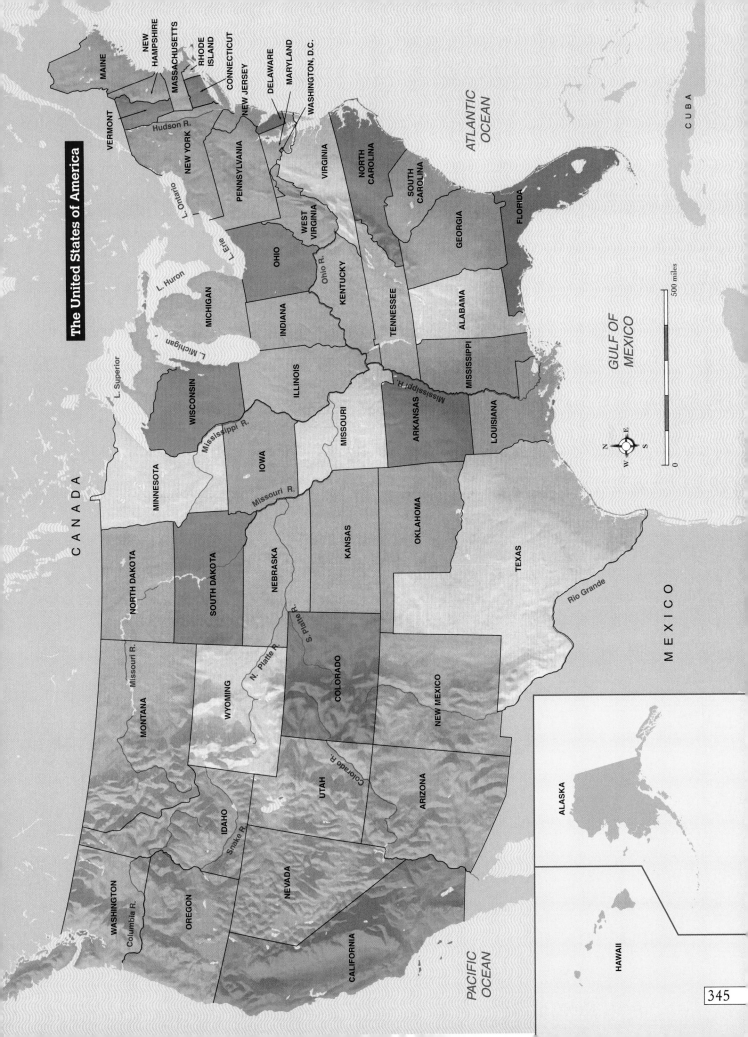

The United States of America

MAINE
NEW HAMPSHIRE
MASSACHUSETTS
RHODE ISLAND
CONNECTICUT
NEW JERSEY
DELAWARE
MARYLAND
WASHINGTON, D.C.

VERMONT
Hudson R.
NEW YORK
PENNSYLVANIA
VIRGINIA
NORTH CAROLINA
SOUTH CAROLINA
ATLANTIC OCEAN
CUBA

L. Ontario
L. Erie
WEST VIRGINIA
OHIO
Ohio R.
KENTUCKY
TENNESSEE
GEORGIA
ALABAMA
FLORIDA

L. Huron
L. Michigan
MICHIGAN
INDIANA
ILLINOIS
MISSISSIPPI
GULF OF MEXICO

L. Superior
WISCONSIN
Mississippi R.
IOWA
MISSOURI
Mississippi R.
ARKANSAS
LOUISIANA

CANADA
MINNESOTA
Missouri R.
NEBRASKA
KANSAS
OKLAHOMA
TEXAS

NORTH DAKOTA
SOUTH DAKOTA
Missouri R.
N. Platte R.
S. Platte R.
COLORADO
NEW MEXICO
Rio Grande
MEXICO

MONTANA
WYOMING
UTAH
Colorado R.
ARIZONA

WASHINGTON
Columbia R.
OREGON
IDAHO
Snake R.
NEVADA
CALIFORNIA

PACIFIC OCEAN

N
W E
S

500 miles
0

ALASKA
HAWAII

345

The World

Glossary/Index

Vocabulary definitions are shown in bold type.

Voting rights
property and, 222
for women, 255

W

Wagon roads—roads or dirt paths made for wagons heading west, 203

Walden (Thoreau), 257, 258

Wampanoag Indians, King Philip's War and, 89

War Department, 172

War for Independence. *See* American Revolution

War Hawks—senators who helped persuade Congress to declare war against Great Britain in 1812, 196

War of 1812, 169, 196–197, 196 (map)
events leading to, 195–196
expansion after, 200–201

Wars and warfare. *See also* Battles; specific wars
British-Native American, 107
French and Indian War, 106–107
with Mexico, 263
among Native Americans, 11
in Ohio Valley, 105–106
between Pequots and settlers, 89
settler-Native American, 82
with Tripoli, 193
Yamasee Border War, 83

Washington (state), 281

Washington, D.C.
Jefferson's inauguration in, 187
in War of 1812, 197

Washington, George, 145, 168
in American Revolution, 132
Continental Army and, 123, 124, 130–131
farewell address of, 180
Hamilton and, 179
inaugurations of, 171, 172
Jay's Treaty and, 178
Ohio Valley fighting and, 105–106
Pinckney, Eliza, and, 75
as president, 171
ratification of Constitution and, 149
at Valley Forge, 130, 131
Wheatley, Phillis, and, 96

Wayne, Anthony, 178

Wealth, equality and, 222

Wealthy
music and, 99
in Northeast cities, 97

Webster, Daniel, 297

West
Civil War in, 313, 321 (map)
cultures of, 15–17
land cessions in, 140, 141 (map)
Northwest Territory and, 142
paintings of, 259
Plains Peoples in, 15
routes to, 212 (map)
settlement in, 108, 114
Union forces in, 313–314
War of 1812 and, 195

West, Benjamin, 141

Western Hemisphere
Europeans in, 36
exploration of, 2
Monroe Doctrine and, 218
Spanish colonies in, 39–45

West Indies
rum/molasses trade and, 78
slaves in, 78
tobacco from, 71

West Jersey, 64

West Point, 132

West Virginia, 312

Westward expansion, 201, 202–205
manifest destiny and, 278–281
slavery crisis and, 292
territorial acquisition and, 281

Wharves(wharf)—the location where ships dock in port, 270

Wheat, in South, 236

Wheatley, Phillis, 96, 99

Whig Party, 301

Whigs, Northern ("Conscience"), 301

Whipping, of slaves, 238, 239

Whiskey, excise tax on, 176

Whiskey Rebellion—the 1794 rebellion of Pennsylvania farmers who refused to pay the excise tax on whiskey, 176

Whitefield, George, 90

White House, in War of 1812, 197

White Plains, battle at, 130

Whites
lower class southerners, 237
in Ohio Valley, 206
in South, 236–237
as unfree workers, 76–77

Whitman, Walt, 258

Whitney, Eli, 193, 235

Wigwams—Native American dwellings usually made with an arched or cone-like framework covered with bark, mats, or hides, 13

Wilderness, The, Battle of, 322

Wilderness Road, 203

Williams, Roger, 61

Wilmot, David, 286–287

Wilmot Proviso—a resolution of 1846 that said that slavery would not be allowed in any territory acquired from Mexico, 287

Winthrop, John, 60

Witch trials, in Salem, 90

Women
abolition and, 254
Adams, Abigail Smith, and, 129
in American Revolution, 132
during Civil War, 319
equality for, 253
frontier life of, 207
housework and, 266–267
as poets, 99
work of, 11, 266–267

Women's movement, abolitionism and, 233

Women's rights, 255

Woodland People, 10–13

Work. *See* Labor

Workers
child labor and, 273
craftspeople as, 98
female, 255
immigrant, 274
mill girls as, 273
in mills and factories, 269–270

World, 346 (map)
Magellan's trip around, 24

X

XYZ Affair—the refusal of the French foreign minister to meet with John Adams's diplomats until paid $250,000, 181

Y

Yahi people, 9

Yamasee Border War—a war between the Yamasee and white settlers in South Carolina, 83

Yorktown, battle at, 132–133

Young, Brigham, 280

Yuma Indians, 16

Acknowledgements

Photo Credits

3 (t)©The Image Bank/Getty Images, (bl)©BP/TAXI/Getty Images, (br)©The Granger Collection; **4** (t)©PhotoDisc/Getty Images, (b)©John McAnulty/CORBIS; **6** (l)©HIP/Scala/Art Resource, NY, (r)©Ohio Historical Society; **7** ©University of Arizona; **8** ©Richard A. Cooke/CORBIS; **9** ©Courtesy the Phoebe Apperson Hearst Museum of Anthropology and the Regents of the University of California; **10** ©Mary Evans Picture Library; **11** ©North Wind Picture Archives; **13** (t)©CORBIS, (b)©North Wind Picture Archives; **14** ©CORBIS; **16** ©Geoffrey Clements/CORBIS; **17** ©North Wind Picture Archives; **20** (t)©Mary Evans Picture Library, (b)©Greg Probst/CORBIS; **21** ©Bettmann/CORBIS; **23** (t)©Mary Evans Picture Library, (b)©Bettmann/CORBIS; **24** ©Mary Evans Picture Library; **25** ©Bettmann/CORBIS; **26** ©Bettmann/CORBIS; **27** ©Mary Evans Picture Library; **28** ©Mary Evans Picture Library; **29** ©Mary Evans Picture Library; **30** ©Mary Evans Picture Library; **31** ©Mary Evans Picture Library; **32** ©Mary Evans Picture Library; **33**(t)©Mary Evans Picture Library, (b)©The Granger Collection; **37** (t)©North Wind Picture Archives, (bl)©The Library of Congress, (br)©J.C. Kanny/Lorpresse/Corbis Sygma; **38** (t)©The Great North West Trading Co., (b)©Denver Public Library, Colorado Historical Society, and Denver Art Museum; **39** ©North Wind Picture Archives; **41** (t)©CORBIS, (b)©North Wind Picture Archives; **42** ©Stapleton Collection/CORBIS; **43** ©North Wind Picture Archives; **45** ©Denver Public Library, Colorado Historical Society, and Denver Art Museum; **47** (t)©Mary Evans Picture Library, (b)©North Wind Picture Archives; **48** (t)©Bettmann/CORBIS, (b)©The Granger Collection; **52** (t)©Bettmann/CORBIS, (b)©Kevin Fleming/CORBIS; **54** (t)©North Wind Picture Archives, (b)©Bettmann/CORBIS; **55** (t)©The Granger Collection, (b) ©The Granger Collection; **56** ©North Wind Picture Archives; **57** ©North Wind Picture Archives; **58** ©North Wind Picture Archives; **59** ©Bettmann/CORBIS; **60** (t)©North Wind Picture Archives, (b)©Bettmann/CORBIS; **61** (t)©Bettmann/CORBIS, (b)©Bettmann/CORBIS; **62** (t)©Bettmann/CORBIS, (b)©The Granger Collection; **63** ©North Wind Picture Archives; **64** ©Francis G. Mayer/CORBIS; **65** ©North Wind Picture Archives; **69** (t)©The Granger Collection, (bl)©Bettmann/CORBIS, (br)©The Library of Congress; **70** (t)©Jeremy Horner/CORBIS, (b)©Tony Arruza/CORBIS; **71** ©The Granger Collection; **72** (t)©The Granger Collection, (b)©Michael Freeman/CORBIS; **74** (t)©The Granger Collection, (b)©CORBIS; **78** ©Bettmann/CORBIS; **79** (t)©CORBIS, (b)©CORBIS; **82** ©The Granger Collection; **83** ©The Library of Congress; **86** (t)Morristown National Historical Society, (b)©Kevin Fleming/CORBIS; **87** ©North Wind Picture Archives; **88**©Bettmann/CORBIS; **89** ©The Granger Collection; **90** (t)©Bettmann/CORBIS, (b)©Bettmann/CORBIS; **92** ©North Wind Picture Archives; **94** (t)©The Granger Collection, (b)©Philadelphia Museum of Art/CORBIS; **95** ©Bettmann/CORBIS; **96** ©The Library of Congress; **98** (t)©The Granger Collection, (b)©The Granger Collection; **99** ©North Wind Picture Archives; **103** (t)©Francis G. Mayer/CORBIS, (bl)©Bettmann/CORBIS; **104** (t)Time Life Pictures/Getty Images, (b)©Bettmann/CORBIS; **105** ©CORBIS; **106** (t)©North Wind Picture Archives, (b)©Bettmann/CORBIS; **108** (t)©North Wind Picture Archives, (b)©Bettmann/CORBIS; **110** ©Bettmann/CORBIS; **111** ©North Wind Picture Archives; **112** ©Bettmann/CORBIS; **114** ©The Library of Congress; **115** ©Bettmann/CORBIS; **116** ©Bettmann/CORBIS; **117** ©The Library of Congress; **119** ©The Library of Congress; **120** (t)©Lee Snider; Lee Snider/CORBIS, (b)©Richard T. Nowitz/CORBIS; **121** ©Bettmann/CORBIS; **122** (t)©CORBIS, (c)©David Muench/CORBIS; **122** ©The Granger Collection; **124** (t)©Francis G. Mayer/CORBIS, (b)©Bettmann/CORBIS; **126** (l)©CORBIS, (r)©The Library of Congress; **127** ©Bettmann/CORBIS; **128** (t)©Bettmann/CORBIS, (b)©Bettmann/CORBIS; **129** ©The Library of Congress; **130** (t)©North Wind Picture Archives, (b)©Bettmann/CORBIS; **132** (t)©Bettmann/CORBIS, (b)©The Granger Collection; **133** ©CORBIS; **135** ©Bettmann/CORBIS; **137** (t)©Christie's Images/CORBIS, (bl)©Bettmann/CORBIS, (br)©The Library of Congress; **138** (t)©The Library of Congress (b)©Dennis Degnan/CORBIS; **139** ©David Muench/CORBIS; **140** ©The Library of Congress; **141** ©Bettmann/CORBIS; **144** (t)©CORBIS, (b)©National Archives; **145** ©The Granger Collection; **147** ©Photodisc/Getty Images; **148** ©Bettmann/CORBIS; **149** ©Bettmann/CORBIS; **150** (b)©The Library of Congress; **151** ©The Library of Congress; **154** (t)©National Archives, (b)©Bettmann/CORBIS; **159** ©Hulton Archive/Stringer/Getty Images; **169** (t)©Francis G. Mayer/CORBIS, (bl)©Bettmann/CORBIS, (br)©CORBIS;**170** ©The Granger Collection; **172** (t)©Bettmann/CORBIS, (b)©The Library of Congress; **173** ©Bettmann/CORBIS; **175** ©Bettmann/CORBIS; **176** ©Bettmann/CORBIS; **177** (t)©CORBIS, (b)©National Archives, Courtesy of the New York State Historical Association, Cooperstown; **178** (l)©Stapleton Collection/CORBIS, (r)©Bettmann/CORBIS; **179** ©Archivo Iconografico, S.A./CORBIS; **180** ©The Library of Congress; **181** ©Bettmann/CORBIS; **182** ©The Library of Congress; **186** (t)©Bettmann/CORBIS (b)©Bettmann/CORBIS; **187** ©The Library of Congress; **188** ©The Library of Congress; **189** (l)©Bettmann/CORBIS, (r)©Bettmann/CORBIS; **191** ©Bettmann/CORBIS; **192** Time Life Pictures/Getty Images; **193** ©Bettmann/CORBIS; **194** ©Naval Historical Foundation; **195** ©The Granger Collection; **196** ©Bettmann/CORBIS; **197** (t)©Bettmann/CORBIS, (b)©Bettmann/CORBIS; **201** (t) ©CORBIS, (bl) ©Bettmann/CORBIS, (br) ©CORBIS; **202** (b)©Bettmann/CORBIS; **203** ©Shelburne Museum, Shelburne, Vermont; **204** (t)©CORBIS, (b)©Bettmann/CORBIS; **205** ©CORBIS; **206** ©Bettmann/CORBIS; **207** ©Bridgeman Art Library, Gift of Mrs D. Carnegie; **208** ©Bettmann/CORBIS; **209** ©Bettmann/CORBIS; **210** (t)©Denver Public Library, Colorado Historical Society, and Denver Art Museum, (b)©The Granger Collection; **211** ©Texas State Library and Archives Commission; **212** ©CORBIS; **213** ©Mary Evans Picture Library; **216** (t)©Bettmann/CORBIS; **218** (t)©The Library of Congress, (b)©The Library of Congress; **220** ©Lee Snider; Lee Snider/CORBIS; **222** ©The Library of Congress; **223** (t)©The Library of Congress, (b)©Bettmann/CORBIS; **224** ©Bettmann/CORBIS; **226** (t)©The Library of Congress; **228** ©Bettmann/CORBIS; **229** ©Max D. Standley; **231**©Bettmann/CORBIS; **233** (t)©Bettmann/CORBIS, (bl)©Bettmann/CORBIS, (br)©Bettmann/CORBIS; **234** (b)©Bettmann/CORBIS; **235** (c)©Bettmann/CORBIS, (b)©Bettmann/CORBIS; **236** ©CORBIS; **237** ©CORBIS; **238** ©Bettmann/CORBIS; **239** (b)©The Granger Collection; **240** ©The Granger Collection; **241** ©The Granger Collection; **242** ©The Granger Collection; **243** (b)©Northern Illinois University; **244** ©CORBIS; **248** (t)©Rick Gayle/CORBIS, (b)©CORBIS; **249** ©Bettmann/CORBIS; **250** ©The Granger Collection; **251** ©CORBIS; **252** ©Bettmann/CORBIS; **253** ©Bettmann/CORBIS; **254** (t)©Bettmann/CORBIS; **255** (t)©Bettmann/CORBIS, (b)©Bettmann/CORBIS; **256** ©Bettmann/CORBIS; **257** (l)©Bettmann/CORBIS, (r)©Bettmann/CORBIS; **258** (t)©Bettmann/CORBIS, (b)©Bettmann/CORBIS; **259** ©The Granger Collection; **263** (t) ©CORBIS, (bl)©CORBIS, (br)©North Wind Picture Archives; **264** (t)©Bettmann/CORBIS, (b)©Hulton-Deutsch Collection/CORBIS; **265** ©North Wind Picture Archives; **266** (t)©Mary Evans Picture Library, (b)©North Wind Picture Archives; **267** (t)©Bettmann/CORBIS, (b)©Mary Evans Picture Library; **268**©Bettmann/CORBIS; **269** ©Bettmann/CORBIS; **270** (t)©Mary Evans Picture Library, (b)©North Wind Picture Archives; **271** (t)©Museum of the City of New York/CORBIS, (c)©Francis G. Mayer/CORBIS, (b)©Underwood & Underwood/CORBIS; **272** ©Stapleton Collection/CORBIS; **273** ©North Wind Picture Archives; **274** ©CORBIS; **278** (t)©Bettmann/CORBIS, (b)©Denver Public Library, Colorado Historical Society, and Denver Art Museum; **279** ©The Granger Collection; **280** ©Bettmann/CORBIS; **281** (t)©The Granger Collection, (b)©The Corcoran Gallery of Art/CORBIS; **283** ©The Corcoran Gallery of Art/CORBIS; **284** (t)©North Wind Picture Archives, (b)©Bettmann/CORBIS; **285** Hulton Archive/Getty Images; **286** ©Bettmann/CORBIS; **287** ©David J. & Janice L. Frent Collection/CORBIS; **288** (t)©Bettmann/CORBIS, (b)©Bettmann/CORBIS; **289** ©CORBIS; **293** (t)©The Granger Collection, (bl)©Picture History LLC, (br)©Bettmann/CORBIS; **294** ©The Library of Congress; **297** (cl)©Bettmann/CORBIS, (br)©Library of Congress, Rare Book and Special Collections Division; **298** (t)©The Library of Congress, (b)©North Wind Picture Archives; **301** ©The Granger Collection; **303** ©Bettmann/CORBIS; **304** ©CORBIS; **305** (t)©CORBIS, (b)©Bettmann/CORBIS; **306** (t)©North Wind Picture Archives, (b) ©The Library of Congress; **307** ©The Granger Collection; **310** (b)©The Library of Congress; **311** (l)©The Library of Congress, (r)©The Library of Congress, **312** ©Minnesota Historical Society/CORBIS; **313** (t)©Museum of the City of New York/CORBIS, (b)©The Library of Congress; **314** ©Francis G. Mayer/CORBIS; **316** ©CORBIS; **317** ©CORBIS; **318** ©CORBIS; **319** (t) ©Bettmann/CORBIS, (b) ©CORBIS; **320** ©The Library of Congress; **321** ©CORBIS; **322** (t) ©The Library of Congress, (b) ©The Library of Congress; **323** ©Bettmann/CORBIS

(t) top, (b) bottom, (l) left, (r) right

364